Controlling From Afar

The Daoguang Emperor's Management of the Grand Canal Crisis, 1824–1826

Jane Kate Leonard

CENTER FOR CHINESE STUDIES
THE UNIVERSITY OF MICHIGAN
ANN ARBOR

MICHIGAN MONOGRAPHS IN CHINESE STUDIES
ISSN 1081-9053
SERIES ESTABLISHED 1968
VOLUME 69

Published by
Center for Chinese Studies
The University of Michigan
Ann Arbor, Michigan 48109-1290

© 1996 Center for Chinese Studies
The University of Michigan
All rights reserved

Printed and made in the United States of America

This book contains material which first appeared in Jane Kate Leonard,
"'Controlling from Afar': Open Communications and the Tao-Kuang
Emperor's Control of Grand Canal Grain Transport Management, 1824–26,"
Modern Asian Studies 22,4 (1988): 655–699.
© 1988 Cambridge University Press
Reprinted with the permission of Cambridge University Press.

Library of Congress Cataloging-in-Publication Data

Leonard, Jane Kate, 1939–

Controlling from afar : the Daoguang emperor's management
of the Grand Canal crisis, 1824–1826 /
Jane Kate Leonard.
p.   cm. —
(Michigan monographs in Chinese studies, ISSN 1081-9053 ; no. 69)
Includes bibliographical references and index.
ISBN 0-89264-114-2 (alk. paper)
1. Grand Canal (China).
2. Grand Canal Region (China)—Description and travel.
3. Inland water transportation—China.
4. Canals—China.
I. Title. II. Series.
HE500.Z5G7346   1996
386'.48'0954—dc20   95-50275
CIP

To My Family
for Their Loving Patience
Benny, Mom, Joe, and Kate

Contents

Illustrations   vii
Acknowledgments   ix
Maps   xi
Chronology   xxv

Prologue   1

Chapter One.   The Grand Canal   5
    The River
    The Technology
    The Origins of the Canal
    The Yuan–Ming Redesign
    The Grand Canal in Qing Times

Chapter Two.   The View from the Palace   51
    Political Reality in the 1820s
    Imperial Administrative Leadership
    The Creation of Greater China
    The Economy and the Canal Zone

Chapter Three.   Streamlining Grand Canal–Grain Transport Management   79
    The Emperor at the Center
    Regional Managers of the Canal–Grain Transport System
    The Grand Canal–Yellow River Directorate
    The Grain Transport Directorate

Chapter Four.   The Grand Canal Crisis   109
    Overview of the Unfolding Crisis
    Prelude: The Autumn Crossing Emergency
    The Disaster at Gaojia Great Dike and First Response
    Root Causes

Chapter Five.　　　Racing Against Time: Reconstruction and
　　　　　　　　　　　the 1825 Spring Crossing　135

Chapter Six.　　　 Muddling Through: Transfer-Shipping　151
　　　　　　　　　　Silt Barriers and Lighterage
　　　　　　　　　　The Transfer-Shipping Initiative
　　　　　　　　　　Qishan to the Rescue
　　　　　　　　　　Assessment of Transfer-Shipping

Chapter Seven.　　The Emperor's Critique of Canal–Grain
　　　　　　　　　　　Transport Management　177
　　　　　　　　　　The Watershed
　　　　　　　　　　Raising the Issues
　　　　　　　　　　Controlling From Afar
　　　　　　　　　　The Dynamics of Central-Regional Decision Making

Chapter Eight.　　 Canal Restoration　203
　　　　　　　　　　Yinghe's Plan: Silver for Tribute
　　　　　　　　　　Taming the River

Chapter Nine.　　　The Sea Transport Experiment　227
　　　　　　　　　　Forcing the Issue
　　　　　　　　　　Compromise
　　　　　　　　　　Operational Planning
　　　　　　　　　　Songyun's Memorial
　　　　　　　　　　Riding the Black Ocean Waves

Conclusion　247

Epilogue　255

Notes　257
Glossary　287
Reference List　291
Index　327

Illustrations

Figures

1. Fishing Craft on Hongze Lake   xxvi
2. Flash Lock   15
3. Detail of Winch Lifting the Baulks of a Flash Lock   16
4. Plan View: Vessel Passing Over Glacis with Capstans   16
5. Pulling Vessel Up and Over Double Glacis with Capstans   16
6. Bamboo Gabion   18
7. Dredging Boat   19
8. Silt Scraper   20
9. Trackers Pulling Canal Boat   37
10. The Hongze Strategy: Lake Water Cascading through the Canal–Yellow River Junction   43
11. Train of Canal Lighters   74
12. Southward Descent into Yellow River from Grand Cana at Yangzhuang   183
13. Grand Canal (Bai River) Approaching Tongzhou   89
14. Guard Post on Grand Canal   96
15. Grain Junk (*Tiangong kaiwu*, 1637)   102
16. Grand Canal Lighter   103
17. Shanghai Sandboat (*shachuan*)   234

Maps

1. Grand Canal and Connected River Systems   xiii
2. Major Rivers, North and Central China   xiv
3. Confluence of Huai, Yellow Rivers and Grand Canal   xv
4. Strategic Communications, Third Century B.C.– Second Century A.D.   xvi
5. Grand Canal ca. 600–1300   xvii
6. Grand Canal during the Yuan Dynasty, 1280–1367   xviii
7. Huaiyang Canal and Grand Canal–Yellow River Junction ca. 1820   xix
8. Canal Head and Clear Passage at Grand Canal–Yellow River Junction   xx
9. Hongze Dike and Drainage System and the Grand Canal–Yellow River Junction   xxi
10. Qing Empire (1644–1911)   xxii
11. Grand Canal and Junction Region Affected by 1824 Floods   xxiii

Acknowledgements

A great many people helped me during the course of this research project, none more important than the staffs of the following archival collections: Qing Archives, National Palace Museum, Taibei; Harvard-Yenching Library; British Library: the Departments of Maps (Ann Taylor), Manuscripts, Prints and Drawings (Lindsay Stainton), the India Office Library, its Department of Prints and Drawings (J. P. Losty), and the Oriental Collection (Francis Wood, Xiaowei Bond, and Lars Laamann). Particularly helpful were the jolly crowd in the reading room and photographic department of the India Office Library on Blackfriars.

I am grateful for grant support from the following institutions: American Council of Learned Societies; American Philosophical Society; the Department of Far Eastern History, Australian National University; and the History Department, University of Melbourne. I am particularly grateful for the generous research support from the University of Akron: two Faculty Research Grants and one Summer Research Fellowship.

I want to thank Yao Ti, bureau chief of the China International Travel Service in Yangzhou, for personally guiding me around Huai'an, Gaoyou, Hongze and Gaoyou lakes, and along the old banks of the Yellow River and Grand Canal in northern Jiangsu. I am also deeply appreciative of the hospitality of Mr. Zheng, the CITS branch head, and Zhu Yanjing, Gaoyou municipal government, during my visit to Gaoyou in 1988.

I have profited enormously from wonderful colleagues who have been generous with their time, expertise, and friendship: Wang Gungwu, the late Jennifer W. Cushman, E-tu Zen Sun, John Watt, Bob Gardella, and the entire history faculty at Melbourne University whose interesting ideas and shrieks of laughter in the departmental tea room made my stay in Melbourne both productive and pleasurable. My colleagues in Qing history in Ohio have been extremely helpful during the last stages of this project: Barry Keenan, Sam Chu, and David Kelley. I am especially grateful to Pei Huang for critiquing the manuscript and sharing with me his vast expertise on Qing politics and institutions. I am also deeply indebted to Chang Hao for his suggestions on the manuscript and his insights on the linkage between practical governance and Confucian thought.

I have been able to convey the complexities of the Grand Canal–riverine network and of Chinese hydraulic technology because of fine maps and drawings. Many thanks to Joseph W. Stoll, Cartography Lab, University of Akron, for his ability to make nineteenth-century Chinese maps understandable and accessible. Special thanks to my daughter Kate for bringing the Grand Canal to life with her drawings and also for tramping around with me on the old site of the Grand Canal–Yellow River junction in northern Jiangsu. Finally, thanks to my husband Benny who never looses sight of the big picture and does so with whimsy and good humor.

JKL
Akron, Ohio
February 15, 1996

Maps

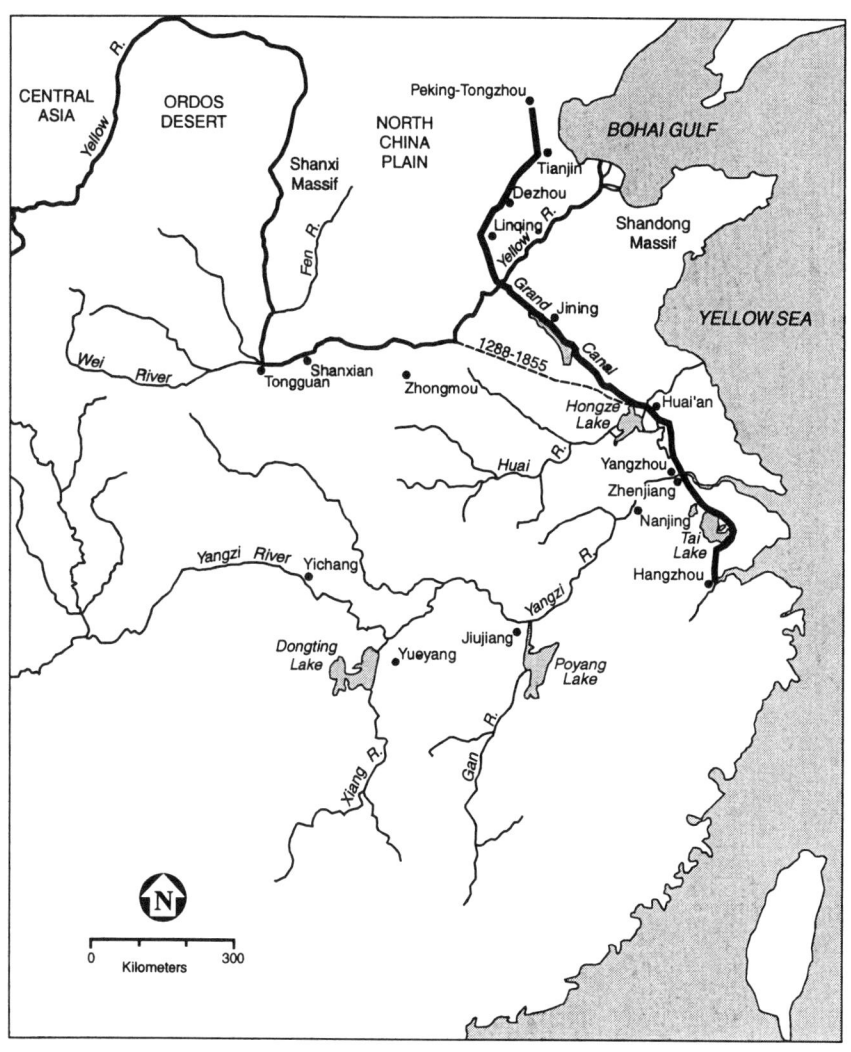

1. Grand Canal and Connected River Systems.

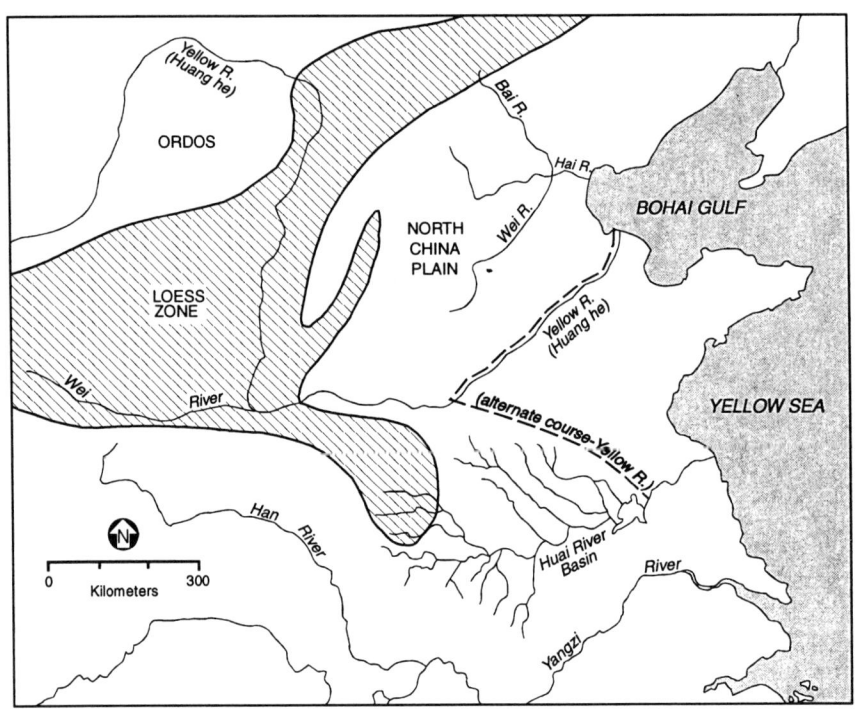

2. Major Rivers, North and Central China.

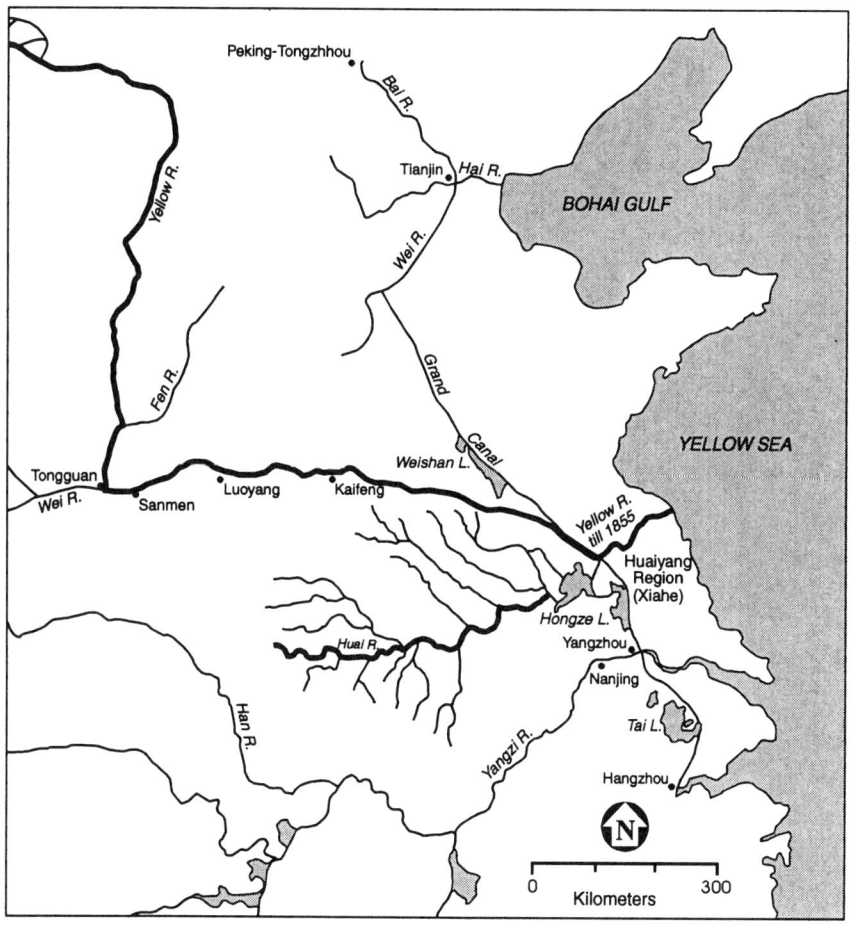

3. Confluence of Huai, Yellow Rivers and Grand Canal.

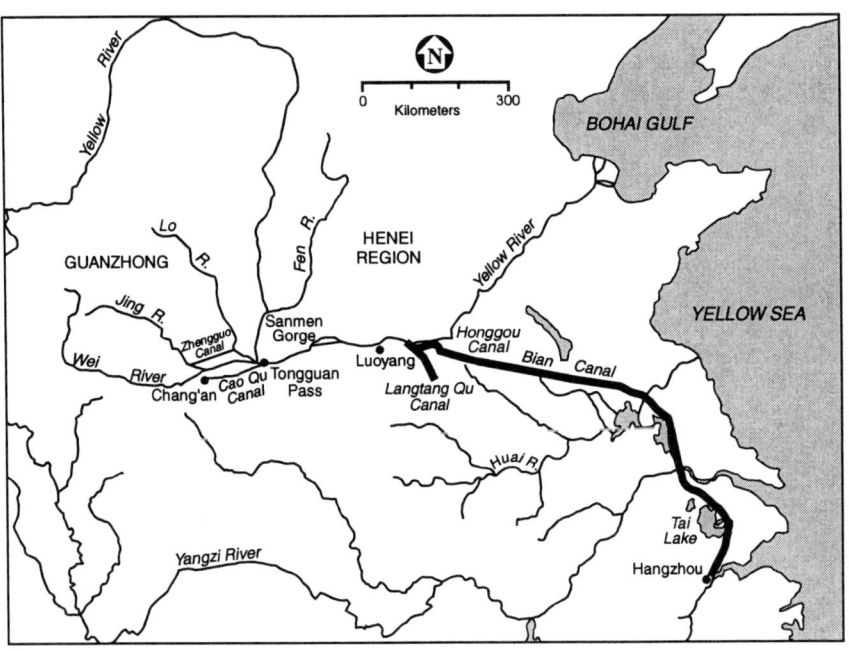

4. Strategic Communications, Third Century B.C.– Second Century A.D.

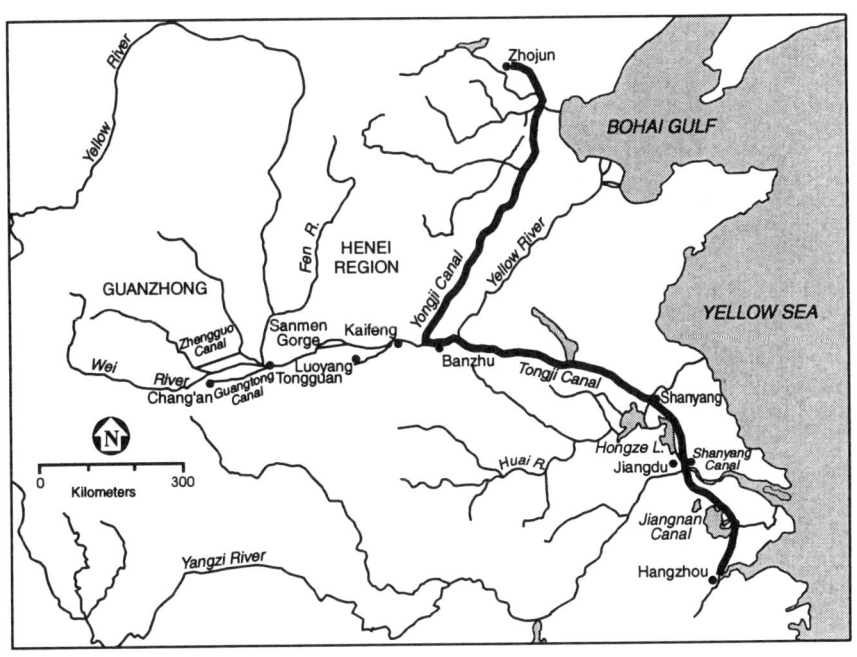

5. Grand Canal ca. 600–1300.

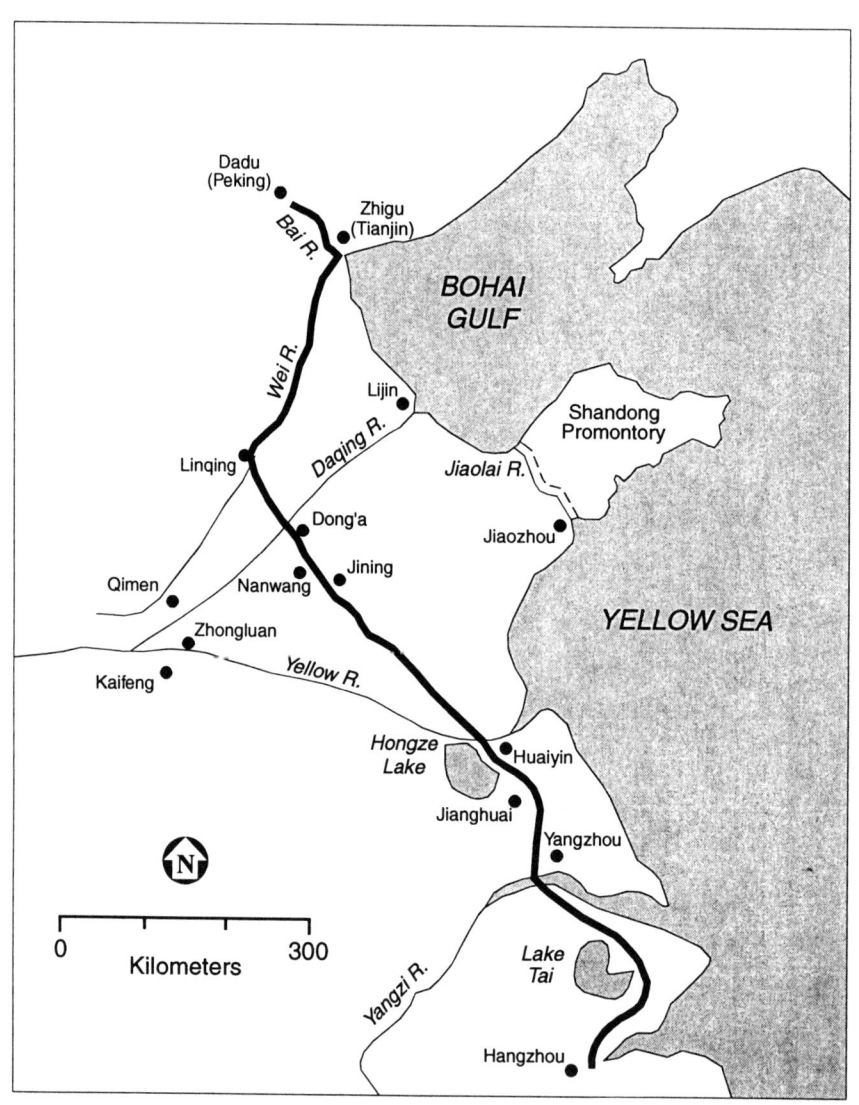

6. Grand Canal during the Yuan Dynasty, 1280–1367.

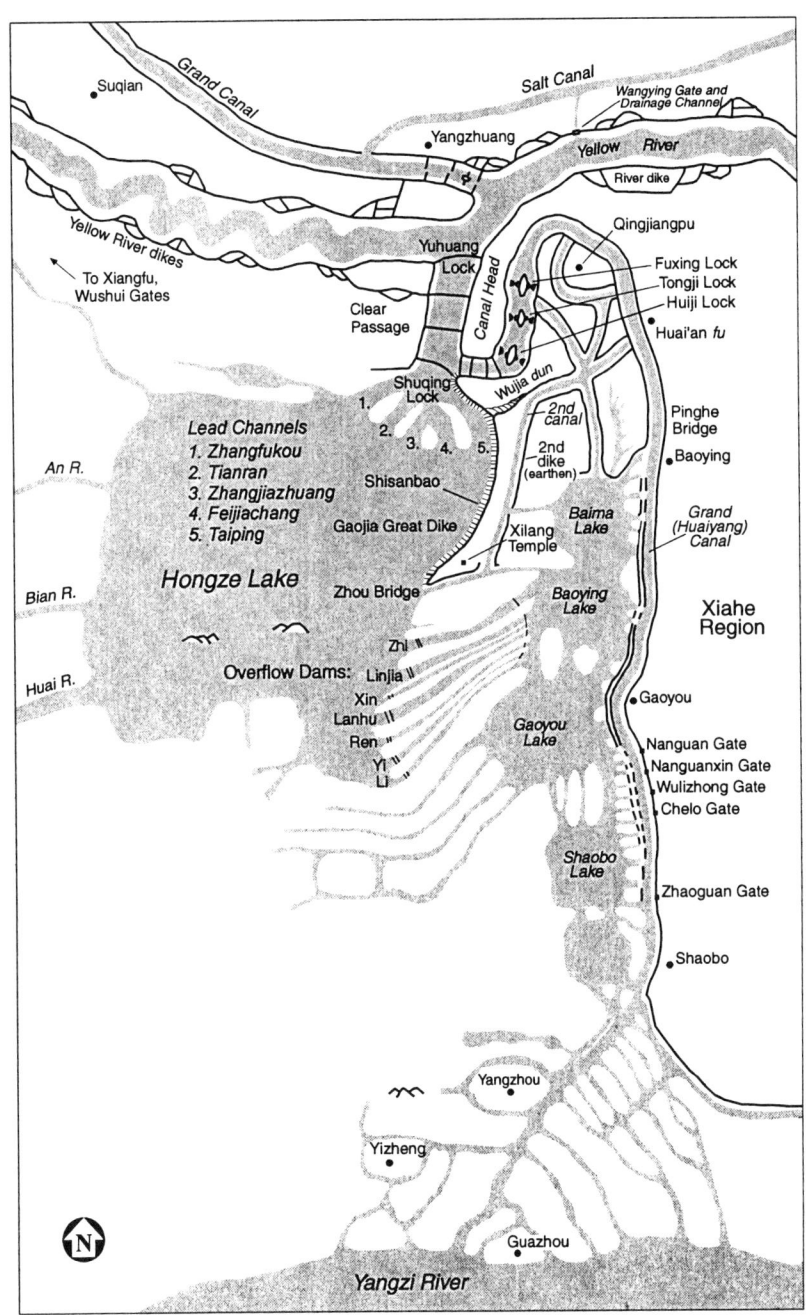

7. Huaiyang Canal and Grand Canal–Yellow River Junction ca. 1820.

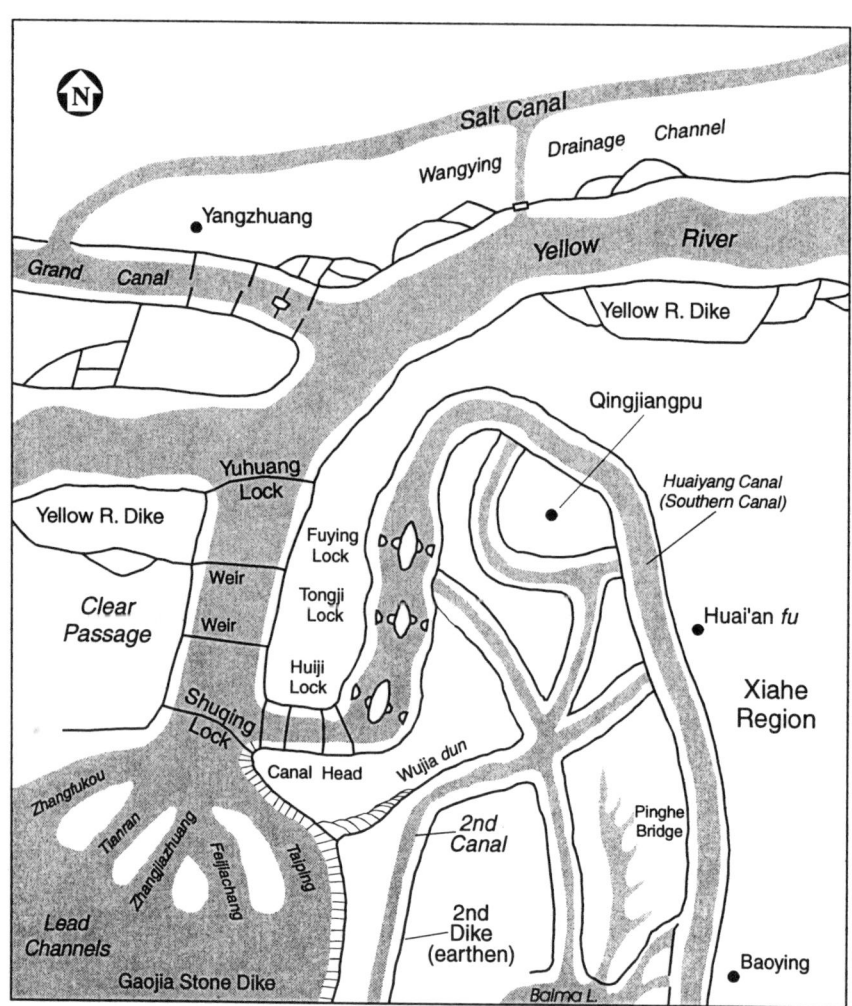

8. Canal Head and Clear Passage at Grand Canal–Yellow River Junction.

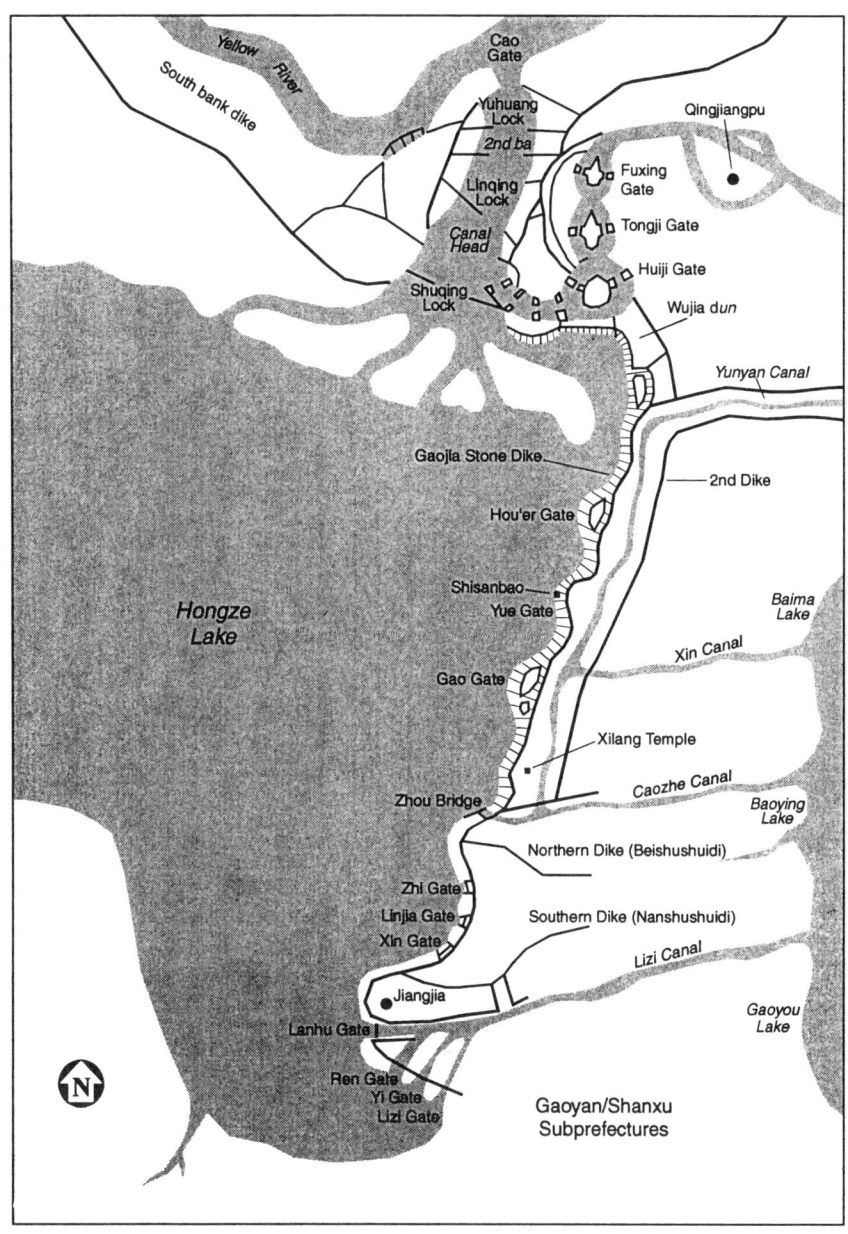

9. Hongze Dike and Drainage System and the Grand Canal–Yellow River Junction.

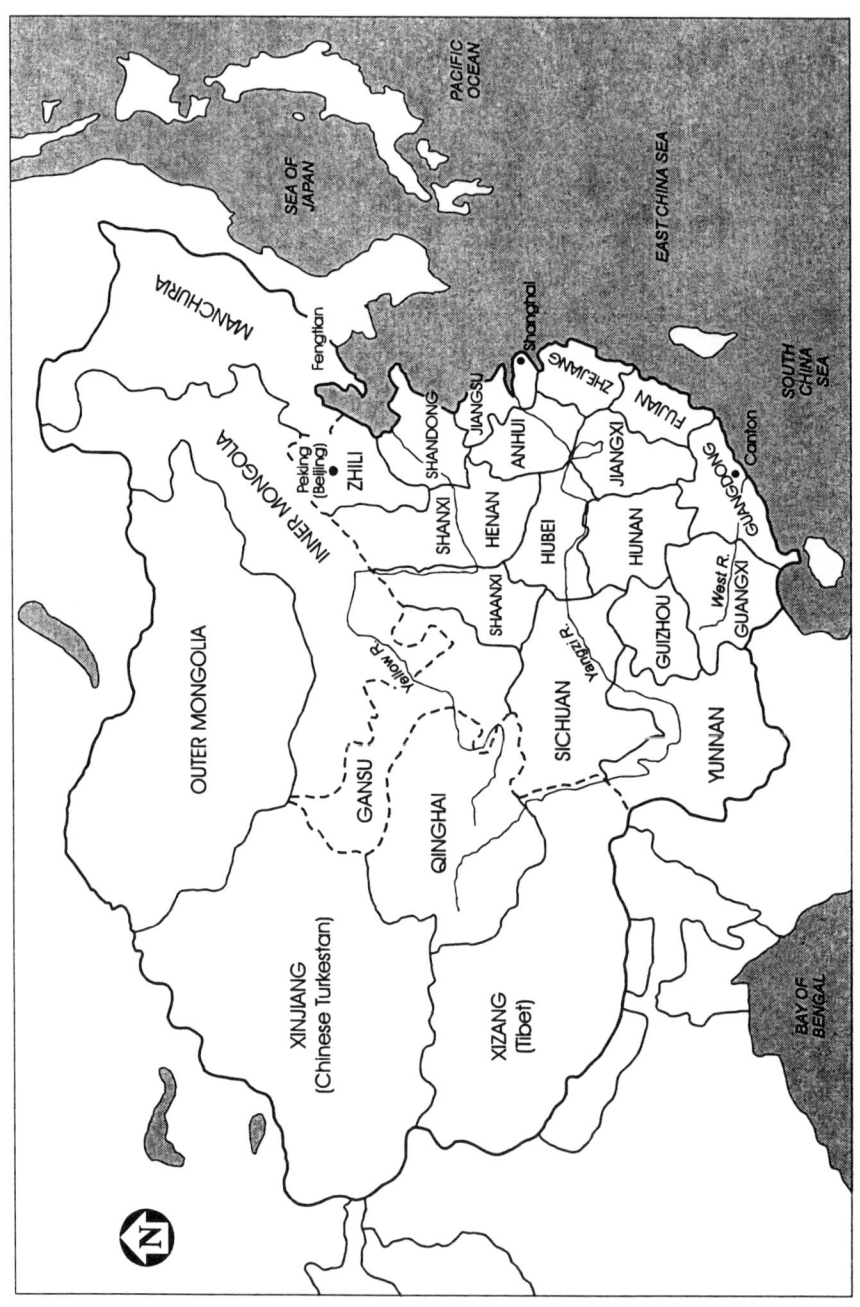

10. Qing Empire (1644–1911).

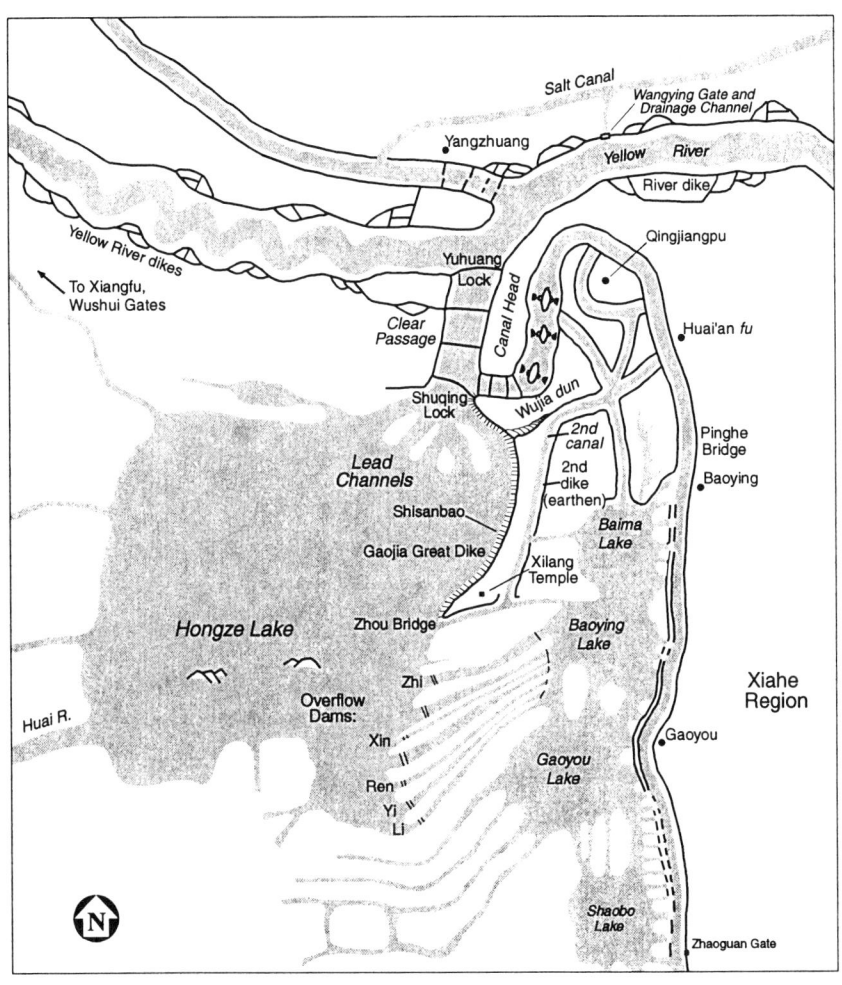

11. Grand Canal and Junction Region Affected by 1824 Floods.

Chronology of the Grand Canal Crisis

1824 (DG4)	9—11	Delayed southward crossing of grain fleets.
	11.23	Collapse of Gaojia Great Dike. Flooding in northern Jiangsu reported to the Daoguang Emperor.
	11.24	Dispatch of Imperial Commissioners Wang Tingzhen and Wen Fu to northern Jiangsu to investigate the disaster and forge reconstruction plans.
		Appointment of new regional officials to manage the canal crisis.
1825 (DG5)	2.1—9	Yuhuang Lock gate opened. First northbound grain fleets cross the Yellow River.
	2.5	First imperial call for a discussion of sea transport.
	4.2	Imperial authorization of a three-province plan for private lighterage of grain tribute.
	4.27—5.10	Breakdown of grain shipping in northern Jiangsu.
	5.12	Seasonal closure of Yuhuang Lock gate.
	5.19	Qishan appointed Liangjiang governor-general.
	5.22	Second imperial call for discussion of sea transport.
	6.29	Imperial decision to use both canal and sea transport in 1826.
	9.8	Imperial authorization of sea transport regulations for 1826.

	9.8	Transfer-shipping completed at the Grand Canal–Yellow River junction.
	10.25	Completion of the 1825 grain transport cycle.
	11.28	Imperial justification of sea transport and transfer-shipping given in response to Songyun's critique.
1826 (DG6)	2.1—8	Departure of first sea shipments of grain tribute from Shanghai.
	2.1	Emperor and Qishan debate the priorities for the reconstruction of the canal-riverine hydraulic system in northern Jiangsu.
	2.21	Arrival of first sea shipments of grain tribute in Tianjin.
	5.16	Successful completion of transfer-shipping through the canal–Yellow River junction.
	6.17	Successful completion of the 1826 sea transport experiment.
	11.25	Collapse of Gaojia Great Dike.

A note about dates. Here and in chapters 4 through 9, Western dates are used to refer to Daoguang reign years: 1824-DG4; 1825-DG5; 1826-DG6. To mark especially important developments or communications, lunar dates indicating reign year, month, and day, e.g., (5.2.1), are inserted into the text.

Fig. 1 Fishing craft on Hongze Lake.

Prologue

Dull gray clouds hovered ominously over Hongze Lake on the last wintry days of 1824. The lake's benign face, lined with small fishing craft, darkened as the winds rose and the storm clouds gathered. The gently swaying reeds that protruded from its margins began to bend restlessly in the wind, and waves marred the surface, anticipating the intensity of the storm to come. The rain began to fall in torrents, and the lake, dangerously swollen from the autumn floods of the Huai River and seepage from the Yellow River, inched up the rock-faced wall of the Gaojia Great Dike that lay along the lake's eastern perimeter. As the storm grew in violence, the wind and waves pounded the great dike and, as if the frantic efforts of dike workers were nothing, tore two huge breaches in the dike wall that sent flood waters cascading down into the Gao-Bao lakes to the east, into the Grand Canal itself, and beyond the canal into the flood-prone, low-lying Xiahe region between the canal and the sea. The flood washed away the secondary earthen embank-ments to the east of the lake that reinforced the great dike; it destroyed vital sections of the Grand Canal from Shaobo to the canal–Yellow River junction at Huai'an; and it devastated the farmlands of the Huaiyang region.

When word of the disaster reached the Daoguang Emperor in Peking, he and his inner court advisers immediately took over the management of the crisis as was the Qing imperial tradition in matters affecting Grand Canal communications. Within the day, he had dispatched trusted agents to northern Jiangsu to assess the dimensions of the disaster and spearhead the search for solutions that would restore the canal and stabilize strategic grain shipments to the capital. Thus began the Grand Canal crisis of 1824 to 1826, a crisis that marked the final phase of the Yellow River's meandering, before the northward shift of the river's course in 1855 and the series of aftershock floods that disrupted Grand Canal communications until the end of the century.

For the Daoguang Emperor, the crisis was of paramount significance, both as a portent of things to come and as a test of his leadership. It constituted one of the first major challenges to his rule in the early years of his reign; and occurring as it did simultaneously with the suppression of rebellion in southwestern Turkestan, it revealed the grim realities of the times, and it instructed the new emperor in the art of what was possible and what was not. The emperor manfully embarked on a two-year program of canal reconstruction and makeshift approaches to grain transport that created an uneasy stability in the canal-riverine network until the autumn flood waters of 1826 destroyed the great dike again.

Although the crisis was caused by the geological process of silt deposition and defied human solution, the emperor and his government were nonetheless held directly and personally accountable for restoring the canal system and the yearly shipments of grain tax to the capital. Imperial responsibility for the operation of the canal–grain transport system had originated in the early imperial age because of the strategic and logistical significance of Grand Canal communications to the establishment of centralized rule and to a complex web of issues connected with internal security and frontier defense. As a result, the management and maintenance of the Grand Canal system assumed a premier place among the responsibilities of imperial leadership. These responsibilities increased and intensified in the Qing period (1644–1911) due both to the Qing emperors' greater involvement in the practical aspects of daily administration, compared to that of the Ming period, and to the logistical imperatives associated with Qing fusion of the borderlands with China proper into a new, vastly expanded empire of Greater China. For these reasons, Qing imperial management of the canal system was invested with much greater strategic weight than had been the case in previous dynasties, and it emerged as a select area of administration whose management was guarded jealously by the Qing emperors. Indeed, the canal became a metaphor for the imperial state and its imperial leadership, and its successful operation was regarded as a test of the viability of both. It was an issue on which the future of the dynasty seemed to hang.

This study examines the Daoguang Emperor's management of the Grand Canal–grain transport crisis from 1824 to 1826, especially the pivotal decisions made in 1825. It looks at the crisis through imperial eyes to discover how the emperor defined its significance, orchestrated the decision-making process to achieve its resolution, and how he identified the major obstacles that hindered his ability to manage from afar this vital branch of administration, which his imperial forebears had dominated since the early reigns. The crisis is contextualized in the long history of Grand Canal communications (chapter 1) and the administrative history of the Qing emperors (chapters 2 and 3). The purpose is to recreate the Daoguang Emperor's vision of the reality he faced in the 1820s. How did he approach the management of the vast logistical system that centered on the Grand Canal? How did practical administrative leadership fit into his vision of Confucian monarchy? Did he have sufficient technical know-how and political savvy to manage this vast sprawling bureaucratic operation with all its tedious and mundane workings? What kind of working relationship did he have with regional officials who faced the day-to-day challenges and dangers of the threatening riverine network that impinged on the canal? It is hoped that an exploration of these issues will shed some light on the organizational capacity of the Qing state, as well as provide insights into the particularities of the Daoguang Emperor's rule during the first decade of his thirty-year reign—a period of turmoil and uncertainty when demographic crisis was eating away at the vitals of imperial government at the local level.

The focus on the 1820s and the early Daoguang reign is important for an understanding of the last century of Qing rule. Scholars have tended to view this emperor, indeed the whole imperial state, as tentative and faltering at this time, even though the first twenty years of his reign have been little studied. This interpretation has been shaped by decades of Opium War scholarship whose Eurocentric assumptions have generally discredited the reign and have discouraged careful study of its early years. Negative views have been perpetuated in more recent scholarship as well. There seems to be a tendency on the part of scholars to blame the emperors alone for disasters and decline, just as traditional Chinese historians did in the past, rather than to probe the meaning of complex processes of structural change that eroded the foundations of Qing state and society at the turn of the nineteenth century. It is hoped that this study will provide a more nuanced understanding of these watershed years, one that goes beyond the clichés about dynastic decline, the failure of imperial will, and inherent weaknesses in the traditional system, to one that centers instead on the operation of complex and long-established institutions in an environment of profound economic and social change. Such a focus will enable scholars to abandon historical myths associated with the Daoguang reign and come to a more realistic assessment of these crucial years.

1

The Grand Canal

The River

There was absolutely no solution to the Grand Canal crisis in 1824. The crux of the problem was the Yellow River and the unrelenting process of silt deposition that forced a massive shift in this mighty river's bed in fairly predictable six-hundred-year cycles. The cycle had run its course by the early nineteenth century. Since 1288, during the Mongol period, most of the river's meandering course had flowed southeastward from northern Henan, usurping the Huai River bed near Huai'an and flowing eastward across northern Jiangsu into the Yellow Sea. The process of silt deposition over the centuries had raised the lower course of the Huai–Yellow River bed to such dangerous heights that by the Qing period it was only a matter of time until the increasing momentum of meandering and flooding would lead to a northward shift of the river back around the western foothills of the Shandong Massif to the Bohai Gulf (map 1).

There was no reversing this inevitable geological process. The early Qing emperors knew this when they embarked on massive public works schemes in northern Jiangsu in the early years of the dynasty. The Daoguang Emperor knew it in the 1820s too, but it was also clear to him that the river would probably shift while he was the caretaker of the Grand Canal, and he alone would be responsible for shepherding the empire through the tragic consequences: the human misery caused by flooding, the disruption of strategic canal communications, and grain shortages in the capital at Peking. As it turned out, the shift of the river was not completed until 1855, five years after his death.

China's topography, climate, and soil conditions conspired to make control of the Yellow River—with its silting, meandering, and flooding—a constant and unsolvable problem. The river has its source in the dry plateau of northeast Tibet and flows across North China for nearly five-thousand kilometers before emptying into the Pacific Ocean. The river is divided into two distinct parts. The upper reaches extend from its source north and eastward around the Great North Bend to the Shanxi Massif, then south to the eastward bend at its confluence with the Wei River (map 2). From the Ordos area at the top of the Great Bend to Tongguan, the river drains an area of around 770,000 square kilometers, flowing through easily erodable loess soil where it picks up 90 percent of its silt load.[1]

The second part of the river begins at the gorges between Tongguan and Sanmen, where it emerges from the western mountains and flows down across the alluvial North China Plain until it runs into the Shandong Massif and must flow either north or south of Shandong to reach the sea. The eastern half of the river does not actually have a large drainage area because the river lies above the plain, especially east of Kaifeng (map 3). This phenomenon is caused by the gradual raising of the Yellow River bed due to the yearly deposition of silt. Every cubic meter of water in the lower reaches carries approximately 38 kilograms of soil. In the early twentieth century, it is estimated that the river carried an average of 1.6 billion tons of silt in the lower reaches each year, of which 400 million tons were deposited on the river's bed. As a result, the silt builds up on the river bed in the lower reaches at a rate of ten centimeters each year.[2] In some places, the silting can be much greater, requiring that existing dikes be raised several meters for stretches of thirty to fifty kilometers, to prevent flooding of adjacent farmland.[3] Therefore, the 155,000 square kilometers of alluvial plain that border the eastern part of the river do not drain into it. Only the land adjacent to the last 700 kilometers (nearly 3,000 square kilometers) does so, while the Dawen River, the major tributary of the Yellow in this region, drains 12,000 square kilometers of the Shandong Massif. It was, in fact, the silting process that actually created the North China Plain. In neolithic times, the Shandong Massif was an island, but the process of silting gradually built up the eastern part of the plain and ultimately connected Shandong with the mainland.[4]

The Yellow River, to recapitulate, consists of the upper reaches where it collects the silt, and the lower reaches, the North China Plain, where it deposits the silt. In the former, it flows faster and discharges twice as much water at Tongguan as it does at its eastern end. In the latter part, the Yellow is essentially an elevated river, flowing on an upraised bed of silt between two dike walls. The river bed functions as a ridge separating two drainage basins. During its travels through the alluvial plain, the river loses water through evaporation and seepage, and over the centuries, its silt load has grown because of deforestation in the upper reaches of the river.[5]

Loess soil—a highly porous, fertile loam—provides the silt. The drainage area of the Yellow River has about 390,000 square kilometers of loess with an average depth of 30 meters. Silt deposition is a geological process which is virtually irreversible even with the use of modern technology. Dikes, built along the banks of the lower reaches of the river, have been the main method for controlling the river and preventing floods since Eastern Zhou times in the eighth century B.C.[6]

Major factors affecting the Yellow River are climate and the pattern of rainfall. The plain through which the river flows receives from 500 to 625 millimeters of rain each year, with more rain falling in the eastern than the western part. Seasonal monsoon winds, along with tropical cyclones and variations in ground elevation, determine rainfall distribution with 80 percent occurring in the summer and autumn months, from June to September. In the winter, from November to March, as temperatures drop in Central Asia, the air cools and sinks, producing dry winds from the northwest that carry the moist ocean air back out to sea. In the summer, as the Central Asian air mass warms and rises, humid warm air is drawn back in from the southeast. This wind system, in combination with low pressures from southwest China and tropical cyclones from the Pacific east of the Philippines, is responsible for the heavy rains in the summer and autumn. Still, rainfall can fluctuate erratically, with disastrous consequences if the dry periods coincide with sowing and replanting.[7]

This climate with its characteristic pattern of rainfall produces four main flood seasons which fall in January, April, July, and October. During January and April, the floods, caused by melting snow, are light, while the floods in July and October are extremely heavy. Water control and utilization facilities, such as dikes, embankments, reservoirs, and sluice gates, must be built to withstand torrential flows in summer and autumn and, at the same time, retain water for later use.

The river, the rainfall pattern, and the silt all combine to produce conditions in the lower reaches of the Yellow River that cause continual change in its bed, its course, and its exit to the sea. The course of the Yellow River has changed nine times, in cycles of approximately six-hundred years, first flowing north of the Shandong Massif and then to the south. From the Later Han to the early Song period, the river followed a northerly course. From the late thirteenth to the mid-nineteenth centuries (1288–1855), it followed a southerly one, usurping the bed of the Huai River. From the mid-nineteenth century to the present, the river has reverted to a northerly course into the Bohai Gulf except for a brief period after 1937, when the dikes were intentionally destroyed to halt the advancing Japanese.[8]

The Yellow River's pattern of continual movement has caused devastating floods across the eastern plain throughout China's history. Yet, if controlled, its endemic meandering and flooding were not without their benefits to agriculture. These benefits were recognized as early as the eighth century B.C. and led to the retention of flood water for irrigation and the use of a thick enriching blanket of silt, left by the floods, to fertilize the soil. So, although generations of Chinese political-administrative managers realized they never could control the Yellow River completely, they devised ingenious techniques to minimize the danger of floods while maximizing the benefits to agriculture. These techniques included measures to control the inundation of cropland adjacent to the Yellow and Huai Rivers.[9]

The Grand Canal

When the Yellow River flows south of Shandong, it impinges on both the Huai and Yangzi rivers, which, like the Yellow, flow from west to east across central China. The Huai River, draining an area of 275,000 square kilometers, lies parallel to and between the Yellow River to its north and the Yangzi to its south and flows across northern Jiangsu through Hongze Lake to the sea. The Huai defines the northern border of what is called Huaiyang, or that area lying between the Huai and the Yangzi rivers. When the Yellow River shifts course and enters the sea south of the Shandong Massif, as was the case from the late thirteenth to mid-nineteenth centuries, it takes over the bed of the Huai near Huai'an, crowding out and diverting the Huai waters into Hongze Lake and the lakes and marshes that extend from Hongze southward to the Yangzi River near Yangzhou: Baima, Baoying, Gaoyou, and Shaobo lakes (map 7).[10]

The gradual expansion of the chain of lakes in northern Jiangsu since the thirteenth century gradually led to endemic flooding eastward from the lakes to the sea that destroyed everything in its path, including sections of the Grand Canal and the low-lying Xiahe, the region "below the canal." In late imperial times, these disastrous Huai–Yellow River floods sparked government construction of massive lake embankments, dikes, and two strategic drainage networks that channeled water into the Grand Canal and then drained it either into Xiahe or further south into outlets that led to the Yangzi. The role of the Yangzi outlets was expanded during the Qing period, increasing the Yangzi's importance as a safety valve for the waters of the Huai River and the expanding lakes region.[11]

The Technology

Chinese attempts to control the Yellow River are almost as old as Chinese civilization itself and date back well before the dawn of the imperial age in the third century B.C. Prior to the development of canal communications, the earliest experiments in water control sought to protect against flooding while at the same time providing for the irrigation and silt fertilization of adjacent crop land. These projects relied principally on the application of three technological innovations: dikes, retention basins, and sluice (water) gates. Dikes, or embankments, were generally constructed of hardened, or tamped, earth although stone revetments, or linings, were used at discrete locations depending on the river's configuration and the degree of threat posed by either bank erosion or sedimentation. Weirs—submerged embankments—were used in conjunction with dikes to even the river bed and manipulate the flow around river bends to guard against the erosion of embankments and the clogging of sluice gates critical for draining off dangerously high flood waters. Sluice gates, set in earthen embankments and dikes, were used during the flood season to divert waters into adjoining drainage and irrigation networks, and in the dry season they admitted water from adjacent lakes and streams to augment river flow and thereby reduce silt deposition. Later, as canal building developed in the Han period (206 B.C.–A.D. 220), sluice gates were used in conjunction with locks to maintain water levels sufficient for barge traffic. Retention basins were constructed close to rivers by placing parallel sets of dikes on each side of a river to capture and control surplus water.[12]

Two basic strategies influenced the use of dikes on the Yellow River. The classic Daoist approach employed a wide-diking system that placed low dikes and retention basins some distance away from the river bank. This approach recognized the impossibility of controlling the Yellow River and sought instead to channel flood waters into adjacent retention basins for later use in irrigation. A drawback to this approach was its dependence on periodic excavation of huge accumulations of silt from the retention basins in order to maintain maximum storage capacity.[13] Additionally, diversion of flood waters into retention basins slowed the current downstream, and this, in turn, led to increased deposition of the river's silt load.

The second approach to flood control, sometimes characterized as Confucian, utilized a narrow-diking system that positioned dikes close to the river banks to constrict the flow of water and increase its speed. This approach lessened the siltation that invariably accompanies slow river velocity and scoured the silt already deposited in the river channel. This method was an asset during the dry season because it kept the diminished supply of water flowing quickly.

The narrow-diking concept was developed by the late Ming river engineer, Pan Jixun, who asserted that siltation was the major cause of floods. If silt deposition could be minimized and river channels kept open, floods and meandering could be reduced dramatically. The narrow dikes Pan advocated were to be flanked by an outer perimeter of parallel dikes that created a wide catchment basin between the two. Flood waters could spill into the catchment, while the outer dikes kept the excess from flooding adjacent cropland. Moreover, the sediment that built up in the catchment acted to reinforce the bases of both the narrow inner dike and the outer one as well. Pan's narrow-diking strategy became a pillar of Qing hydraulic plans designed to control the Yellow River and protect the Grand Canal from its destructive floods.[14]

This method, however, was not without its drawbacks. Narrow-diking was even more dependent on a rigorous schedule of dredging than was the wide-diking approach. Dikes, embankments, and sluice gates had to be in tip-top condition to withstand the tremendous water pressures narrow-diking created during the peak flood season. The upkeep of these installations required efficient, coordinated action by the imperial state and by local peasant communities. But timely maintenance work of this sort often was not attended to during periods of economic hardship or government inefficiency. Narrow-diking also led to enormous sediment build-up in the lower reaches of the Yellow River, which forced the river to back up during the flood season and caused dangerous flooding and sedimentation further upstream in a corridor across Henan, southwestern Shandong, and northern Jiangsu.

Qing water control problems, such as those of the mid-1820s canal crisis, centered in this critical corridor. As flood waters backed up as far westward as Henan, the surplus flow caused dangerous meandering within the dikes as well as flooding across outer dikes. When the excess flowed southward, it followed the geographical slope of the land and diversion canals into the already filled lake reservoirs, silting and raising their beds, putting at risk the lake dikes and drainage channels on the east side of the lakes, and threatening the security of the Grand Canal, the agricultural lands of Xiahe, and the salt fields of Huaiyang.

With the formation of the Chinese empire in the third century B.C., the strategic needs of the imperial state sparked momentous developments in water conservancy, its goals, management, and technology. The earlier concern with flood control gradually gave way to a primary emphasis on strategic canal communications, which reflected the expanding state's drive to speed the movement of troops and grain supplies across a vastly enlarged territorial base. This area stretched beyond the old capital region of Guanzhong, located near the imperial city of Chang'an at the confluence of the Wei, Fen, and Yellow rivers, to newly developing agricultural centers in the eastern part of the China Plain, the Huai–lower Yangzi valleys, and the Sichuan basin (map 4). As the agricultural potential of these core regions was realized, the state placed a premium on the control of their grain reserves and the development of canal communications to facilitate the transport of grain to the capital and grain-deficient areas.

Imperial planners began to develop important techniques for mobilizing human and material resources for the construction of canal works. Developments in strategic communications from the Han to early Tang periods sought to draw grain from the new agricultural centers in the east back to the capital in Guanzhong, but the centrifugal pull of these regions proved overpowering and dictated that the eastern plain, not Guanzhong, ultimately would become the strategic pivot of the Chinese empire. Canal communications, the state granary network, and the growing prominence of the eastern capital at Luoyang all testified to this logistical reality by the middle Tang period.[15]

The political objective of initial projects in the Qin–Han period was to make the capital region of Guanzhong rich and powerful, and three kinds of projects were undertaken to achieve this goal. The first centered in the Guanzhong area itself and attempted to make the region self-sufficient in grain. These projects combined irrigation with canal works in order to spur production of food grains and provide faster delivery to the capital. The spectacular Zhengguo canal and irrigation scheme, built by the Qin state in 246 B.C., prior to its conquest of the warring states of the late Zhou period, achieved both these strategic objectives (map 4). The main canal lay north of and parallel to the Wei River, and it linked the Jing River in the west to the Lo River farther east. Lateral irrigation canals radiated outwards, irrigating and silting the adjacent cropland. The grain produced here was shipped via the Lo, Yellow, and Wei rivers to the capital. The Zhengguo irrigation system, which still exists today, transformed Guanzhong into a fertile, grain-producing region, and from its riches the Qin built a firm political-military base from which they conquered the states of the North China Plain and established the first empire in 221 B.C. A similar irrigation-transport canal (Cao Qu) was built south of and parallel to the Wei River in the early Han period, and restored in the Tang to expand grain production along its 150-kilometer length.[16]

The second group of projects centered not on Guanzhong but on the eastern plain, and highlighted the construction of transport canals to ship grain produced in the plain and the Huai area to grain storage facilities along the central reaches of the Yellow River near Luoyang. The most important works of this kind were the two canals that reached into the Huai River drainage and lay parallel to and south of the Yellow River near Luoyang.[17] These canals represent the first attempts to connect the southeast with the state granaries located on the Yellow River.[18]

The third and least successful of the early projects were those built to improve transport on the central sections of the Yellow River in order to facilitate the shipment of grain from the eastern plain to the capital at Chang'an. Nearly insurmountable barriers plagued transport on this section of the river. The primary obstacle was Sanmen Gorge, the treacherous section of the Yellow River lying midway between Luoyang and Tongguan (map 4). Sanmen contains a dangerous series of rapids, broken by three protruding rock formations that made barge traffic almost impossible without huge losses. Efforts were made from the Han to the Tang periods to find a solution to this problem. These included the excavation of tracking paths on either side of the gorge to enable gangs of haulers, or trackers, to tow the vessels through the rapids, detour roads around the obstruction, and bypass routes that utilized adjacent rivers, canals, and portages, such as the elaborate bypass network designed to connect the Yellow River with the headwaters of the Fen River. But nothing in the Chinese technological repertoire worked. By the end of the Tang, the strategic axis of the empire inevitably shifted eastward towards the emerging grain-producing centers of the eastern plain, the Huai, and the lower Yangzi valley. Efforts to tame Sanmen Gorge were abandoned, and the Guanzhong region lost the strategic prominence it had commanded since ancient times.[19]

The increasing momentum of canal-building projects from the Qin to the Tang period sparked explosive developments in hydraulic engineering that included innovations in canal design as well as the creative adaptation of earlier water-control technologies to the problems of transport. Chinese canal builders faced two main challenges. The first was the problem of leveling canal beds, and the second was the need to adjust water levels in canals that passed through areas of uneven terrain. To achieve the former, Chinese engineers expanded the use of weirs and other "river-training" devices to facilitate water flow into lateral irrigation canals. To achieve the adjustment of water levels from one terrain level to the next, they modified the adjustable sluice gate to function as a lock. This was then used in conjunction with the glacis, capstan, windlass, and winch.

Fig. 2 Flash locks (K. Leonard after Wm. Alexander).

The water gate, previously used as a sluice on the sides of canal embankments to admit water from adjacent waterways, was turned into a lock by positioning it across the channel of a canal or river to raise or lower water levels. The flash, or double stanch, lock—first used around the first century B.C.—was a water gate mounted in two solid wood or stone abutments, each having a vertical groove down the middle into which horizontal planks, or baulks, were inserted or lifted out to achieve the desired water level (fig. 2). The name "double stanch" referred to the two grooved abutments that anchored the gate (fig. 3), and the term "flash lock" indicated the ability to remove the baulks and release water in a flash, to wash vessels into the next level of a canal. Pound locks, which were used widely only in the Northern Song period (A.D. 960–1126), were nothing more than two flash locks set across a waterway a short distance apart to impound, or hold, and adjust water levels between the two points. It is not certain when pound locks were first developed, but it is clear that after the resumption of Grand Canal communications in the Yuan period (1280–1367), they were less frequently used than flash locks.

Fig. 3 Winch lifting baulks of a flash lock.

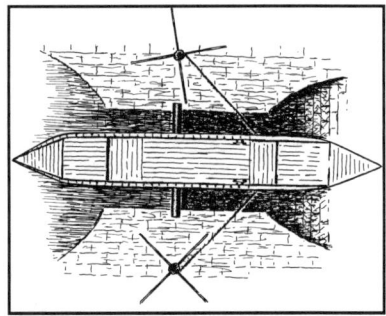

Fig. 4 Plan view: Passing over glacis with capstans (Staunton 1797, folio 34).

Fig. 5 Pulling vessel over double glacis with capstans (K. Leonard after Wm. Alexander).

The flash lock was used in conjunction with the glacis, a ramp-like inclined plane, or slipway, which functioned to slide, or ease, the movement of vessels from one level to the next. The glacis consisted of either a single or a double slipway (fig. 5). When the terrain change was steep, the lock and glacis were supplemented by capstans or winches that were mounted on either side of the gate and fitted with large ropes to haul vessels up or down the slipway (fig. 4).

Canal engineers employed flash locks most extensively on the Shandong section of the canal from the Yuan to the Qing dynasties. Flash locks were opened at certain times of the day, and ships would wait and then pass through the gate and down an inclined plane, or glacis, to the lower level. After the ships passed and the baulks were replaced, sluice gates upstream were opened to draw water from feeder canals into the main canal, thus replenishing the water supply. This procedure also was applied when moving craft up to a higher level, except that ropes attached either to man-powered capstans or winches were used to haul each boat up over the glacis and through the gate. Flash locks were positioned fairly close together so that the changes from one terrain level to the next were quite slight. The painter-draughtsman, William Alexander, who accompanied the Macartney mission to China, 1792–94, made detailed drawings of flash locks and carefully explained their operation in his diary of the trip.[20]

The most spectacular achievements in canal engineering were innovations in design that enabled Chinese canal builders to utilize the geographical contours and water supplies of existing river systems to facilitate the construction of canals. The simplest form was the lateral transport canal, which traveled parallel and adjacent to one major river from its source to its terminus, drawing water from the river and its tributaries. A more elaborate version, the derivation lateral canal, also ran parallel to one river system but did so in a serpentine pattern, using water from numerous feeder rivers or branch canals. The contour canal, in contrast, was designed to link one river system and its watershed to another across a geographical divide. This type of canal followed one river from its source and then moved along contours across a saddle between hills into the valley of a second river system, which it followed to its terminus. Similarly, the summit canal connected two different river systems, but it was designed to scale terrain differentials of much greater magnitude, moving up one side of a divide in serpentine steps, crossing the divide, then moving down by similar steps to the terminus of a second river. Because of the difficulty of maintaining water levels in summit canals, pound locks generally were used at the summit sections where the canal crossed the divide. An example of a summit canal with pound locks is the Nanwang section of the Grand Canal in Shandong province between Jining and Nanwang (map 6).[21]

Ingenious inventions accompanied the development of canal technology and improved the planning, maintenance, and defense of newly constructed waterways. These inventions included survey and sighting techniques for charting canal beds, dredging mechanisms, and, most importantly, new methods for reinforcing dikes made of tamped earth. Earthen dikes were used more widely in China than those of stone, and they were as crucial to the protection of canals as they were to river control. Earthen dikes were cheap and fairly durable, particularly when vulnerable parts were reinforced by mortared rock revetments, loose rock fragments and bricks, and gabions and fascines made from *sao*—bundles of stalks, grasses, and wood.

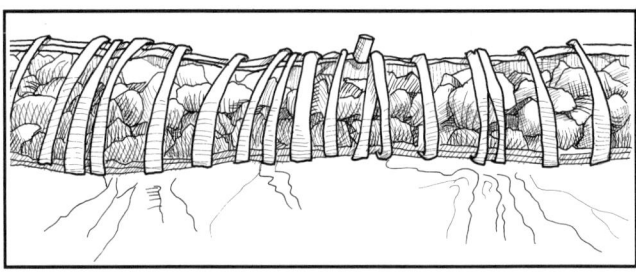

Fig. 6 Bamboo gabion.

Bamboo gabions were ingenious cylindrical crates made of woven bamboo and filled with rocks and *sao* materials that were anchored alongside dikes and embankments with hemp ropes (fig. 6). Because of their porosity, these gabions were able to absorb and withstand the shock of the sudden surges of water pressure so characteristic of autumn floods. Equally ingenious were the huge square and cylindrical fascines, enormous *sao* bundles, that were bound together by hemp and bamboo ropes. Fascines were used to block breaches as well as to reinforce dikes and embankments and buttress the abutments of water gates. These devices were hauled or rolled into place with ropes pulled by legions of laborers.[22] Fascines were particularly important for lining and reinforcing the junction passages leading from the Grand Canal near Huai'an to the Yellow River.

Fig. 7   Dredging boat (K. Leonard after Needham 1971, 4, Pt. 3, 338).

Additionally, dredging boats, fitted with iron-clad buckets manipulated by a spar and winch attached to the main mast, scooped up silt and dumped it in their holds (fig. 7). Large rake-like harrows and scrapers were pulled along between two boats to loosen the silt on river and canal beds so that the scouring effect of the current would carry the silt away (fig. 8).[23] One of the most ingenious devices, the flying dike, or overflow gate, was an embankment, dam, and drainage gate all in one. It consisted of a long, shallow, stone-clad spillway, reinforced by earth and fascines, and connected to a network of flood dispersion channels. In a flood emergency, a small breach was made purposely to wash away the embankment, debris and all, and to carry it into the adjacent drainage channels, thereby controlling the dispersion of flood waters while saving the stone spillway.[24] An impressive set of flying dikes was built into the containment dikes on Hongze Lake during the Qing period, and it was precisely those dikes and connected embankments that were destroyed along with the Grand Canal in the mid-1820s (maps 7, 11).

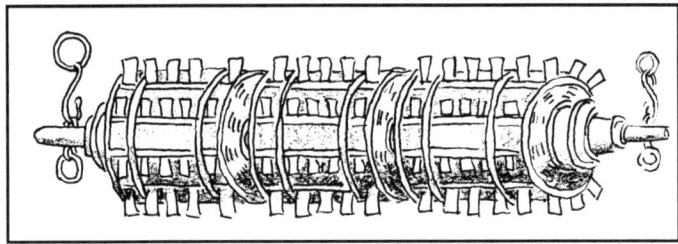

Fig. 8   Silt scraper (Lin Qing 1836, 2:30).

The technology that was created for canal construction is impressive in its simplicity and efficiency. It was admirably suited to a canal system that relied, except for very large works, on local peasant communities for its maintenance and operation. It was also well suited to the multipurpose character of China's canal networks, which had important subsidiary functions in irrigation and flood control. These attributes were noted with admiration by Western travelers in the seventeenth and eighteenth centuries, who asserted that the efficiency of the system compared favorably to similar works in Western Europe at the time. And the basic technological innovations of the sluice gate, glacis, capstan, winch, and practical adaptations of basic canal designs remained the mainstays of Chinese canal engineering up until the twentieth century.[25]

Innovations in bureaucratic management of water control projects paralleled these technological advances in hydraulic engineering and led to the tradition of state sponsorship and organization of projects perceived as essential to the logistical security of the state, and to the well-being of peasant agriculture. A growing emphasis on the former stimulated the construction and expansion of canal communications in the early empire. Structural changes in the economy accompanying the iron age in the late Zhou period (8–3 centuries B.C.) gave imperial planners from the Qin to the Tang periods a vastly expanded stockpile of material and labor resources with which to build and manage large-scale, canal-centered hydraulic projects. As a result, they designed new governing techniques to mobilize and utilize these resources. The number of officials and agencies charged with water conservancy and grain transport was expanded, and their responsibilities were outlined carefully in administrative codes to include the construction and maintenance of large-scale projects. These officials mobilized peasant labor to build and repair these projects, as well as smaller community-based works, and they began to develop and enforce a system of equitable water rights. By Tang times, canal communications and related conservancy projects were issues of the highest priority. They were regarded as a crucial responsibility of the imperial state and a measure of imperial leadership. The pivotal relationship between the state's strategic needs and state management of the empire-wide system of canal communications is aptly demonstrated in the history of the Sui–Tang (A.D. 581–906) and subsequent dynasties.

The Origins of the Canal

The creation of an empire-wide canal system in the Sui–Tang period marked the culmination of a centuries-long process of experimentation in water-control engineering and management that enabled the Chinese state to achieve the strategic control and logistical integration of a greatly expanded empire. This fledgling empire was faced with the double challenge of defending its northern frontiers while absorbing the emerging agricultural centers of eastern and southern China. The expansion of canal communications helped accomplish these tasks. Earlier state-directed efforts to tame the major river systems for the protection and benefit of agriculture were refocused on the construction and management of canal communications. These initiatives were paralleled by the organization of a state-controlled system of grain transport designed to draw grain reserves from the east and south to imperial capitals along the central reaches of the Yellow River. So important were Grand Canal–grain transport operations to the security of the empire that the central government undertook their management, expansion, and improvement up until the end of the imperial age.[26]

The geographic obstacles to canal building in China were formidable and resulted from a unique topographic pattern that has both challenged and spurred the development of canal communications since earliest times. The pattern is shaped by the great Asian plateau and the contours of China's mountain and river systems (map 1). The Asian plateau, which sweeps across and dominates the Asian continent from southwest Asia to the northeast Pacific, falls away to the sea eastward across the face of China. The major mountain ranges and river systems of China reinforce each other in their west-to-east contours and, consequently, cut China into parallel east-west tiers that pose daunting obstacles to north-south communications and to the unification and integration of north and south China. These geographic barriers were overcome in China's early history by state commitment to the construction and control of a unified canal system capable of transporting grain surpluses from core agricultural regions in the east and south to important political-strategic centers in the north.

The Grand Canal underwent two major periods of development. During the first period, from the Sui–Tang to the end of the Northern Song dynasty, the main section of the Grand Canal consisted of the central reaches of the Yellow River that flowed from Tongguan in the northwest to Luoyang on the eastern plain.[27] Two lateral branches fanned out from the Luoyang end of the axis, one to the northeast, which reached to Zhojun in the present Peking area (map 5), the other reached southeast to the Huai River near Hongze Lake. The configuration of this first Grand Canal network was designed to link up the three principal agricultural areas of that era: Guanzhong (the capital region around Chang'an in the northwest), the eastern plain, and the Huai–lower Yangzi region. From its secure base on the central reaches of the Yellow River, the central government was admirably positioned to organize the defense of the northwestern frontiers while simultaneously expanding its grip over central and south China.

During the second period of its development, from the late thirteenth century to the end of the Qing dynasty, the Grand Canal was repositioned to follow a straightened north-south line from the Peking area in the northeast, southward across the western edge of the rugged Shandong massif to Huaiyin where it joined the southern leg of the old Sui–Tang canal and followed it further southward to Hangzhou in the lower Yangzi valley (map 6). The Mongol dynasts of the Yuan period engineered this massive change in order to draw China's fiscal resources further north and closer to Inner Asia, thereby facilitating their control of both China and their Central Asian empire.[28] This move gave the late imperial governments of Ming and Qing the network to expand and develop their control of the Inner Asian borderlands—a process that was largely completed by the end of the Qing dynasty.

From 605 to 610 A.D., the Sui emperor Yangdi carried out a series of dazzling projects that launched the first Grand Canal network. These projects welded together and expanded China's preexisting canals and waterways to form one unified, state-controlled system of canal communications. The construction of the Grand Canal was a pivotal aspect of the Sui emperors' drive to centralize and unify China after the centuries of upheaval that followed the collapse of the Han empire. It expressed a new strategic vision of empire and a new set of imperatives that flowed from revolutionary changes that had occurred in China in the post-Han period. These changes included the vast expansion of the territorial base of empire, demographic movement from the western plain to the east and south, corresponding economic development and expansion in these regions—both in agriculture and commerce—and, finally, innovations in political-military institutions that accompanied nomadic penetration of North China.[29]

In response to these changes, the Sui dynasty and their Tang successors embarked on a radical program of institution-building that was designed to expand central authority over a much larger and more culturally and economically diverse area. The construction of the Grand Canal was vital to this centralizing process because it, along with a public granary system, allowed the imperial government to overcome the logistical problems inherent in mobilizing grain resources in the east and southeast from northern-based capitals whose location was dictated by the security needs of the northern frontier. As a result of their centralizing reforms, the Sui–Tang dynasties were able to achieve the political and logistical integration of North and South China. The fiscal and political consequences of this feat for the future of imperial rule in China cannot be overstated.

The Sui–Tang canal consisted of three parts. The pivotal east-west axis comprised the Wei and Yellow Rivers from Chang'an, the heart of the ancient capital region of Guanzhong, to Luoyang, located east of the treacherous Sanmen Gorge near the agricultural centers of the eastern plain. Work on this central axis launched the Sui program of canal-building in 584, three years after the founding of the dynasty. The Sui founder, Wendi (r. 581–604), built a 160-kilometer-long canal (Guangtong Canal) south of and parallel to the Wei River in order to connect the capital with the Yellow River at Tongguan and thereby bypass the silt-prone Wei (map 5).

Construction of the remaining two branches of the Grand Canal proceeded at an unprecedented pace under the driving force of Sui Yangdi's leadership (605–618). Between 605 and 610 the southeast branch of the Grand Canal was created from three preexisting canals that were modified, improved, and linked together. It extended from the Luoyang region on the Yellow River to Hangzhou, south of the Yangzi River. The first section, finished in 605, extended from the Yellow to the Huai River and was called the Tongji Canal.[30] The second part of the southern branch (Shanyang Canal), begun in 605, extended from Huaiyin to Yangzhou (then Jiangdu) on the north bank of

The Grand Canal 25

the Yangzi, a distance of 190 kilometers.[31] The Japanese Buddhist monk, Ennin, was dazzled by this part of the Grand Canal during his travels in the ninth century. He marveled at the fleets that filled the canal, of boats lashed two or three abreast drawn by water buffalo, following one another in great caravans.[32] The third and terminal section of the southern branch of the Grand Canal (Jiangnan He) stretched southeast of the Yangzi for four hundred kilometers along the eastern side of Lake Tai to Hangzhou (maps 4, 5). The completion of this section in 610 gave the imperial state access to the grain resources of the lower Yangzi valley, and it provided an opening to the sea and to the prestigious luxury trade with the kingdoms of Southeast Asia—the remote and exotic Nanhai (Southern Sea).[33]

As the southern canal was nearing completion, Sui Yangdi's Korean adventures began to take shape, and he embarked on the construction of the northeastern branch of the canal (Yongji Qu) to facilitate the supply of his armies. Completed in 608, this canal, the only wholly new section, extended northeast, joining the canalized Wei River (map 5) and then on to Zhojun, running north of and parallel to the Yellow River.

Both the southern and northern trunks of the Grand Canal converged on the Yellow River east of Luoyang, then followed the Yellow and Wei rivers westward to Chang'an. On this route, the canal passed Luoyang, the treacherous Sanmen Rapids, and Huazhou, the city at the junction of the Wei and Yellow Rivers near Tongguan (map 4). The completed canal network set the stage for the establishment of the Tang empire in 618.

The ambitious Sui program of canal building was linked closely to the establishment of an empire-wide granary system, which the state used to stabilize grain prices and to facilitate the distribution of emergency famine relief to avert internal unrest and rebellion. The price and availability of grain were issues that affected both internal security (in the not infrequent periods of famine and natural disaster that drove the Chinese to rebellion) and external security (connected to the defense of the northern frontiers). Symbolically, too, the Grand Canal also was intimately connected to the new imperial age, as exemplified by Sui Yangdi's grandiose imperial canal tours. Like the construction of splendid capitals and the creation of awe-inspiring rituals that expressed the universalist imperial order and its cosmic links, the canal tours provided the opportunity "to display the wealth and majesty of the new monarch throughout the empire."[34]

The Tang dynasty added little to the basic structure of the Grand Canal, although its rulers continued to maintain the canal works with vigor and commitment. The dynasty's principal contribution lay in the bureaucratic organization and management of the Grand Canal and grain-transport systems, which were part of its program of institution building, designed to centralize and unify the imperial state. The Tang emperors fought to improve grain transport in order to guarantee sufficient grain supplies for the capital, Chang'an. To this end, they made bold efforts to overcome the barriers posed by Sanmen Gorge and to expand both the state-sponsored granary system and the grain-delivery system.

Tang expansion of the public granary system included the establishment of relief granaries (*yicang*) in all prefectures as well as price-regulating granaries (*changpingcang*), whose stores were bought and sold by local officials to stabilize prices and guarantee the availability of food grains for peasant producers. Taken together, these steps reveal the expansion of the state's role in the economy, and they show the linkage of economic stability to imperial perceptions of the state's political-military security.

Later in the dynasty, after the eastern plain and lower Yangzi regions had emerged as the dominant agricultural centers, and when the capital's precarious grain supply system was in crisis, more attention was given to improving the grain procurement process. Improvements were made in grain collection from the peasant community, including delivery to the canal anchorages, storage in imperial granaries, and final shipment to the two capitals of Chang'an and

Luoyang, which were used alternately, depending on grain availability in Chang'an. These innovations took the system out of the hands of the regular "territorial," or "field," administration and vested authority in a new, specialist agency charged solely with grain-transport functions. This agency reorganized shipping patterns and divided the transport route into a number of discrete stages, each with its own storage facilities. Boats from the grain-producing prefectures could deposit their cargoes at these intermediate depots, thus avoiding the long, expensive, and risky trip to the capital. The agency had complete authority over grain shipment and storage, including control over transit granaries, fleets of grain barges, and carts for overland haulage. Large surpluses were built up in the granaries located on the Yellow River, and the amount of grain shipped to Chang'an doubled in the 730s and 740s, when nearly four-million bushels of grain reached the capital. In local prefectures, new regulations placed added responsibility on rich families to fund local transport and to act as guarantors for grain boats and their cargoes. These changes greatly facilitated collection and shipment at the local level.

The Tang dynasts placed as much strategic value on the canal system as had their Sui predecessors. They continued to maintain and improve the canal and expand institutions related to grain transport and storage, binding the three principal economic regions of the empire to the capitals in the north. As the dynasty faltered in the late eighth century and the northeast became autonomous, intense efforts were made to protect the southern branch of the canal, to safeguard grain shipments from the Huai–Yangzi region, and thus to assure the fiscal solvency of the state. It was only in the late ninth century that a series of rebel movements succeeded in severing the capital at Luoyang from the south.

The canal building of the Sui–Tang period was a spectacular undertaking with consequences for the later imperial age. It is not an exaggeration to say that the canal system laid the political and economic foundations for Tang power. But the Grand Canal was more than a potent force for unification in early imperial China. It also left an indelible mark on the imperial institution itself, linking the canal and the state together until the end of the imperial age in the early twentieth century. It was axiomatic that economic power and stability were the foundations of the political order. This assumption mandated imperial organization and control of grain reserves, canal communications, and the granary and grain-delivery systems. Later, the management of these core institutions became a pivotal responsibility of imperial rule, tying the survival of the canal to that of each successive dynasty. The canal, indeed, became a symbol of imperial rule during the remainder of the imperial age.

The Tang experience also reveals the tensions created by the need to plant the political-strategic center of empire in the northwest in spite of the gradual shift of the empire's demographic and economic base to the east and southeast. The Northern Song dynasty responded to this strategic problem by founding its permanent capital in Kaifeng, east of both the Sanmen Rapids and Luoyang. It was under Song leadership that the canal reached its peak efficiency, transporting 424,000 tons of grain to Kaifeng annually, compared with the 165,000 tons shipped to the Tang capital in the late seventh century. The canal ceased to function after 1126, when Song forces broke the dikes of the southern branch of the Grand Canal to slow the advance of the invading Jin armies into the Huai–Yangzi region. It was not until the Mongol conquest and the establishment of the Yuan dynasty that a radically altered grain transport system brought about the redesign of the Grand Canal and reaffirmed its pivotal role in strategic imperial communications.[35]

The Yuan–Ming Redesign

The Grand Canal achieved its final form in the late thirteenth century (1279–93) during the Yuan dynasty. The Mongols had relocated the imperial capital in northeast China in the Peking area at Dadu (map 6), away from the traditional sites of Chang'an and Luoyang.

This move was intended to facilitate communications between Mongol-dominated China and the greater Mongol empire, which stretched from Kharakorum to Western Asia. It reflected the Mongols' unique approach to rapid and direct strategic communications. The logistical imperatives associated with the supply of this burgeoning capital, as well as with the Mongol maritime expeditions mounted against Japan, Vietnam, and Java (1281–93), required the design of an efficient and streamlined system. These imperatives sparked the organization of an elaborate grain-shipping network that relied primarily on maritime transport, although inland waterways remained an important, albeit subordinate, part of the system.[36]

The grain-transport process was reorganized several times during the dynasty, but the agency primarily responsible for its management was the Directorate of Maritime Transportation, an office, significantly, under the jurisdiction of the Board of War. The directorate was headquartered in the southeast coastal region, from which vantage point it could superintend grain shipment to the capital, as well as supply the naval expeditions dispatched to maritime Asia. Because both these transport tasks were invested with great strategic significance, the Mongol regime lavished support on the directorate, enabling it to expand in manpower and naval capability.[37] Although it was free from neither corruption nor profiteering, the directorate was an effective and powerful force behind the Yuan sea transport system from 1282 to 1330.

Masterminded by two ex-pirates, who had aided the Mongols in the conquest of South China, the directorate transported two shipments of grain per year—one from March to May, the other from June to September—following a route from the lower Yangzi valley, around the treacherous coast of the Shandong promontory to the granary depot of Zhigu (Tianjin area; map 6) in the north, close to the new capital of Dadu. The shipping process evolved from a two-month voyage, undertaken by a melange of government and private boats that timidly hugged the coastline, to a ten-day, deep-ocean voyage by a powerful fleet of large ocean-going junks, capable of rounding the promontory with only one stop at Jiaozhou (map 6) while carrying as much as eight thousand *shi* of rice per boat.[38]

In spite of the predominance of the sea transport system and its superiority in shipping large amounts of grain, canal transport was not abandoned. Indeed, the Mongol regime dramatically reshaped the Grand Canal route to run in a straight north-south line from Hangzhou to the Peking area and made revolutionary advances in hydraulic engineering that enabled them to overcome the daunting obstacles posed by rugged terrain and elevation changes in Shandong province. The Mongols undertook these difficult and innovative canal projects because of what they and their Ming and Qing successors perceived to be the vulnerability of the sea route to natural hazards. The canal provided a backup system of transport that could guarantee adequate supplies of grain to the capital in the event that sea transport failed.

After the Mongols completed the conquest of the Southern Song in 1279, the only functioning sections of the Grand Canal that remained were the southern parts from Huaiyin, in northern Jiangsu, to Hangzhou (map 6). Those parts that linked Huaiyin to the Kaifeng region (Henan) and to Jining (Shandong) had either been destroyed or had deteriorated during the intervening years, following the retreat of the Song dynasty to the south in the early twelfth century. Additionally, the Yellow River was in the last (and most unpredictable) stages of its shift from a northern to a southern course to the sea. Although most of the river arced southward to the old canal near Huaiyin, usurping the Huai bed, a northern branch, the Daqing River (map 6), still flowed into the Bohai Gulf and posed dangerous problems of meandering and flooding in eastern Henan, western Shandong, and northern Jiangsu. This condition plagued the Mongol canal planners well into the fourteenth century.

The Mongols undertook the reconstruction of the canal with characteristic energy and dispatch, completing their canal-building agenda during the first twenty years of their rule. The first venture followed the Yellow River westward from Huaiyin to Zhongluan (map 6), then proceeded nearly a hundred kilometers overland to Qimen, where it joined the Wei River and followed it northeast to the granary depot at Zhigu. Because this route held little promise of speed, economy, or volume of grain cargoes, the Yuan simultaneously embarked on a project to build a direct north-south route from the old Grand Canal at Huaiyin to the new capital at Dadu. The route required extending the canal for 610 kilometers from Huaiyin to Linqing. Its new course snaked up and around the lakes and marshes of southern Shandong, including Nanyang, Dushan, Zhaoyang, and Weishan lakes, crossed the Shandong Massif from Jining to Dong'a, then descended to Linqing. Because this stretch of canal required the construction of numerous flash locks to ease the passage of vessels from one terrain level to the next, it earned the nickname, "the Canal of Gates." From Linqing, the canal followed the canalized Wei River to Zhigu, where it joined the Bai River and followed it north to Dadu.[39]

The completion of the Shandong section of the Grand Canal was a spectacular achievement that expressed the Mongols' energetic drive for open and effective strategic communications. It reshaped the Grand Canal into a straight north-south course across the Shandong Massif, linking the rice-growing lower Yangzi valley directly to the new capital in northeast China—a region that has remained the strategic center of China to the present. Although Grand Canal transport was not the predominant system of grain transport used in the Mongol period, the Yuan reconstruction and extension of the canal set the stage for the Ming and Qing revival of a grain transport system that relied exclusively on the Grand Canal. The Yuan Canal, therefore, laid the groundwork for strategic communications during the late imperial age.

The Ming dynasty made few structural changes in the canal. Instead, it left its mark on strategic thinking about canal-based transport and expanded central bureaucratic management of the canal.[40] Both developments intensified the significance of canal transport, compared with sea transport, and led to greater central direction of regional management of the canal–grain transport network.[41] Although the bureaucratic machinery functioned imperfectly, the Ming approach to canal management paved the way for the Qing emperors' meticulous, day-to-day supervision—the hallmark of canal management during the Qing period.

The Ming drive to refine and dominate the Grand Canal system reflected profound changes in strategic outlook that resulted from the challenges and crises of the first four decades of Ming rule, from 1368 to 1415. At the beginning of this period, the Ming geopolitical focus was the south and the maritime world. The Ming emperors undertook vigorous initiatives to erase the terrible image that the Yuan dynasty had created with its invasions of Japan, Champa, Annam, and Java, and its imposition of a direct and aggressive form of overlordship that had radically altered longstanding and benign traditions in Sino-Nanyang relations.[42] To counter these effects, the early Ming emperors planted their capital firmly in the south at Nanjing (map 3) in the lower Yangzi valley; they moved quickly to open peaceful tributary communications with the Nanyang, or Southeast Asian, states; and they initially perpetuated the Mongol system of sea transport to give logistical support to their maritime adventures, especially the dazzling expeditions of the Yongle reign (1402–24). Finally, in an act which was, in fact, reminiscent of the Mongols, the Yongle Emperor invaded and imposed a bloody occupation on Annam from 1406 to 1428.[43]

Yet active involvement in the maritime world yielded few positive results and placed great fiscal strains on the Ming state. All the Ming leadership had to show after four decades of effort was a failed tributary-trade policy, angry resistance to Ming rule in Annam, mounting expenses associated with the maritime expeditions, and general revulsion at the Ming state's militant expression of overlordship in maritime Asia—an overlordship that too closely resembled the earlier pattern of Mongol aggression. All this, and the resurgence of Mongol power in the north, sparked a sweeping reappraisal of Ming strategic priorities that redirected attention once again to the Inner Asian borderlands. The result was a major logistical withdrawal from the coast and maritime affairs, the abandonment of the Annam "quagmire," and the relocation of the main capital to Peking in the north.[44] Similarly, foreign relations, defenses, and logistical supply networks were redirected northwards.

The Yongle Emperor undertook the reconstruction of the Grand Canal (1411–15) to conform to these new strategic priorities. The canal again, as in Sui–Tang times, became the pivot of strategic communications and logistical supply, and sea transport was abandoned.[45] The emperor's program centered on the two sectors of the canal that posed the greatest threat to safe, efficient grain transport: the mountainous Shandong "Canal of Gates" and the Southern, or Huaiyang, Canal lying between the Huai–Yellow River and the Yangzi River (map 7). The problems with the former centered on augmenting and manipulating water supplies to maintain adequate levels in the canal, while those of the latter focused on the destructive effects of the Huai–Yellow River on the Huaiyang Canal.[46]

The reconstruction of the Huaiyang Canal was assigned to one of the Ming dynasty's most gifted administrators, Chen Xuan, who was then serving as the chief commander of the sea transport system.[47] Chen masterminded the changeover to inland, canal-based transport. To protect the Huaiyang Canal from the overflow from the lake reservoirs on its western side (map 7), he organized the construction of a dike system along the east shore of the lakes that was periodically extended and strengthened throughout the dynasty. The main part of the system was a stone-faced dike, the Gaojia *yan*, built along the eastern perimeter of Hongze Lake for 15 kilometers.[48] This dike was later rebuilt and extended in the late Ming and early Qing periods, reaching a length of 68 kilometers and a height of 9 meters, with a base thickness of 50 meters and a crown thickness of 6 meters. Because of the downward slope of the land eastward and the gradual siltation of the lake bed, the lake lay from four to eight meters above the plain.[49] To facilitate the evacuation of water from the lake reservoirs, the Ming devised a drainage network in the sixteenth century that drew water from the lakes into the canal through sluice gates built into the sides of the canal's western embankment; then, depending on conditions, the floods exited to the sea via the Yangzi River or else were discharged into the Xiahe region through sluice gates on the eastern canal dike.[50]

By the late Ming period, the imperial state faced two challenges to river control in the corridor from Henan to the sea. First, the siltation of the Yellow River caused flooding and meandering that made it difficult to transport grain up the short stretch of the river from Huai'an to Xuzhou used as part of the canal route. Second, flooding across the Yellow River's south bank led to seepage into and siltation of Hongze Lake, raising the lake ever higher, putting the lake dikes at risk, and increasing the threat of floods in Huaiyang. These problems sparked a radical new approach to river control, devised by the practical-minded river engineer, Pan Jixun. As explained earlier, Pan rejected the conventional wisdom of the time about dispersing the river in its lower reaches into several channels. He rightly pointed out that this method increased siltation because it decreased the velocity of the current. Pan argued that the current should be constricted, or concentrated, to increase velocity, which would minimize siltation and naturally scour out preexisting silt from the river bed.

From 1565 to 1580, Pan undertook to narrow and dredge the Yellow River bed and to intensify the Huai flow from Hongze to its confluence with the Yellow River by raising the lake dikes and streamlining the diversion channels leading from the lake into the river (maps 7, 8). This use of the clear lake water to flush out the canal–Yellow River junction became the crux of hydraulic policy in the Qing period. Pan was not completely successful in carrying out all his plans, but his approach became the dominant one used later by Jin Fu (1633–1692) and other Qing hydraulic engineers until the early nineteenth century, when the practical possibilities of this approach were exhausted, and the Yellow River loomed high above the Huai plain, poised for its northward shift.[51]

The Grand Canal 35

Ming engineers made the last major addition to the Grand Canal in 1604, when they constructed a short bypass canal between Suqian on the Yellow River and Xiazhen on the Shandong border. This canal shortened the distance that canal boats normally traveled on the Yellow River and eliminated altogether the passage through the dangerous rapids south of Xuzhou, which had proved very costly in terms of lost grain, vessels, and human life. A century later, the Qing state extended the bypass canal from Suqian southeastward to Yangzhuang village (map 7) on the north bank of the river opposite the canal junction near Huai'an. This move eliminated all travel on the Yellow River other than the direct crossing to the river's north bank.[52]

The Ming regime developed a large and complex bureaucratic organization that insured, at least in theory, imperial control of every facet of Grand Canal–grain transport operations. The government monopoly of these operations reflected both the strategic weight attached to them and the growth of imperial absolutism that characterized the Ming period. The Ming emperors devised an administrative system that placed executive power exclusively in their hands, enabling them to deal directly with the central ministries and with a network of censorate, military, and circuit-prefectural (*daofu*) officials at the middle and lower levels of regional government.[53]

Grand Canal–grain transport management reflected this emperor-centered model. A regionally based directorate located at Qingjiangpu (map 7), headed by a canal commissioner after 1450, coordinated the tasks of a wide range of central and regional agencies, which included the Public Works, Finance, and Military ministries, special regional grain and canal officers, provincial officials, and finally, at the lowest levels, peasant communities adjacent to the canal. The commissioner became one of the most important regional officials in the Ming imperial state because of his direct appointment by and access to the emperor. Yet, for all its prestige, the commissioner's position suffered from the same weakness that afflicted the regular territorial bureaucracy. He had little executive authority. In spite of his ability to report directly to the emperor, he had no staff of his own but relied instead on a range of officials from other agencies to carry out the tasks connected with the canal and grain transportation.[54]

The military dominated the canal directorate when it was first organized by Chen Xuan in the Yongle reign. Though civil officials gradually took over its leadership, the military continued to play a major role in the grain collection and delivery process. The military organization charged with the shipping of grain was one of the many sprawling parts of the canal–grain transport system.[55] Over the course of the Ming period, the military collection network was expanded, with the number of collection stations increased to facilitate the delivery of grain tax by peasant producers.[56]

By the end of the dynasty, the strategic importance of this critical supply system had increased as the Ming faced major threats on the northern frontier, especially in Manchuria (map 10). As northern supply networks broke down, frontier garrisons grew increasingly dependent on grain shipped by canal to the capital and thence overland. Although sea transport might have proved beneficial as a supplement to canal transport at this time, the Ming planners were unwilling to expose strategic grain supplies to the double risks of the ocean voyage around the Shandong promontory and piracy, which was rampant in the sixteenth and early seventeenth centuries.[57] The grand seafaring traditions of the early Ming state lay forgotten as the Ming leadership continued to cling to the canal as the only viable means of supplying the capital.

The Grand Canal in Qing Times

By the Qing period, the strategic and historical significance of the Grand Canal was embedded in the rich cultural matrix of values, institutions, laws, and precedents that comprised the Chinese imperial state. The images of the canal—its trains of grain junks lashed together "nose to tail," its gangs of trackers pulling junks through the shallows, the legions of laborers engaged in the seasonal tasks of reconstruction and maintenance—all evoked the power of the imperial state, its strategic-logistical contours, and its demonstrated ability to mobilize human and material resources to secure peace and stability throughout the empire.

Fig. 9 Trackers pulling canal boat.

Heirs to these images and symbols, the Qing emperors invested Grand Canal communications with even greater strategic significance than had the dynasties that preceded them. Their concern with the canal stemmed, first, from the bloody resistance to their rule they had encountered in the seventeenth century in the provinces that lay along the canal and, second, from their unique view of empire, which went beyond the limits of China proper to encompass the Inner Asian borderlands in a vast multi-ethnic empire of Greater China (map 10). To guarantee its control and security, the Manchu emperors fashioned a new military-logistical system, in which the capital at Peking functioned as a pivot connecting the two main axes of the empire—the borderlands and the Chinese heartland. The capital was also, from the Qing point of view, a Manchu ship in a sea of Chinese. Its grain supplies depended utterly on open communications with the Yangzi valley and on the smooth uninterrupted operation of the Grand Canal–grain transport system.

The Qing emperors scrutinized canal communications with great care throughout the dynasty, considering them essential to their logistical and fiscal control of the capital. They shrewdly shaped agricultural, military, and coastal policy to pacify and secure the canal zone and relied exclusively and unwaveringly on a state-run, canal-based system of inland transport rather than sea transport. The commitment to canal transport, initially, was shaped by what they perceived as the greater safety of inland shipping. This assessment reflected not only centuries of experience prior to the Qing, but also unique conditions in the Qing period itself.

The Ming logistical retreat from the coast and maritime world had left the coastal region vulnerable and unprotected in comparison with the Yuan and early Ming periods. The coast hovered between a state of lawlessness and autonomy due to the capricious and restrictive approach of the Ming to coastal shipping and commercial interests. Piracy developed as a direct consequence of Ming coastal policy and left many parts of the region devastated for over a century. What is more, the Ming retreat from maritime affairs and naval development increased the regime's ignorance of ocean sailing, which in turn exaggerated the not insignificant risks of navigating northward around the Shandong promotory, a route that was essential if grain was to reach the capital by sea. Added to piracy and the dangers of ocean sailing was the troubling appearance of Western traders, mainly Portuguese and Dutch, who had a far different approach to maritime trade on China's coast than had the traders of maritime Asia.[58]

The preference for inland, canal-based shipping was intensified in the Ming–Qing transition because of the Manchus' landed orientation and because of the strategic importance of the canal zone. They faced the threat of piracy on the southeast coast and Taiwan (map 10), led by the Zheng regime (1645–83), which was committed to the downfall of

The Grand Canal   39

the Manchus. The Zheng assault on the lower Yangzi cities of Zhenjiang, Yangzhou, and Nanjing (map 1) in 1659 epitomized all the dangers the Chinese associated with the maritime world: piracy, the penetration of the lower Yangzi valley, and the blockage of the Grand Canal at the Yangzi River junction.

Although the Qing regime accomplished the pacification and integration of the coastal region with supportive policies, especially the legalization of maritime trade, problems persisted on the coast: rebellion in Taiwan; continued Western trade in the coastal ports; the clandestine infiltration by Christian mendicant friars propagating a heterodox faith; the scourge of piracy along the coast from Zhejiang to Guangdong (map 10) in the late eighteenth and early nineteenth centuries; and, finally, the increasing momentum of British trade, which outstripped the Canton system's ability to manage it.[59] All of these developments served as ominous reminders of the dangers of the maritime world and reaffirmed the wisdom of inland, canal-based transport and its hallowed position as a fundamental and unchanging institution of imperial government.[60]

During the Jiaqing and Daoguang reigns (1796–1850), as a result of the growth of coastal shipping and private trade between the lower Yangzi and northeastern ports and the growing crisis in grain transport caused by the meandering and flooding of the Yellow River, emperor and officials alike began cautiously to reconsider sea transport.[61] When they undertook the 1826 sea-transport experiment, the Daoguang Emperor himself openly refuted the old myths about the dangers of ocean sailing, noting that private shippers routinely used the sea route from Shanghai to the northeastern ports of Shandong, Zhili, and Fengtian and that the sea route need not be feared as it had in the past.[62] Yet, in spite of the Qing leadership's growing willingness to put aside old fears and use sea transport during the last stages of the collapse of the canal, new security threats made it impossible to do so. Taiping penetration of the lower Yangzi valley from 1853 to 1864 severed Grand Canal communications and river traffic to Shanghai, while Western enclaves on the coast after the Opium War (1839–42) eroded Qing control of coastal communications.

The risks and danger evoked by the maritime world and ocean sailing, combined with the Qing leadership's greater strategic emphasis on the canal, gave the tradition of canal-based transport renewed ritual-political force and the status of a fundamental institution of the imperial state. In retrospect, it is difficult to measure the precise depth and embeddedness of feelings about the significance of canal-based grain transport. It does emerge, however, as a consistent and powerful theme in imperial and official writings, sometimes sincerely, sometimes to mask other political-economic motives. In either case, it had merit in the eyes of the Manchu regime until the very end.

Modern scholars, impressive for their ability to project the modern Eurocentric experience back to an earlier age, have long decried the system of government-controlled canal transport for its waste, corruption, and inefficiency, and they have condemned imperial commitment to the canal as backward-looking and mindless, especially when Yellow River floods continually disrupted regular canal shipments in the early nineteenth century. These culture-bound judgments obscure the powerful symbolism attached to the canal and the centuries of historical experience that highlighted the real risks associated with ocean sailing. Early Qing history shows how these powerful images and imperatives sparked gargantuan hydraulic engineering works and important changes in canal management that improved and streamlined the canal-transport system for much of the dynasty.

Because of the strategic significance of the canal to the empire, and because Qing control of the canal zone was fiercely contested in the early reigns, the Qing emperors took an activist role in the day-to-day administration of the canal–grain transport system, a role made possible by innovations in the decision-making process. As will be discussed below in chapters 2 and 3, their administrative direction gave them a tight hold over the canal system; it enabled them to streamline aspects of this incredibly complex bureaucratic organization; and it enabled them to build and maintain massive public works projects designed to "defend the canal" from Yellow River floods and maintain yearly shipments of grain tribute to the capital. Yet for all their energy, skill, and flexibility, the Qing emperors were destined to fight a bold but losing battle.[63]

The successful operation of the canal–grain transport system hinged on the state's ability to control the Yellow River and the process of siltation that accompanied its flow across the China plain to the sea.[64] During the late Ming and Qing periods, the problems intensified in the corridor along the lower reaches of the river from Henan eastward, including the Huaiyang region to the south (map 3). The narrow-diking system introduced by Pan Jixun in the sixteenth century exacerbated siltation at the mouth of the river, clogging it and causing it to back up, generating a constant pattern of meandering and flooding further upstream. When these backflows spilled over the south bank of the Yellow River, they flowed into Hongze Lake through two drainage gates, Xiangfu and Wushui, on its north side (map 7).[65] These channels had originally been designed to divert clear lake water into the river to scour silt from its bed. However, as the river bed rose and backflows increased, seepage from the river entered the lake, raising its bed with silt and reducing its holding capacity. Additionally, floods often overflowed into the canal junction, clogging it with silt and making it impassable for canal shipping.

Hongze Lake was the collecting basin for the Huai River drainage to the west, as well as a receptacle for excess water from the Yellow River. As explained earlier, when its water reached dangerous heights, it was diverted into the adjacent lakes to the south and, finally, into the Southern, or Huaiyang Canal, from which it was either drained into the Xiahe region, east of the canal, or diverted southward into the Yangzi (maps 3, 7). Each successive flood brought more silt into the whole network which, in turn, reduced the holding capacity of its lake reservoirs, Hongze, Baima, Baoying, Gaoyou, and Shaobo lakes, and the navigability of the junction passageways.[66]

The Qing regime approached these seemingly irreversible conditions with characteristic energy and with a holistic strategy that saw the critical relationship of the parts to the whole canal-riverine network. The strategy, put into practice in the Kangxi reign (1662–1722), was based on Pan Jixun's narrow-diking scheme. Hydraulic engineering work centered on the improvement of two facilities that guaranteed the safe passage of grain fleets throught the canal–Yellow River junction. The first was the expansion of the drainage facilities north and south of the Yellow River; the second was the dual use of Hongze Lake to contain the Huai summer floods and divert flood water through the canal's junction passage into the Yellow River. The latter process of flushing the junction passage helped to float the grain boats safely through the junction and scour the junction passage and adjacent river bed. This dual use was termed the "Hongze strategy" and was the pivot of hydraulic engineering in the Huaiyang section of the canal (see fig. 10).

The Huaiyang Canal lay a few meters below the level of the Yellow River, and this disparity increased as the silt on the river bed rose over the course of the dynasty. The junction was fitted with a series of three flash locks, Fuxing, Tongji, and Huiji, located at the canal head, which raised the passing vessels closer to the level of the river (map 8). The ships then passed out of the Huaiyang Canal into a final corridor called the Clear River, or Clear Passage (Qinghe), which extended from the Shuqing Lock gate at the neck of Hongze Lake through a series of weir-like structures to the final Yuhuang Lock gate and into the Yellow River. The Clear Passage functioned as the final and largest lock in the junction. Its water level was raised to that of the river by opening up five lead, or diversion, channels (*yinhe*) from Hongze Lake: Zhangfukou, Tianran, Zhangjiazhuang, Feijiachang, and Taiping (map 8).[67]

The Grand Canal

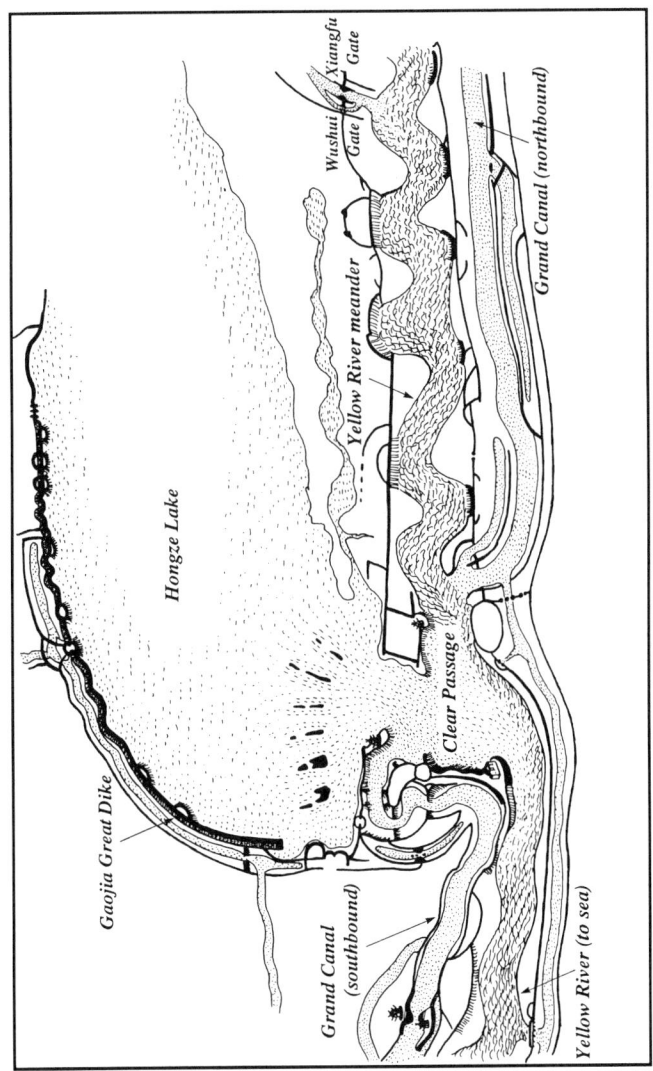

Fig. 10 The Hongze strategy: Lake water cascading through the Grand Canal–Yellow River junction (BLOC 2362).

The flow of the entering lake water was constricted, raised, and quickened through the passage with the aid of weir-like projections so that when vessels passed out into the Yellow River through Yuhuang gate, the force of the clear Hongze water both scoured silt out of the passage and countered the inrush of silted Yellow River water, saving the Clear Passage and canal head from silt damage.[68]

The Qing leadership struggled continuously with the construction of the junction facilities over the course of the dynasty. It was a long and arduous task requiring experimentation and frequent changes in the location of the junction mouth and in the configuration of the installations within the junction.[69] On each outer side of the junction passage, protective dike embankments and deflection dikes, reinforced by reed fascines, held the Yellow River at bay, while tracking or hauling roads on the embankment causeways allowed trackers to drag the grain boats through the junction when the water levels were low and the silt high.[70] According to British travelers who viewed the canal in the late eighteenth and early nineteenth centuries, the passage through the junction took about three hours.[71]

Besides the improvement of junction facilities, the Qing engineers devised a complicated drainage network for the Yellow River corridor from Henan to the sea. These projects were designed to protect the southern end of the Shandong Canal and its fragile water supply system while at the same time providing drainage networks and deflection devices to draw the Yellow River away from its south bank, the canal junction, and the Huaiyang region. One of the most valuable drainage channels, which was to figure importantly in the 1820s canal crisis, was that leading through the Wangying gate into the Salt Canal (Yanhe) north of and parallel to the canal–Yellow River junction (map 8).[72]

A second major drainage channel lay south of the Yellow River and east of the lakes, where land elevation drops in a southeastward direction toward the sea. This network was designed to achieve the controlled release of flood waters and Yellow River seepage from

Hongze Lake into the Grand Canal, and divert it either into the Xiahe region or the Yangzi outlets (maps 7, 9).[73]

At the beginning of the Qing, neither the Yangzi outlets nor the Xiahe drainage network could handle the volume of flood water flowing in from the lakes region.[74] The Yangzi outlets were limited in number and scale, and the Xiahe channels operated with minimal efficiency, even when they were well-maintained, because of the bowl-shaped topography of the area. Xiahe was, in effect, a sink without a drain. Prior to the Qing period, the state's strategic need to protect the canal took precedence over the needs of agriculture and the salt industry, which depended on the matrix of canals across Xiahe for irrigation, flood control, and shipping. Flood waters were routinely drained into Xiahe from overflow gates in the eastern canal dike. The Qing regime, however, took greater responsibility for water control in Xiahe in order to protect the livelihood of the region, which they considered essential to the pacification of the area. The Kangxi Emperor undertook the reconstruction of flood control facilities in Xiahe in the period of economic restoration; and later, in the eighteenth century, the state expanded the Yangzi outlets. Drainage regulations coordinated the opening of overflow dams on the lake dikes with those on the Yangzi outlets and, when necessary, the gates on the eastern canal dike leading into Xiahe. The Qing state improved and expanded the overflow gates throughout the canal-riverine system, especially the stone-buttressed overflow gates in the dikes containing Hongze Lake and those on the eastern dike of the Grand Canal between Shaobo and Gaoyou, including Nanguan, Nanguanxin, Wulizhong, Chelo, and Zhaoguan gates (map 7).[75]

Dikes and embankments also played a crucial role in drainage, flood control, and the operation of the junction facilities south of the Yellow River. Dikes lined the south bank of the Yellow River, the eastern perimeter of Hongze, the Huaiyang Canal, and the fragile, complex junction facilities.[76] The dike system containing Hongze Lake was the pivot of the entire water-control network and shipment process through the junction. It was approximately two-hundred kilometers in length, and its cornerstone was the large stone-faced section on the eastern side of the lake, now called Gaojia Great Dike (Gaojia *dadi*, or *yan*; map 9). The great dike, originally built in the early Ming period, extended southward for 68 kilometers, from the Yellow River junction to Zhou Bridge.[77] It was buttressed by a network of earthen embankments that lay behind it to the east. These were designed to slow the rush of flood water from the lake and divert it away from the canal junction to the north and into the Huaiyang drainage network.

Overflow gates built into the sides of Gaojia dike and other lake embankments were a crucial part of the dike structures, especially the Zhi, Linjia, Xin, Jiang, Lanhu, Ren, Yi, and Lizi gates.[78] They were designed for easy opening when flood waters reached dangerous heights. By opening these gates before the flood waters actually ruptured and destroyed the dikes, Qing engineers were able to reduce the damage to the stonework on the dikes and, at the same time, channel the water into drainage canals rather than into peasant fields. The combination of dikes and overflow gates became extremely important as Hongze expanded and as Yellow River seepage and siltation in the lake increased and reduced its holding capacity. Therefore, to hold more water plus the silt, the dikes had to be raised layer by layer over the years. This created a lake that lay several meters above the plain to the east.[79] And as the overflow gates became submerged in mud, they had to be dredged out or repositioned on higher ground and rebuilt.[80]

The Qing planners, following Pan Jixun's approach, decided to make the high water in Hongze work for them to facilitate grain shipment through the canal–Yellow River junction. During the early Qing, when the lake was clear and largely unsilted, they channeled its water out into the Yellow River through the junction in a constricted and focused course that would both scour out the junction and resist the inflows of the Yellow River with its damaging silt (fig. 10). This became the "customary method" for crossing grain boats at the junction and was termed "accumulating the clear to attack the Yellow." This method depended on high levels of clear Huai water in the lake, on ever higher dikes, and on more efficient overflow gates to manage the dispersion of flood waters when levels became dangerously high.

This strategy for navigating the junction was, of course, risky. It utilized high water levels but had to guard against excessively high levels that could burst Gaojia dike, damage the canal, and flood the Xiahe region. It depended absolutely on a well-dredged drainage network that could carry off flood waters quickly during emergencies. The twin goals of holding back floods and channeling clear, unsilted water through the junction were increasingly difficult to achieve by the late eighteenth century, when silt levels compromised the whole system and ominously portended an imminent shift in the Yellow River's course.

The scale and increasing complexity of the canal-riverine system in northern Jiangsu made state responsibility for its construction, maintenance, and repair absolutely essential throughout the dynasty. The Qing regime followed a rigorous cycle of maintenance and repair to guarantee the successful operation of the canal–grain transport system. The cycle was determined by seasonal imperatives connected to the grain shipment calendar and to the pattern of rainfall and floods. The dikes, embankments, and gate structures on the Yellow River and the lakes, as well as the connected drainage networks and overflow gates were dredged and repaired in winter and spring when the Huai and Yellow rivers were at their lowest. In contrast, the dredging of the junction and the Huaiyang and Shandong canals was completed in the summer and autumn, after the grain fleets had passed northward and before their return in the tenth lunar month. The repair of ships was sandwiched in between the shipping cycles of the various fleets, each of which was slightly different depending on a fleet's province of origin and distance from the capital.[81]

The cycle had to be maintained on schedule; its seasonal imperatives were uncompromising. Its dictates were embedded in administrative law and the traditions of the imperial ancestors of dynasties past. The Qing emperors bowed to these regulations, for to do otherwise was to court disaster. They also reshaped canal-transport administration to insure disciplined adherence to the regulations, which they viewed as a rudder in a sea of natural calamities and administrative complexity.

In spite of the scale and complexity of the canal's water-control network, and advances in the bureaucratic management of the system, the Qing state was losing its battle against silt by the late Qianlong reign. The canal, lakes, rivers, and drainage canals were all silted and their beds upraised, and overflow gates were mired in mud. Hongze Lake, the symbol of this sisyphean drama, mirrored the problems of the whole system: more seepage from the Yellow River, higher silt levels, less holding capability, and higher water levels. Hongze was perilously high, yet not high enough to use against the Yellow for the junction crossing. Frank admission of the seriousness of the silt problem was demonstrated in 1785 when, for the first time, Yellow River backspills were used to cross grain boats at the junction.[82] Backspills were used when lake water flowing into the junction was too weak to resist the inflow of silted river water as Yuhuang Lock gate was opened to cross the grain boats. In such a case, the boats were pulled through the junction on the silted river water, or backflows, that rushed into the junction passageway. Even though this practice intensified silt damage to the junction and canal head, there seemed to be no way out, and the practice was continued with increasing frequency in the Jiaqing reign (1796–1820).

The deepening canal crisis hovered over the imperial house like a grim specter, casting doubt on the regime's logistical hold over its vast empire and its ability to cope with a problem that, in fact, had no solution. In response to growing instability in canal–grain transport operations, the Qing emperors intensified their search for options, temporary though they might be, in the face of the Yellow River's impending shift. They continued to monitor the canal–grain transport process with scrupulous care and to intervene in its administration, directing discourse with regional officials on such options as the repair and reconstruction of water-control facilities, lighterage (*panbo*) on the Huaiyang Canal, transfer-shipping (*panba jieyun*) which used lighterage for the entire trip to the capital, temporary commutation of grain quotas to raise money for repairs, and, lastly, sea transport of grain tribute from the south. Yet, emperor and officials alike knew the situation could not be reversed or solved for the future because the "Yellow River could not be controlled by human means."[83]

By the mid-1820s, makeshift methods of transfer-shipping on the canal were used increasingly, as were Yellow River backflows to make the junction crossing. Meandering and flooding intensified throughout the 1840s as the Yellow River began its shift northward. The final shift occurred between 1851 and 1855, with the main branch of the river moving north in 1852.[84] Devastating floods continued for the rest of the dynasty as this mighty river established its new bed, while invading rebels and foreigners watched from the sidelines. But all that lay in the future at the time that the Daoguang Emperor embarked on his new reign in 1821 and struggled with the Gaojia dike disaster from 1824 to 1826.

2

The View from the Palace

Political Reality in the 1820s

The Daoguang Emperor's leadership during the Grand Canal crisis in the first decade of his reign was profoundly shaped by his perception of political reality in the 1820s. Shifting images of past experience, present challenges, and expectations for the future intermeshed to form his view of the times. His daily review of incoming memorials revealed the formidable problems that required solution if the dynasty were to survive. The economy, which had fared so well in earlier reigns, showed signs of dislocation and instability because of inflation, fluctuations in the monetary and market systems, and a downward spiral in grain prices that made the yearly collection of land taxes even more problematic than it had been in the two previous reigns. These ominous signs portended danger to the "state's fiscal resources and the people's livelihood" (*guoji minsheng*).[1]

The organizational resilience and effectiveness of the state also seemed diminished, with neither focus nor momentum. The Heshen scandals of the late eighteenth century had rocked bureaucratic confidence, while systemic weaknesses, exacerbated by demographic crisis, had paralyzed regional government at its lowest levels. The very fabric of the state seemed to have worn thin, loosened, and unraveled, incapable of suppressing the unrest and violence that erupted with increasing frequency throughout the empire—on the coast, in the borderlands, and in the interior of China itself. By the time of the Daoguang succession (1821), the Qing state had witnessed over three decades of intermittant outbursts of popular revolt and lawlessness. Piracy had plagued the coast from Zhejiang to Guangdong (map 10). Sufi extremism and clumsy Qing military leadership had ignited the volatile region of Altishahr in southwest Chinese

Turkestan (map 10). And the very heartland of China proper had experienced peasant, tribal, and Muslim rebellions. All three issues—economic instability, bureaucratic malaise, and deteriorating internal security—if left unresolved, could intensify and threaten the very foundations of the Qing state.²

Yet, while these issues loomed large in the emperor's assessment of his situation, powerful recollections countered and overshadowed them. Three historic threads gave inspiration and direction to the new emperor as he defined his agenda and his approach to the exercise of imperial power. The first was the administrative legacy of the Qing monarchy, which had achieved a level of bureaucratic discipline and efficiency unmatched in earlier dynastic periods. The second was the dazzling accomplishments of Qing empire building which resulted in a vastly expanded empire of Greater China. In this expanded China, the peoples and territories of the Inner Asian borderlands were bound in a new and much more intimate relationship to China proper. The third was the Qing emperors' long tradition of active stewardship of the economy, which, while undertaken to enhance security and the logistical control of the empire, had nonetheless sparked unprecedented prosperity, growth, and structural change in the various regional economies of China. All three spoke of the power and achievements of Qing rule. They ordered the past, set the agenda for the present, and etched an uneasy but essentially positive view of prospects for the future of the new emperor's reign, if he continued in the footsteps of his ancestors.

The Daoguang Emperor had ample time to reflect on the accomplishments of his imperial forebears and the challenges of his times as he waited on the sidelines until age thirty-nine before ascending the throne in 1821. Since his birth in 1782, he had been reared and educated to fit the Manchu image of kingship, and his childhood name, Mianning, captured the dynasty's hope for a future of "Unbroken Peace," a future that was, unfortunately, not to eventuate. Mianning participated in the great summer hunts in Jehol with his grandfather,

The View from the Palace

the Qianlong Emperor, and his father, the Jiaqing Emperor. Here the imperial princes and sons of the Qing nobility were initiated into the Manchu manly arts and the traditions of comraderie, discipline, and austerity associated with military campaigning.[3] The School for Princes and its Confucian tutors grafted the Manchu military ideal onto the age-old tradition of Confucian monarchy, with its intense emphasis on the cosmic, moral, and political imperatives associated with imperial rule.[4] In 1799, when the Jiaqing Emperor finally assumed all the powers of emperorship at the death of the aged Qianlong, Mianning, then seventeen, was secretly designated heir to the throne. Coming of age in the troubled years of the late Qianlong and early Jiaqing reigns, he witnessed the brewing storm over Heshen and the crisis that accompanied his fall. He was old enough also to understand the reappraisal of Qing rule implicit in the Jiaqing reforms, as well as to observe imperial response to unrest and rebellion and concern over fiscal weakness.

As Mianning grew to adulthood, he developed a reputation as a serious student with interests in Confucian learning and writing, and he composed volumes of prose and poetry before assuming the throne.[5] He projected a personal style of austerity, down-to-earth practicality, and great decency in his relationships with friends. He also had significant personal courage, as his response to the Eight Trigrams' assault on the imperial palace demonstrated on October 8, 1813. Returning to Peking from Jehol ahead of the Jiaqing Emperor and his entourage, he was present in the Forbidden City when a gang of rebels gained entry to the palace grounds through the connivance of traitorous eunuchs. As the alarm was sounded, the prince rushed to the scene. When he and his young brother, Miankai, spotted the rebels scaling the wall near Longzong Gate and poised to enter the Great Interior, he seized a musket and shot two of them, even though the use of firearms within the palace precincts was forbidden. After ensuring the safety of the empress, he joined the group of princes, eunuchs, and palace guards that hunted down and captured the remaining rebels.[6] His spontaneous response and courage in the face of personal danger marked him as a worthy successor to the Jiaqing Emperor, and as one who could be relied on to restore the dynasty's fortunes in the face of crises spawned by the Heshen scandals and the fiscal strains unleashed by demographic crisis in the first decades of the nineteenth century.[7]

Imperial Administrative Leadership

As Mianning watched and waited for his turn to ascend the dragon throne, he must have looked back with intense pride at the way his imperial ancestors had exercised and expanded the powers of Confucian monarchy. These non-Han monarchs, heirs of the tribal leader Nurgaci, had worn the mantle of kingship with verve and flourish while moving swiftly and ruthlessly to correct institutional weaknesses in the imperial state they had inherited from the Ming. Their bold innovations in the political process vastly expanded imperial control over the practical aspects of administration in sectors of government considered crucial to the perpetuation of Qing rule.

The early Qing monarchs manipulated the powers of emperorship with great ingenuity. Publicly, they assumed all the trappings and symbols of traditional Confucian monarchy and performed the cosmic, state, and ancestral rites with scrupulous care. They drew a hostile literati class into Qing service through public acts of benevolence and generous patronage of scholarship, bibliographic collection, and art. They personally mastered the core of Neo-Confucian learning to enhance their own image as sage and moral leaders, and they created ideological unity throughout the empire by adopting the most conservative and authoritarian aspects of Neo-Confucianism as the basis of public ethics and morality. All these cosmic, moral, and political responsibilities were displayed and performed to perfection to demonstrate Qing legitimacy in the best tradition of Chinese imperial rule.[8]

While publicly adopting all the monarchical traditions of the past, the Manchu emperors secretly pursued their own agenda and crafted radical new political institutions to achieve it. Their ultimate aim was the restructuring of the empire to include the borderlands in an expanded multi-ethnic state, and they supported this adventure by restoring and stabilizing the economy and fiscal system. Crucial to the achievement of their goals was a decision-making process that gave them a free hand to innovate and respond to political reality as they perceived it. Unfortunately, the imperial state they inherited from the Ming dynasty had structural weaknesses that undermined administrative efficiency.

By late Ming times, the emperor had come to dominate imperial government and was the symbolic expression of the state. His dominance was expressed in cosmic, moral, and raw political terms. Much of his role as Confucian monarch centered on the public performance of state rituals that emphasized his awesome power and political charisma (*de*) which theoretically radiated outwards, creating order and stability throughout the world.[9] But in addition to these elaborate ceremonial functions associated with his public persona, the emperor had access to almost unlimited power in the late imperial period, if he chose to use it. The expansion of imperial authority had resulted from changes in the state structure from Song to Ming times that led to the elimination of top-level official-executive posts in both central and regional government. This enabled the emperors to monopolize the top agencies of the central government as well as to reach down directly to lower-level circuit and prefectural officials, with no intermediate-level posts, such as governorships, to interfere with the control of regional administration.[10] The elimination of central and regional executive officials vested much more power and responsibility for the day-to-day affairs of government in imperial hands and greatly expanded the emperor's control over the political-administrative process.[11]

Yet in spite of the expansion of imperial power during the Ming period, there was, in fact, no institutional provision for imperial monitoring of the administrative process on a day-to-day basis. The elimination of executive posts weakened the state, leaving a power vacuum at both the regional and central levels. Imperial dominance of the political process also inhibited and curtailed official action. The emperor's usurpation of official functions curbed official initiative, advisory functions, and the exercise of remonstrance. It also spawned a great unwillingness to challenge administrative law, especially the traditions of the dynasty's ancestors. The emperors essentially turned the best and brightest officials into functionaries who had to approach political action and change with great care and circumspection.[12] Officials could not be seen to lead in the formulation of new policies or ideas because this, in itself, violated imperial prerogatives and challenged the traditions of the imperial ancestors. Ironically, the growth of imperial authority actually weakened the state by overburdening the emperor and intimidating bureaucratic officials. In response to these constraints, both emperor and official tended to seek refuge in administrative precedents and the ponderous workings of the outer court bureaucracy.

Far-reaching changes in Confucian monarchy in the Qing period eliminated these systemic weaknesses and gave both emperors (with their inner court advisers)[13] and regional officials more room to maneuver to effect change.[14] The founders of the Qing state took a hard look at the institutions they had inherited from the Ming and, with great skill, identified the major weaknesses of the Ming structure: first, the emperor was out of touch with and remote from changing day-to-day realities facing regional government; and, second, that administrative law, interpreted by the central outer-court administrative agencies, guided the affairs of state, not imperial initiative. This spelled danger because it meant that the power center at the capital was unresponsive to changing conditions in the provinces, a situation that could ultimately challenge and undermine the dynasty itself.

To correct these problems, the Qing rulers created permanent executive posts, governors and governors-general, in the provinces in contrast to the temporary duty assignments (*chaiqian*) of the Ming period. They then reorganized government communications to place decisional power in the hands of the emperor and his inner court advisers who worked directly and secretly with top regional officials. These changes began gradually in the Kangxi reign and crystallized during the Yongzheng (1723–25) and early Qianlong reigns (1736–38), and they enabled the inner court to bypass the slow-moving, precedent-bound central administrative agencies.[15] These agencies generally crafted administrative strategies based on precedents contained in the Qing administrative code, rather than on concrete conditions. These rules defined how things ought to be, but not necessarily how they were in actual fact.

The emperor imposed his control over the decisional process by his daily review of incoming palace memorials from the provinces. He registered his response to these reports with a personal endorsement, or rescript, placed directly on the memorial. If an issue raised in a memorial was deemed routine, the matter was referred to the appropriate administrative agency for handling. If, instead, urgent or potentially threatening problems were reported that bore on crucial areas of government, the emperor, with the advice of his inner court advisers and the benefit of deliberations of other expert officials in the capital, responded with the dispatch of a secret edit, or court letter.[16] The despatch of a court letter signaled the inner court's intention to participate in specific administrative decisions, and it initiated the direct, semi-secret dialogue between emperor and regional officials that was the principal channel for non-routine decision making in the Qing period.

The daily review of secret memorials with his Grand Council advisers gave the emperor a profound sense of the rhythm of the empire and regional government, and it enabled him to monitor regional affairs and work quickly and efficiently with regional officials to solve urgent problems that threatened the dynasty. The flow of information and planning options from the provinces provided the imperial center with a realistic picture of regional conditions in those select areas of government that were of special concern to the imperial leadership.[17] Armed with this knowledge, the Qing emperors could be selective and focus their energies on high-priority and dangerous issues, leaving routine and mundane matters to functionaries in the central administrative agencies. In the Qing period, these select issues included: 1) the maintenance of ideological-ritual orthodoxy; 2) the creation of a strong military and logistical network capable of maintaining internal and external security; and 3) the promotion of social-economic stability through low taxes and fiscal restraint, the careful maintenance of a bimetallic monetary system, regulatory mediation in the private economy, and investment in the hydraulic infrastructure. Because of innovations in the decisional process, the Qing emperors were able to attend to these core issues with discipline and dispatch.[18]

The Qing decisional system also empowered regional officials, who were brought directly into the decision-making process with the emperor and his closest advisory officials in the capital. It expanded their responsibility for crafting practical solutions to emerging problems and contributed to the disciplined administration of imperial policy at the regional level.[19] If officials had a hand in creating administrative strategies and stood behind them, the chances of successful implementation were greatly enhanced. If regional officials were not behind a policy or felt it was unworkable, as was the case with grain tax commutation in 1825, it did not stand a chance of rigorous enforcement.[20] Finally, Qing decisional communications fostered a consensual interplay between the imperial center and regional officials in the creation of governing strategies that reduced the potential for imperial abuse of power and recklessness and maximized the experience, creativity, and accountability of regional officials. With this balance between center and region, the emperor was able to "control from afar" (*yaozhi*) through the efforts of regional officials, maximizing both regional initiative and central imperial control.

Overall, the use of court letter and the consensual discourse it fostered created what may have been the greatest legacy of early Qing imperial activism—the tradition of decisional flexibility in response to changing political realities, rather than adherence to any single administrative policy or strategy. This tradition empowered later emperors to set their own agendas and use the court letter freely to supersede and bypass outdated administrative law. The daily imperial review of governing problems also produced a much stronger and more consistent pattern of imperial administrative leadership than had been the case in the Ming period. This pattern was maintained until the regency in 1861, after which the grand councillors carried this responsibility alone and thereby "prolonged the life of the dynasty despite the ascendancy of figurehead emperors."[21] It is inconceivable to imagine any of the preregency Qing emperors whining as the Ming emperor Wanli did about having to attend to daily matters of state.[22] Nor can one imagine high officials in the Qing period resorting to public demonstrations to force the emperors to get down to the business of governing, as they did in the Ming.[23]

In broad historical perspective, it is clear that the secret communications system enabled the Qing emperors to expand the administrative responsibilities associated with Confucian monarchy, fastening administrative leadership to the roles of cosmic mediator and moral leader and creating a new Son of Heaven who functioned both as the charismatic symbol of the state and a hard-working, practical administrator. Moreover, the imperial activism this innovation unleashed not only reversed the increasing remoteness of the emperor from the daily affairs of government that had characterized Confucian monarchy since the Song period, but it also fostered a standard of conscientious governance unmatched in earlier dynastic eras.

These changes in Qing administrative leadership took place within and were reinforced by new trends in the Confucian Statecraft (*jingshi*) tradition. By the late eighteenth century, these currents included an approach to government that emphasized small-scale reforms and piecemeal institutional changes to meet the needs of changing times. This tradition placed a premium on technical expertise and operational rationality as well as personal moral cultivation, and it provided ample precedents for reforms that would strengthen both "the states resources and the people's livelihood."[24]

Statecraft literature was certainly available to the Daoguang Emperor and his advisers, and leading officials in the canal crisis in the 1820s, such as Tao Zhu, were proponents of this tradition. He Changling, the organizer of the 1826 sea-transport venture, sponsored the compilation of the famous 1826 Statecraft collection, *Huangchao jingshi wenbian*.

As the new Daoguang Emperor reviewed the achievements of two hundred years of Qing rule in the 1820s, the significance of the patterns of Qing monarchy was clear. He had the institutional tools to effect change; he had an inspiring model of aggressive and flexible imperial leadership to follow; and he also had high standards of administrative achievement to live up to.

The Creation of Greater China

As the Daoguang Emperor looked back over the years of Qing rule, he would have reflected with pride on the achievement of two pivotal goals. The first was the integration of the northern and western borderlands into a new multi-ethnic empire. The second was the strengthening of the economy to enhance the dynasty's grip on this greatly expanded empire. These Qing goals revealed a new view of empire, one that drew its inspiration not from the Chinese tributary ideal, but from the geopolitical imperatives that the new Manchu dynasty faced in Inner Asia, the Grand Canal zone, and at the intersection point between the two at Peking. The major challenge, as the Qing emperors saw it, was to fuse the two legs of empire—China and the borderlands—together into one stable, unified whole.[25]

The View from the Palace

The tributary model, inherited from China's past, conceptualized the empire as a series of zones radiating outward from the capital and consisting of an inner zone administered by the imperial government and an outer zone of foreign satellite states.[26] This model recognized the power of the center, the seat of universal empire, to command material resources from the tributary zones, both inner and outer. This power was symbolized by tribute required of foreign states and by special taxes in kind on regional commodities within China, the most important of which was grain tribute, or grain tax in kind, from the lower Yangzi valley.

The Qing dynasts adopted the cosmological and ritual aspects of the tributary ideal with its concepts of universal empire and overlord-tributary ties. But, because this ideal emphasized pre-Qing definitions of frontiers and the distinctions between indigenous Chinese and foreigner, it did not satisfy the Qing emperors' assessment of their own needs and priorities, an assessment that took account of their non-Han origins, their role as conquerors of both Inner Asia and China proper, and their drive for logistical control of both.

From the vantage point of their newly conquered capital at Peking, the Manchus saw a very different strategic map than that evoked by the tributary model, one that was drawn to highlight two distinct zones extending outwards from the capital. The one, the Inner Asian borderlands, stretched north and west from Manchuria to the Pamirs and Tibet (map 10); the other, connected to it and equally important, was the Grand Canal zone, extending southward from the capital to Hangzhou and up the Yangzi to Huguang (the Hunan-Hubei region), tying the grain-producing provinces of the Yangzi valley to Peking, the lynchpin of the empire (map 1). The strategic connections between the two, and the security of both, dominated imperial concerns in the Qing period.

The Manchu emperors, throughout the Qing era, responded with creativity and inspiration to the strategic imperatives that flowed from their view of empire. They devised a multiplicity of new military, political, and economic forms of organization to tie the Inner Asian borderlands to the Qing state; they fashioned new approaches to the administration of the canal zone to tighten their control of this strategic area; and they also organized the management of the adjacent coastal frontier to enhance the security of the canal zone. These innovations allowed the Qing regime to reshape the structure of the empire so as to guarantee their hegemony in both Inner Asia and China.

The Banner military organization was the cornerstone of Qing borderland policy. It enabled the Manchu leadership to mobilize human and material resources in Manchuria and Eastern Mongolia and to spearhead the conquest of China proper and the remaining Inner Asian borderlands: Mongolia, Chinese Turkestan (Xinjiang), and Tibet. Banner officers provided the leadership for the newly crafted military administrations for each border region, and Banner soldiers served as the occupation forces.[27]

Equally important was the Lifan Yuan, an agency that helped plan the conquest of the border regions and then managed a wide spectrum of tributary relations with peoples inside and outside of these fledgling dependencies. Later in the dynasty, as conditions in the dependencies changed, this agency played a key role in the development and revision of imperial policy regarding their control. Its shaping influence continued to be felt in the nineteenth century, when Manchu officials—such as Songyun and Changling, who had apprenticed in this agency and served in Inner Asia over the course of three reign periods—played a decisive role in revising policies to resolve cultural, economic, and political conflicts between Han and non-Han subjects, and between subjects and foreigners in the border dependencies, especially Xinjiang.[28]

Working closely with non-Han leadership in the Lifan Yuan and the Banner forces occupying Inner Asia, the Qing emperors crafted an impressive array of institutions that guaranteed Qing hegemony in the borderlands and led to the gradual political, economic, and cultural integration of these regions into the empire of Greater China. These institutions ranged from the directly governed provincial and Banner organizations in Manchuria to the military protectorates formed in Mongolia and Xinjiang, which utilized a variety of forms of indirect rule at the local level. In Mongolia, indirect rule depended on Lamaist monastic organizations and specially created Mongol Banners. In Tibet, the Qing presence overlay the indigenous local order. In Xinjiang, a staggering diversity of institutions existed side by side, including military and civilian agricultural colonies, Mongol Banner organizations, tributary arrangements with roving bands of Kazakh and Kirghiz, and virtually autonomous Islamic oasis communities ruled either by hereditary or bureaucratic *begs*. This amalgam of institutions reshaped and redefined the political and cultural relationship between the Qing state and the Inner Asian borderlands, confirming the inhabitants of these regions as non-Han subjects, not as foreign barbarians.[29]

Over the course of the dynasty, the problems associated with the security of the Inner Asian regions changed continually as did the administrative strategies designed to solve them, but this did not slow the Qing drive to integrate these regions and peoples into a more unified Greater China. The process continued unabated into the nineteenth century, with the suppression of Islamic revolt and the reorganization of trade in Altishahr during the Daoguang reign, and later, in the 1880s, with the annexation of Xinjiang as a province.[30]

In the eyes of the Qing emperors, the drive into the borderlands and the control of China proper both depended on control of the Grand Canal zone. This was the highway that linked the capital to the agricultural heartland, and it was the route by which grain revenues were conveyed to the capital to supply the civilian and military bureaucracies on whom its security depended. The grain conveyed to the capital through this corridor was, as the Daoguang Emperor reminded regional officials in 1824, "the capital's sole supply."[31] Yet control of the canal zone hung in the balance for nearly forty years (1644–83), as

Qing forces encountered bloody resistance to their rule and mounted brutal suppression campaigns in the lower Yangzi valley.[32]

The mainstay of the resistance was the Zheng maritime empire based in the southeastern coastal region, which drew its support from flourishing coastal and overseas trading networks. The Zheng regime staunchly supported both the Ming loyalist forces that rallied around the fleeing Ming princes (1645–62) and, later, the Sanfan rebels (1673–81). In doing so, the Zheng helped prolong the resistance against the Qing forces; but, more importantly, it also demonstrated clearly to the Qing leadership that the Grand Canal zone was vulnerable to insurgency movements based on the coast.[33]

As a result of the wars of conquest, the Qing leadership had come to view the China coast as the eastern perimeter of the Grand Canal zone, not primarily as a frontier separating China from the foreign maritime world. Peace in the canal zone depended on peace and stability on the coast; and, from the Qing perspective, the successful pacification of both for the long term depended absolutely on economic prosperity and stability. After the conquest, the Kangxi Emperor moved quickly to help rebuild the coastal economy by assisting in the resettlement of the population and by ending a centuries-long repression of the coastal trade that was the dynamic core of the local economy. To strengthen and solidify the role of local commercial interests, he initiated a unique pattern of administration that placed power and responsibility for the management of maritime trade and coastal defense in their hands. These innovations radically altered the relationship of the coastal region to the state. They also altered the relationship of the Qing state to the foreign maritime world because the management of foreign maritime trade was structurally separated from the conduct of formal interstate relations.[34]

The Qing system of port management placed nominal responsibility for the management of trade in the hands of a court appointee, the Hoppo, who really was just there to "skim off the cream." Real responsibility for the day-to-day management of trade, as well as marine defense, was shouldered by locals who played official and semi-official roles in customs and port administration that ranged from clerks and powerful *hong*-merchant brokers to key officers in the Green Standard navy. The diversity in customs administration from one port to the next (about which later Western traders complained so bitterly) reflected the diversity of local interests—interests that the system was designed to support without interference from the customs superintendents or provincial authorities.[35] The subtlety and complexity of the Qing pattern of coastal administration is documented brilliantly by Ng Chin-keong (1983) in his study of the Amoy trading network. He shows how Qing policy set the stage for the growth and integration of the Chinese junk trade into the regional coastal economy.

Imperial power was used aggressively during the Kangxi reign to create institutions that were driven by and safeguarded local coastal interests. Thereafter, the Qing rulers turned their attention to other, higher-priority areas of administration that were considered more crucial to their rule, thereby fostering a pattern of deliberate but benign neglect of coastal affairs for the rest of the dynasty. However, when local interests were threatened—either by provincial authorities, pirates, foreign traders, or other disruptive influences—the emperors did intervene on their behalf.[36] Even when demographic change began to threaten local order in the eighteenth century, the early Qing policy of bowing to local economic interests remained in force, and the main lines of this policy were perpetuated until the Opium War.[37]

Qing coastal policy created an institutional structure for defense and trade administration that was consistent not only with the economic needs of the coastal region but more importantly with the strategic goals of the Qing leadership. This policy gave an internal-security gloss to issues and events on the coast, relating them to the stability of the Grand Canal zone rather than to the foreign maritime world. It can be said, in view of these developments, that the Qing period marks a major watershed in Chinese maritime history. The Qing regime's legitimization of the junk trade and reliance on trading organizations for its management led to the successful integration of this border region into the political, administrative, and economic framework of the Qing empire. These developments also should be seen as completing the Chinese government's logisitical withdrawal from the maritime world, begun by the Ming after the Yongle reign (1402–24).[38] This process sounded the death knell for formal interstate relations between China and the maritime world in all but its most trivial ceremonial and ritual forms.[39]

In other words, the Qing internalized or drew inwards the coastal region just as they were drawing the great expanses of Inner Asia inwards. As a result, the maritime frontier, separating Chinese and foreigners, was pushed farther and farther out into the dim and shadowy regions of the Nanyang, just as the land frontiers were pushed out beyond the Pamirs. The maritime world became an area of little or no strategic or economic consequence in the Qing view of empire. It ceased to be written or read about by anyone who mattered.[40] It continued to be neglected until the Opium War proved that British ships could create conflict on the coast, penetrate the Yangzi, and threaten the Grand Canal as the Zheng regime had done two hundred years before.[41]

The Economy and the Canal Zone

In stark contrast to the coast, the Grand Canal zone—its hydraulic engineering works, its administration, and the prosperity of its communities—was an issue of the greatest strategic import to the Qing leadership. From the early reigns, the Qing emperors closely monitored conditions in the canal zone and directly intervened in those aspects of regional administration that bore on it. They pursued a three-pronged approach that included the reconstruction and expansion of hydraulic engineering works, described earlier, and the streamlining of the canal–grain transport administration, considered below. But the cornerstone of their canal policy was a program of economic initiatives designed to restore and enhance prosperity in the canal zone. These initiatives were but one part of a larger activist strategy for supporting and enhancing the people's livelihood (*minsheng*), which was considered essential to the long-term peace and security of the empire.[42]

The intimate linkage between the people's livelihood and strategic control of the empire expressed fundamental Confucian assumptions about the relationship between economic order and the political-moral order and about the role and responsibility of the state and the people in achieving both. The Confucian view held that economic order and stability were prerequisites for the achievement of moral-political order. The state's charge was to create conditions of security and order so that the people could develop productive resources to sustain the family, community, and state superstructure. The state's strategic sphere and the people's productive sphere were inextricably linked and interdependent. Their integration was required if civilization was to progress toward the achievement of a universal moral order.[43]

The functional relationship between the two spheres defined and served to limit the prerogatives of the imperial state with respect to the economy, or more accurately, the people's livelihood at the subdistrict level. On the one hand, the state had the legitimate right to levy those taxes required to maintain the superstructure and guarantee peace and stability. It was not, however, entitled to enrich itself at the expense of the people, nor to expand its functions at the subdistrict level in ways that might interfere with, or compromise, the people's livelihood, thereby threatening internal security. Nonetheless, the state did have the responsibility for specific tasks that were considered vital to economic stability. Among them were start-up investments in agriculture after periods of turmoil, the construction of a large-scale water-control infrastructure that was beyond the organizational and financial capacity of individual peasant communities, and regulatory acts to assure economic equity and monetary and market stability. These actions were seen as beneficial and essential to the achievement of the "state's plans and resources and the people's livelihood."

The Qing monarchs undertook these tasks with great determination, energy, and discipline, seeking to stimulate prosperity and growth as well as stability in the various regional economies. They saw these initiatives as consistent with and necessary to the expansion of the empire into the borderlands, the long-term pacification and control of China proper, and the correct exercise of Confucian paternalistic rule. Because they linked the survival of the dynasty directly to the people's livelihood, the Qing emperors showed a great willingness to intervene in the economy to promote prosperity and to assure fiscal-economic justice in ways that accorded with the limited prerogatives of the state at the subdistrict level. They were able to do so because of their secret communications links with regional government. These efforts created an environment throughout the Qing period in which economic enterprise expanded, developed, and diversified in *both* the agricultural and commercial sectors. Even when the state's ability to ameliorate the disruptive effects of economic change was limited in the nineteenth century by demographic crisis and the weakness of local government, the desire to do so remained undiminished as did the state's sense of responsibility for the people's livelihood.

From the beginning of the dynasty, the Qing emperors undertook a broad program of economic initiatives to restore agriculture, support trade, and stabilize the economy. These measures included a low, uniform tax levy, incentives for land reclamation, and bold engineering feats to rebuild the water-control infrastructure, as well as support for small-scale water-control projects, called "people's works," that were crucial for the restoration of agriculture. The Qing leadership also responded generously with emergency relief and tax remissions in times of natural disasters and was particularly successful in devising both bureaucratic and nonbureaucratic strategies for the provisioning of local granaries, the stabilization of grain prices, and the delivery of grain supplies for military and relief purposes. Finally, the Qing leadership established a unified, bimetallic monetary system that lent stability and order to both fiscal and market operations.[44]

The Qing emperors reinforced these initiatives with institutional changes that sought to increase bureaucratic discipline at the regional level to protect the people from official exploitation. Changes of this kind included measures to curb gentry privileges, restrict magisterial manipulation of the tax collection process, build links to the peasant community with *baojia* networks, and expand the state's control over specialized bureaucratic functions at the subprefectural level (*ting*).[45] These measures reflected strong misgivings about the efficiency and integrity of local officials. This negative view was intensified later as demographic pressures undermined the operation of local government, creating an unwillingness among the Qing leadership to undertake fundamental reforms of local government and the fiscal system that depended on the administrative action of local officials.[46]

In the early reigns, the regime moved quickly and decisively to restore agriculture and trade after the turmoil of the Ming-Qing transition. The effectiveness of its efforts is seen, for example, in the development of agriculture in Hunan and in the expansion of the coastal and overseas junk trade, which long had been restricted by the Ming.[47] The former transformed Hunan into one of the premier grain-producing centers of China. The latter led to the development and diversification of the coastal economy, the rise of magnet trading entrepots, like Amoy, and the development of Tianjin. Later, after the conquest of Turkestan in 1759, the Qing leadership also undertook "start-up" development of agriculture and commerce in this culturally diverse region to hasten its political integration into the empire.[48]

The character of Qing involvement in the economy changed over time in response to changing realities. After the economy was restored in the eighteenth century, and agricultural and commercial prosperity was achieved, the state generally retreated from direct leadership and support of economic interests.[49] Yet the Qing emperors continued to monitor the economy closely and asserted their right to intervene in and to mediate conflicts arising from economic change in order to quell unrest and to accommodate diverse economic interests.[50] They also continued to aid regions afflicted by economic hardship with a variety of arrangements for loans from government and private sources.[51] Will's important study of the imperial state's response to famine in Zhili in 1743–44 shows both the moral-ideological orientation of the leadership and its organizational capacity to respond quickly and effectively to famine conditions that undermined local economic and political order.[52]

The state's efforts to procure monetary copper clearly reveal the lengths to which it was willing to go to assure the stability of the monetary and market systems. First, the leadership organized a group of specially licensed traders to manage the importation of Japanese copper. Later, after 1715, the state began the systematic development of private copper mines in Yunnan. According to Hans Ulrich Vogel's important study, this latter initiative ultimately led to a complex, multifaceted program of government investment in a range of mining operations and the development of overland and riverine transport routes out of Yunnan.[53] These routes sparked widespread economic development throughout the province by the mid-eighteenth century.[54]

Qing imperial stewardship of the economy was marked by fairly cooperative interaction between the state and private economic interests. The reciprocity and interdependence of these relations reflected the Qing leadership's apparent preference for nonbureaucratic approaches to some fiscal operations and their reluctance to expand bureaucratic involvement in economic affairs, even in those areas perceived as strategically important. This approach was shaped both by deep misgivings about the integrity and efficiency of local-level officials and by the belief that private organizations, and their market networks, were more efficient at distributing commodities and stabilizing prices.[55]

One finds state-private cooperation in a number of important areas: the grain-transport administration's reliance on private lighterage in the Zhili section of the Grand Canal,[56] the state's use of Shanxi bankers for monetary transfers,[57] the use of trading organizations to manage important aspects of coastal and overseas trade,[58] and the "recruitment" (zhaoshang) by the Finance Ministry (Hubu) of private capital to encourage the development of enterprises deemed useful both to the state and private sectors of China's regional economies.[59] Similarly, the state used private grain merchants and shippers to make strategic grain transfers, and traders were given special incentives to expand their networks to the borderlands, buttressing the expansion of Qing political-military control over this region.[60]

In the late eighteenth century, as demographic change undermined the operation of local government, the state turned increasingly to private groups to take over, or "privatize," a number of government functions. This pattern is seen in the private management of water-control projects, in the state's reliance on private wage labor for hydraulic engineering projects and the government grain fleets, and, finally, in its dependence on private lighterage in silt-clogged sections of the Huaiyang Canal to transport government grain.[61] The readiness of the state to work with private groups is again seen in the nineteenth-century reforms of the salt monopoly, which the state opened up to small merchants and traders to expand legal sales and increase government tax revenues.[62]

Besides its close cooperative relationship with private economic interests, the Qing state continued traditional regulatory actions designed to stabilize the market and monetary systems and to insure the availability of important commodities such as salt, food grains, and monetary copper. Because of greater discipline in regional government in the Qing than in previous periods, these regulatory actions, as well as normative fiscal operations, were for the most part carried out effectively.[63]

The Qing state also continued its management and funding of enterprises whose size or strategic significance warranted government action, notably the shipping of grain tribute, or grain tax in kind, and the management of large water-control facilities, such as those in the Grand Canal system and the long dikes on the Yangzi in Hubei.[64] In the former, the state employed an official-military organization—the Grand Canal–Yellow River directorates, discussed below. In the case of the Hubei long dikes, after the state rebuilt them in the early Qing, various combinations of "government supervision and people's repair" (*guodu minxiu*) were devised to maintain them. None of these efforts, however, proved satisfactory in the long run.

In general, these schemes sought greater community management, funding, and labor recruitment. To achieve this, local officials lent political and moral support to private local groups and tried to prohibit interference by *yamen* underlings. They also helped raise capital in a variety of ways. By the late eighteenth and early nineteenth centuries, as fiscal paralysis gripped local government and water-control problems multiplied, local officials lost ground to these powerful local interests. Nonetheless, they continued to assert the state's right to inspect, supervise, and arbitrate disputes that arose over the building and funding of these works. In the end, neither private nor state organizations were able to meet the challenges of a multiplicity of local problems, including popular resistance and environmental degradation.[65]

It is precisely within the context of Qing stewardship of the economy, and related strategic goals associated with the expansion of empire, that Qing management of the Grand Canal–grain transport system should be interpreted. Of all the water-control enterprises that the state undertook, this was the largest and most complex. To assure its security, the Qing emperors not only rebuilt and expanded its hydraulic engineering facilities, they also acted to enhance the economic security of the canal zone communities. They monitored and responded to economic problems quickly and efficiently, particularly to hardships caused by natural disasters, which might breed turmoil and unrest. Most importantly, they expanded their commitment to the reconstruction and expansion of smaller water-control facilities in this network, called "people's works" (*minnian*). These drainage and flood-control projects were undertaken not just to protect the canal but also to protect the livelihood of peasants and traders in the communities that bordered it. Imperial responsibility for these smaller facilities reflected the state's strategic stake in the economic prosperity of the canal zone.[66]

Such smaller works were an integral part of the Grand Canal–riverine system, which was a vast interlocking network of both large and small water-control works. The large-scale works consisted of the canal itself, the junction facilities, the Hongze Lake dikes, and the largest drainage facilities, such as the Wangying–Salt Canal north of the Yellow River in northern Jiangsu, and the Yangzi River outlets off the Grand Canal in the Yangzhou region (map 7). These large works were connected to an elaborate network of smaller facilities for water supply, drainage, and flood control that radiated outwards from the canal to the streams, lakes, and marshes along its entire length from Peking to Hangzhou and up the Yangzi to Huguang (maps 3, 7). The smaller works linked to the canal included the holding reservoirs along the Canal of Gates in Shandong and the canalized Wei River on the Shandong-Zhili border, and the drainage networks essential for flood control in southwestern Shandong, eastern Anhui, and the Xiahe region to the east of the Huaiyang Canal. Both networks were essential to the operation and defense of the canal, but the smaller parts also played an important role in agriculture, which sustained the communities that straddled the canal.

In the Kangxi reign, for example, when the state constructed the Grand Canal and the large lake dikes in northern Jiangsu, it also rebuilt and expanded the smaller drainage and flood-control works in the flood-prone Xiahe region, both to benefit agriculture and trade and to improve the drainage system leading from the lakes to the sea. Similarly, in Huguang, an important grain-tax-producing area, the state constructed the long dikes in southern Hubei on the north bank of the Yangzi that protected the whole region from floods, while

74   *Controlling from Afar*

simultaneously building the smaller Dongting Lake dikes that were essential for the restoration of agriculture.[67] During the 1820s canal crisis, the state continued to support "people's works" affecting the canal. For example, it funded the improvement of small community lead channels (*yinhe*) in eastern Anhui that protected the fields from floods and, simultaneously, increased the clear water reserves in Hongze Lake that were essential for the crossing of grain fleets at the canal–Yellow River junction.[68]

Fig. 11   Train of canal lighters.

The Qing regime obviously expanded its responsibilities for these lesser parts of the canal-riverine network to protect the canal, but also to create and to sustain agricultural prosperity, which it saw as vital to the long-term pacification of Chinese in the canal zone.[69] Yet, the lines between large and small works, and the distinction between the state's and the people's responsibilities for them, were not always clearly drawn. Even though the smaller works were important to the security of the Grand Canal network, the state was unwilling to assume permanent responsibility for their management and cost. Additionally, agricultural needs were often in conflict with strategic needs because agriculturalists needed water from canal reservoirs at precisely the same time that water was needed for canal shipping. When there was a conflict of interests, the state's strategic need to ship grain took precedence over the needs of agriculture. This is particularly clear in the use of reservoir water adjacent to the canal in Shandong and in the canalized Wei from Linqing to Tianjin (map 6).

While Qing policy toward "people's works" reflected the state's strategic interest in the people's prosperity, innovations in the traditional grain tribute system and the eventual use of private wage labor to man the grain junks on the Grand Canal show the Qing regime's responsiveness to changing economic realities. During the early reigns, the Qing had reformed many aspects of the traditional grain-transport system to achieve greater efficiency and to respond to changing economic and ecological conditions. To gain greater efficiency and equity in the collection of grain tax, the Qing emperors required the district magistrate, rather than the peasant taxpayer, to collect and ship the grain to the canal anchorages. They also limited surcharges on this tax, expanded the use of inspection personnel at checkpoints along the canal, and eliminated costly delays in shipping. These changes, along with greater imperial scrutiny of the canal–grain transport administration, greatly improved the efficiency of the grain-transport system as a whole.[70]

One of the most significant economic developments affecting grain transport was the increasing commercialization of the lower Yangzi valley, which led to the growth of private, canal-borne shipping and trade with North China. The economic expansion and diversification that this trade sparked provided greater mobility and more alternatives for the canal-zone population, including the hereditary boatmen who manned the government grain fleets.[71] As David Kelley's excellent study of private labor organizations on the grain fleets shows, the transport troops were drawn into the civilian community and economy, and their state-owned garrison fields (*tuntian*) were absorbed by private landholders. As the ranks of the government shipping crews decreased, the state was forced to accept the use of transient skilled laborers, organized and led by tough-minded leaders of the Buddhist Luo sect and bound together by religious ties and economic need. Labor from these organizations replaced the transport corps on the junks and dictated the terms and conditions of work for the crews of the state grain fleets by the early nineteenth century.[72] Two issues are clear from Kelly's work: first, structural economic change provided the context for this development and, second, the Qing regime gradually adapted to this changed economic environment.

Similarly, the growth of private shipping on the Grand Canal provided the context for the state's increasing dependence on private lighterage for the transport of tribute grains. By the second half of the eighteenth century, the siltation of the entire canal-riverine network in northern Jiangsu was so serious that it obstructed the regular grain junks from Jiangnan and the larger junks from the central Yangzi provinces. In response, the grain transport directorate, in conjunction with field officials in northern Jiangsu, Shandong, and Henan, increasingly hired smaller private craft, or lighters, to carry the grain through silt-damaged parts of the canal. These developments on the Huaiyang Canal were similar to those that had been experienced on the Northern Canal since the beginning of the dynasty. The procedures for recruiting private craft were so common and routinized that hundreds of lighters could be mobilized quickly and efficiently throughout the three-province region of northern Jiangsu, eastern Henan, and Shandong when shipping crises occurred.[73]

The increasing use of private shippers on the Grand Canal shows the ability of the Qing regime's central and top regional leadership to respond effectively to regional realities; it further demonstrates its organizational capacity and its willingness to work jointly with private, nonbureauratic sectors of the canal-zone economy to achieve imperial goals in the early nineteenth century, even in one of its most sensitive strategic-fiscal operations.

In spite of the significant problems that bore down on the empire in the first years of the Daoguang reign, Qing stewardship of the economy had produced unprecedented agricultural and commercial growth that brought the late empire to new heights of material well-being. Qing integration of the borderlands had muted the chronic instability and conflict that had afflicted Chinese–Inner Asian relations for millennia. Both achievements were due to Qing imperial administrative skill, innovation, and tireless dedication to the day-to-day tasks of government. Although fiscal-economic success had bred economic change and demographic crisis, and although political-territorial expansion had stretched the empire's logistical network to the breaking point, the fruits of these accomplishments were still tangible in the 1820s. The Daoguang Emperor surely thought that the Qing tradition of administrative activism and flexibility would prove equal to the tasks ahead.

The test would come in the mid-1820s, with Jahangir's challenge to Qing control of Altishahr and the destructive flooding of the Grand Canal in northern Jiangsu. The former was managed. The latter could not be, because the Yellow River was beyond human control—poised for its massive and destructive shift northward—and because imperial-regional decision making was less effective in addressing long-term problems than short-term crises.

3

Streamlining Grand Canal–Grain Transport Management

The Qing emperors achieved impressive results in the management of the Grand Canal–grain transport system, in spite of overwhelming geological obstacles associated with the precarious flow of the Yellow River. They successfully centralized, streamlined, and coordinated the operations of the four government branches that managed this system at the regional level: 1) the top executive-level posts of the regular territorial, or field, administration of provincial government, 2) low-level regional officials who fused specialist and field responsibilities in the actual operation of the system, 3) specialist, or expert, officials of the three Grand Canal–Yellow River directorates, and 4) specialist officials of the Grain Transport Directorate. The Qing emperors were able to reorganize the system because of innovations in the decision-making process that vastly expanded their role in the administration of canal-zone provinces and gave them great leeway to respond selectively to those problems that undermined canal operations. Their careful scrutiny of conditions in the canal zone and their direction of key aspects of the system lent coherence and discipline to canal-transport operations down to the subprefectural level. Yet, as the Daoguang Emperor's management of the canal crisis will demonstrate, imperial direction of the system relied heavily on the advice of regional officials and their articulation of short-term needs and on the guidelines spelled out in administrative codes and statutes. Imperial power was, consequently, focused and shaped by these two factors, and the decisions that resulted were a curious blend of central goals and regional necessity, past experience and present realities.

The Emperor at the Center

Because the Qing emperors treated the Grand Canal–grain transport system as a high-priority issue, they scrutinized its regional operation with great care throughout the Qing period. Open communications between the emperor and regional leaders were the key to flexible problem solving in its management because this facilitated and maximized imperial direction while, at the same time, enabling the emperors to take account of regional realities and official initiatives. Yet, while this administrative pattern enabled the imperial government to respond effectively to changing conditions, canal–grain transport management also lay on a solid bedrock of disciplined adherence to administrative practice embedded in the administrative code, regulations, and local lore.

The driving force at the center of the canal–grain transport system in the 1820s, as in the past, was the emperor. Because of his position at the pivot of the communications network, he was uniquely placed to monitor conditions in the canal zone from incoming secret reports from regional leaders. And regional officials diligently reported on all matters associated with the cycle of floods, the repair of the canal network, and the step-by-step progress of the grain fleets up and down the canal. Examples of the issues addressed in public edicts in 1824, prior to the canal crisis, include tax deferrals conferred in the wake of natural disasters, repairs made to the Northern Canal in Zhili, minor changes to the transport route in Jiangnan because of silt obstructions, problems with corruption and inspection procedures connected to the delivery and storage of tribute grain at the capital granaries, the rebuilding of Grand Canal dikes and subsidiary people's dikes connected to them in Shandong, and loan advances for the repair of people's works.[1]

When these routine but important issues could be managed in accordance with established administrative practice, the emperor authorized and referred the memorials to the central ministries of the outer court for regular handling and public announcement.[2] If, on the other hand, the memorial reports identified changing conditions, emerging problems, or disasters that might threaten the canal system, the emperor quickly intervened to work out solutions consensually with regional officials, field and specialist, and then monitored the implementation of these solutions.[3] The dispatch of a court letter signaled a departure from the normal decision-making process and opened the way for regional officials, with the emperor's sanction, to adjust the rules to meet changing realities. If a large-scale emergency occurred, then special imperial agents, or commissioners, were dispatched to verify and to reinforce the work of regional officials. When such disasters involved several provinces, the emperor himself acted as a special mediator, coordinating the administrative actions of officials from each of the provinces as they worked together to solve common problems.

Although it was highly authoritarian and emperor-centered, the Qing decision-making process nonetheless was dependent on executive-level regional officials for information gathering and reporting, for the identification and solution of regional problems with which they were familiar, for on-the-spot decisions, and for supervising the implementation of imperial policy. Imperial reliance on these officials gave the latter substantial responsibility for shaping decisions, which not only empowered them, but also increased their willingness to enforce imperial orders with commitment and discipline. So, although the Qing emperors kept a tight grip on this select branch of regional administration, they were in fact forced to share power and encourage official initiative in order to achieve their goals. As the Daoguang Emperor emphasized, he "could not rule from afar" effectively without accurate reconnaissance, workable policy options, and disciplined enforcement of imperial orders at the regional level. What is more, imperial reliance on regional officials was particularly great in canal-transport management because the system was so vulnerable to natural disaster and required fast, on-the-spot decisions—decisions that often could not wait for imperial approval.

To be successful, the decision-making process relied upon speed and the forthright exchange of information between the emperor and regional officials. Open and reliable communications were the key. The emperor's intervention in regional issues asserted his determination to participate in and direct the problem solving process. His insistence on thorough, reliable reports expressed his desire to do so responsibly. The emperor's intervention also placed great responsibility on regional officials for producing planning strategies. It is clear from the dialogue between the imperial center and northern Jiangsu during the 1820s canal crisis, that the very act of reporting a problem committed an official to propose a solution. If an official failed to present planning options with his reports, the emperor used the court letter to remind him to "prepare plans in advance" (*xianshi chouji*) so that dangerous contingencies could be controlled or avoided. Reporting could not be taken lightly because it bound an official to devise specific planning options.

Prior planning was, of course, essential if the emperor was to participate in decisions. He required the submission of planning strategies ahead of time in order to evaluate their appropriateness and to sanction any departures from administrative norms that they might entail. But the emperor's linkage of reporting and planning also expressed his view that regional officials, with their firsthand grasp of local realities, were more capable than he and his central advisers of devising truly effective plans to cope with local problems. The emperor could do no more than direct the process, and then only if he had a comprehensive knowledge of the situation through honest and detailed memorial reports from the field. If the emperor felt he was not receiving reliable or complete information, he pressed harder and sought more details. His queries and his responses to initial reports and planning options served to make imperial priorities clear and directed discourse along lines that he felt were most appropriate and timely. This reliance on expert advice from the provinces was similar to imperial dependence on official experts at the capital in central-government decision making.[4]

Grand Canal–Grain Transport Management 83

This model of regional responsibility, highlighted by official reports and proposals for action, is clearly revealed in the emergency of late 1824, when hundreds of empty grain junks were stalled north of the Yellow River at the canal junction near Yangzhuang, waiting to return to their home anchorages in the south (fig. 12). When regional officials reported that abnormally high waters might impede the crossing, the emperor intervened directly with a court letter requesting specific details about water levels in the river and Hongze Lake and urging regional officials to move quickly to resolve the problem. He wanted the information not so as to make the decisions himself but to give him enough insight to direct the decision-making discourse in a knowledgeable way. Only regional officials who were assessing the situation in person could make the final decisions.[5]

Fig. 12 Southward descent into Yellow River from Grand Canal at Yangzhuang (K. Leonard after Wm. Alexander).

Because of the special problems that faced canal-transport administration, the emperor and regional officials played a much greater role in policy-making than did the central ministries of the outer court, which managed the routine aspects of the system. Outer court involvement included the Finance Ministry for the collection and storage of tribute grain; the Works Ministry for the supervision of seasonal maintenance, repair, and construction necessary for the successful operation of the water-control networks; and the War Ministry, for the organization of river troops and the protection of key parts of the canal. These ministries, for the most part, went by the book, relying on administrative law and established precedent to guide the normative processes of canal–grain transport administration.

Yet, because the routine cycles forecast in the administrative code rarely matched events in the canal zone, with its erratic pattern of rainfall, floods, and silting, the regulations and procedures were often of limited applicability. The code could never be more than a guide, albeit an important one, to be adapted and changed as conditions warranted. The Qing leadership recognized the limitations of administrative law and devised a system that facilitated the imperial use of the edict to respond to regional realities and bypass the central ministries and administrative law when developments threatened the canal system. In short, they used the code and regional reports of realities in tandem to achieve stable and effective management of the canal system. The balance between the two enabled the Qing regime to overcome some of the structural weaknesses of the Ming administration and to vastly improve the operation of the canal-transport sytem.

However, even though the emperor and regional officials moved freely to devise flexible responses, nonetheless, they both attached great importance to the administrative code. To them it contained an agenda driven both by logistical and natural imperatives. It provided a comprehensive and holistic approach to offsetting the effects of nature's unrelenting and capricious seasonal cycles. The northbound crossing of the Yellow River, for example, was timed to occur before the onset of summer and autumn floods, while the return crossing was timed to occur after the floods subsided. Yet, if rains and floods occurred

Grand Canal–Grain Transport Management 85

earlier than normal and threatened the crossing, the regulations contained special procedures for the early opening of drainage and diversion channels. Similarly, the emperor's insistence that the grain fleets begin their journey northward on schedule, and pass the required checkpoints on time, was calculated to insure that the fleets would be ready to move quickly through the junction, "nose to tail" (*xianwei*), if river levels rose earlier than usual. The code, therefore, provided solid ground rules that took into account a variety of yearly natural and bureaucratic challenges. Centuries of successful practice had been generalized and boiled down in the code for use by later generations. Emperor and regional official alike could ignore it only at their peril.

The impeachment of Zhang Wenhao in early 1825 reveals the significance of the code in the eyes of the emperor and shows how regulations and precedents were used as a foundation for flexible administrative action. Zhang was the Southern Canal director during the 1824 autumn crossing crisis described above. He was censured afterwards for contributing to the crisis because he had not followed assiduously the normal procedures for controlling flood waters in both Hongze Lake and the Yellow River. Had he done so carefully and systematically, he could have offset at least partially the abnormally high and fluctuating water levels, and he would have known when the time was right to depart from the regulations. In the edict admonishing Zhang, the emperor contrasted his haphazard performance of the routine tasks of canal administration with the actions of an earlier and far more successful Southern Canal director, Li Shixu (1773–1824).[6] Zhang, he averred, had departed recklessly from the "old regulations" (*jiuzhang, jiugui*) and ignored the advice of others, and thus he had caused delays in the southward crossing of the grain fleets. Li, in contrast, had achieved a balance between adherence to the code and administrative initiative so that the flood waters "brought profit" (*lishe*) and the grain fleets were never delayed. If officials "follow the old regulations" and take the precautions spelled out in the code, the emperor wrote, "we will not suddenly be faced with shipping delays."[7]

The censure of Zhang Wenhao shows how routine and nonroutine aspects of regional administration were supposed to work. The code plotted out the required steps when canal-transport operations proceeded normally. It was the primary anchor in the yearly administrative cycle and was to be followed in an exacting and disciplined way. In contrast, the emperor-led decision-making process provided emergency remedies when challenges to the system threatened its operation. Yet although the system was weighted toward the emperor and his regional allies and to the nonroutine aspects of regional administration, both relied heavily on the normative procedures embedded in the administrative code. The former was geared to the historical moment; the latter to long stretches of historical time and nature's cycles. The emperor mediated between the two to achieve effective administration of the canal–grain transport system.

Regional Managers of the Canal–Grain Transport System

Top-level field and specialist officials shouldered the major administrative tasks of the Grand Canal–grain transport system in the nine provinces that comprised the canal zone: Zhili, Shandong, Henan, Jiangsu, Zhejiang, Jiangxi, Anhui, Hunan, and Hubei. Although their responsibilities and relationships varied according to the special circumstances of each province, as a group they apprised the emperor of changing conditions in the canal zone area and played the principal advisory role on policy questions. At the same time, as regional executives, they were pivotal in the supervision of lower-level officials, from circuit, prefecture, department, and district officials to their specialist assistants at the subprefectural, subdepartment, and subdistrict levels, who actually supervised water-control projects and the policing of the grain-shipment process.

Early in the dynasty, when canal-riverine projects were planned and built, specialist officials, such as Yu Chenglong (1638–1700) and Jin Fu, dominated regional management of the canal system. This was due

Grand Canal–Grain Transport Management 87

to their key role in designing the hydraulic scheme for the Grand Canal–Yellow River system and their ties with and support from the Kangxi Emperor, who was deeply involved in the planning and inspection of these new works.[8] In the mid-eighteenth century, as patterns of regional administration crystallized, executive officials of the regular provincial government (governors-general and governors) began to carry the brunt of responsibility for overall management of canal-transport operations. They did so even in those parts of the canal zone that were most vulnerable to the destructive force of the Yellow River (northern Jiangsu, southwestern Shandong, eastern Henan) and, therefore, most dependent on the skills of the specialists.[9]

The governors-general, the highest ranking regional officials in the civil service hierarchy (1b), dominated canal-transport management in Liangjiang, Huguang, and Zhili. Specialist officials (2a), such as the directors of the canal and grain transport agencies, had slightly lower rank and authority, but stood slightly above governors (2b). This ranking gave governors-general the necessary authority to supervise and coordinate the work of the specialist officials and lower-ranking field officials and to push both to cooperate in order to solve the morass of problems that they faced from the competing demands of canal maintenance, the grain-shipment calendar, and the vagaries of nature.[10]

The governor-general of Liangjiang was assigned responsibility for canal-transport affairs in northern Jiangsu in 1765. This was the site of the most difficult hydraulic problems in the entire canal system: those of the canal junction, the lake reservoirs, and the drainage networks for both the Huaiyang Canal and the Yellow River. This post required an official with superior leadership skills, one who could coordinate and supervise the work of the Southern Canal and grain-transport directors as well as lower-level field officials. For example, he had to see that the Southern Canal director, who managed the canal in northern Jiangsu, neglected none of the myriad tasks associated with repair and maintenance of the junction, the river and lake dikes, and drainage networks leading to the sea. In 1825, when so many of the facilities were weakened and in need of emergency repairs, the new Liangjiang governor-general, Qishan, was specifically ordered to check up on Yan Lang, the Southern Canal director, to see that in the latter's preoccupation with reconstructing the great dike at Gaojia, he did not neglect the repair of the overflow gates on the Huaiyang Canal. The emperor reminded Qishan that if Yan failed to do both, Qishan would be held accountable.[11] Additionally, because Jiangsu-based problems often extended to the Shandong-Henan corridor, the Liangjiang governor-general was often required to work with officials from these neighboring provinces. Similarly, the governor-general of Huguang played the leading role in articulating and managing the problems of the central Yangzi tribute-bearing provinces of Hunan and Hubei. This pattern of accountability of governors-general in canal–grain transport adminstration is consistent with that in other high-priority areas of administration.[12]

The Zhili governor-general, a position that had included the concurrent post of Northern Canal director since 1749, managed grain shipping and water-control projects that affected the silt-prone rivers that made up the Northern Canal: the canalized Wei River from the Shandong border near Linqing to Tianjin and the Bai River from Tianjin north to Tongzhou-Peking, the site of the capital granaries (maps 3, 6, fig. 13). This part of the canal was considered strategically sensitive because of its proximity to the imperial capital, and it faced serious challenges from a matrix of silt-bearing rivers that impinged on the canal as they flowed to the sea near Tianjin via the Hai River. The first major water-control projects in the Kangxi reign were undertaken in this region and centered on the diking of the Lu River, which flows south via Peking to Tianjin. Once this river was harnessed between solid dikes and renamed the "permanently stabilized river" (the Yongding River), the Wei and Bai rivers were used with greater security as the principal route of the Northern Canal.[13] Yet problems of siltation, meandering, and flooding persisted and challenged the Zhili governor-general until the late Qing period. Observers from the Macartney mission described vividly the serpentine configuration of the Northern Canal—caused by the rivers' meandering around silt obstructions—and the need for gangs of trackers to haul the imperial barges through the shallows.14

Fig. 13 Grand Canal (Bai River) approaching Tongzhou (K. Leonard after Wm. Alexander).

In both Henan and Shandong—provinces critical to canal communications—the top field officials were governors, and they dominated canal-transport affairs in their provinces, even though their rank was lower than that of the canal and transport directors. A major task of the Henan governor was "harnessing the Yellow River" as it flowed from west to east across the province. It also appears, from evidence in the emperor's court letters during the canal crisis, that this governorship had explicit supervisory authority over the Shandong Canal and the Shandong Canal director.15 As a consequence, appointees to this governorship were traditionally men with considerable water-control experience. Similarly, because control of the Yellow River was intimately connected with the defense and safety of the canal network in southwest Shandong and northern Jiangsu, the Henan governor was often drawn into the administration of problems that affected this entire region.

During the 1820s crisis, the governor of Henan was a talented and experienced official named Cheng Zuluo.[16] In 1825, he proposed a plan for the relocation of the two-district city of Wuzhi from the south bank of the Yellow River to a new site on the north bank in order to avoid the yearly cycle of devastation and impoverishment caused by Yellow River floods.[17] The Daoguang Emperor regularly sought Cheng's advice on appointments to official posts that required water-control expertise.[18]

The Shandong governor also had important responsibilities in canal management. His three major concerns included: 1) the maintenance of the flash locks (fig. 2) and sluice gates in the Canal of Gates, which stretched across the uneven terrain in Shandong from Linqing to Tai'erzhuang; 2) the fragile and complex system of reservoirs that held water in the wet season and then released it into the canal in the dry season; and 3) flood-control and drainage networks linked to the canal in southwestern Shandong which were highly vulnerable to Yellow River floods and required constant maintenance. Throughout the Qing period, persistent problems afflicted this section of the canal.[19]

Because the "Hedong" (Henan-Shandong) governors shared common water-control problems and a similar grain-shipment cycle, they often collaborated. During the 1825 crisis they joined forces to recruit extra lighters, both private and state-owned, to assist in the transfer of grain cargoes from the canal–Yellow River junction to the capital.[20] Both governors were assisted by the director of the Shandong Canal, whose headquarters at Jining (map 6) placed him close to recurrent canal–Yellow River problems in southwest Shandong, as well as to the difficult hydraulic problems that regularly threatened the canal at its summit section near Nanwang and from the summit to Linqing.

This review of the canal-transport responsibilities of the three top field officials in Shandong, Henan, and Jiangsu highlights the necessity of regional cooperation for planning strategies in areas such as transfer-shipping, and for financial assistance in times of crisis. When canal-transport problems were multiprovincial in scope, the emperor

Grand Canal–Grain Transport Management 91

stepped in and coordinated these joint efforts. He also consciously sought to encourage cooperation with praise and rewards. In early 1825, for example, soon after the disaster, both the Henan governor, Cheng Zuluo, and the Shandong governor, Qishan, memorialized the emperor, offering to contribute provincial funds to Jiangsu to help with relief and reconstruction work.[21] The emperor's response to both lauded their loyalty and dedication to the larger interests of the state, which "transcended provincial boundaries." Of Qishan, he also asserted, "He realized that Shandong was a neighboring province, and he has disregarded provincial jurisdictions. He made financial preparations ahead of time and was thus able to show his concern for state affairs. This is indeed praiseworthy!"[22]

The Jiangsu governor, stationed at Suzhou, and the Zhejiang governor at Hangzhou handled the less demanding water-control and shipping tasks south of the Yangzi in southern Jiangsu (Jiangnan) and Zhejiang, while the top field officials of the Yangzi River provinces of Jiangxi, Anhui, Hunan, and Hubei directed the shipment of their grain-tax quotas down the Yangzi to the canal junction at Guazhou (map 7). The governor-general of Huguang played a particularly important role in articulating the problems of the grain-shipping provinces of the central Yangzi valley. His leadership can be seen as late as the Taiping period in the reforms in grain-tribute collection devised by Hu Linyi between 1855 and 1861.[23]

By focusing responsibility for planning, implementation, and supervision on the highest-ranking field official in each province of the canal zone and making him responsible for coordinating and meshing the specialist and field tasks which bore on canal grain shipment in his jurisdiction, the emperor could direct and facilitate discussion of canal-transport problems, and streamline the chain of command. He could elicit information and planning options that represented a consensus of the views of the entire corps of top field and specialist officials, but he relied most heavily on the top field officials to help him forge a consensus and then to supervise the implementation of a designated course of action. By setting up a framework in which field and specialist officials worked together, the Qing emperors maximized functional expertise and bureaucratic discipline.

In a sense, the Qing system increased centralization at two levels. It maximized centralized direction from the emperor and his inner court advisers, and it also centralized the regional management process at the top levels of the provincial government in the canal zone. It intensified imperial input and direction without sacrificing regional expertise, initiative, and responsiveness to changing local circumstances. As we shall see below, the lower-levels of provincial government also fused together aspects of functional and field administration, and this fusion was critically important to the successful implementation of imperial canal–transport policy.

The Grand Canal–Yellow River Directorates

Even though top field officials bore the greatest responsibility for the canal-transport system after the mid-eighteenth century, specialist (expert) officials played a crucial role in the actual direction of canal reconstruction and grain shipment. The Qing regime adopted the skeletal outlines of the Ming canal and grain-transport agencies, then strengthened and expanded their jurisdiction at the grassroots level, while tying them firmly to both the regular provincial, or field, administration of the canal-zone provinces and to the emperor and his inner court advisers. Their operations were tightly integrated into provincial administration and, at the lower levels, were almost indistinguishable from it.

The Grand Canal–Yellow River directorates undertook responsibility for the design, construction, and maintenance of the canal-riverine hydraulic system, which included the lakes and rivers north of the Yangzi that impinged on the canal or served as part of it—notably the Huai, Yellow, Dawen, Wei, and Bai rivers. This sector of the canal zone faced much greater geophysical obstacles than those parts that lay south of the Yangzi and in the central Yangzi valley. During the Yongzheng reign, the administration of the canal-riverine system was divided into three directorates, with headquarters in the hearts of the three regions considered the most vital to canal communications: the Northern Canal director in Zhili, the Shandong Canal director in Shandong, and the Southern Canal director in northern Jiangsu. This reorganization provided for greater focus on the unique technical problems of each region.

Thereafter, the canal directors generally played a lesser role in policy issues than had their earlier counterparts, such as Jin Fu. While each had the right to memorialize the emperor directly, their planning and problem solving initiatives generally were conveyed to the emperor by field officials to whom they were formally or informally subordinate. They were, nonetheless, held strictly accountable for the repair and maintenance of facilities and projects on the canal-riverine network and were expected to have a thorough grasp of technical issues and the corpus of administrative and regulatory lore that governed its seasonal operation. The directors generally concentrated on the on-site tasks of hydraulic engineering, but by the early nineteenth century, as problems connected to the shift of the Yellow River worsened, a number of canal directors, such as Zhang Jing and Pan Xi'en, assumed a more activist role, and they figured importantly in decisions respecting reconstruction strategies and river control in this period of anxious waiting.

The position of Northern Canal director was held concurrently by the governor-general of Zhili, as noted above. His primary tasks were the elimination of silt obstructions from the canal and overseeing the last stages of the yearly shipment of grain-tax to the capital granaries. During the canal crisis, when the sea transport program was put into effect in 1826, he also played a pivotal role in devising a temporary system for the unloading, inspection, and lighterage of grain cargoes traveling from the coast up the Hai River to the canal at Tianjin (map 3).

The Shandong Canal director was headquartered in Jining, and he had responsibility for both flood and drainage problems in Henan and southwest Shandong and the complex water-supply network and flash locks on the Shandong Canal.[24] Responsibility for the Southern (Nanhe), or Huaiyang Canal, was assigned to the Southern Canal director, whose responsibilities centered on the water-control network in northern Jiangsu, including the Hongze Lake dikes and overflow gates, the canal dikes, the junction facilities, and the main drainage networks leading off the Yellow River and the Huaiyang Canal to the sea.

Each of the three canal directors functioned as both technical expert and chief administrator for the canal-riverine systems within his own jurisdiction. They participated in policy formulation, working consensually with top regional officials who then communicated with the emperor's inner circle to shape planning strategies designed to keep the system operational. As chief project administrators, the directors oversaw the completion of repair and maintenance tasks, directing a diverse corps of lower-level field and specialist officials, from circuit intendant down to assistant magistrates, and legions of guards and laborers.

The circuit intendants were important, middle-level bureaucrats with explicit specialist responsibilities for territories comprising several prefectures. Those in the canal zone with special responsibilities for canal-river affairs reported on local conditions and managed the inspection and fiscal accounting of water-control projects. Some were designated solely as canal-river intendants (*hedao*); others, who had field responsibilities in addition to specialist canal-river tasks, were not so named.[25] The intendant supervised assistant officials at the prefectural, department, and district levels who were responsible for special canal-river tasks. These assistant positions were defined in terms of the field offices to which they were attached, yet they were accountable to the canal-river intendant for specific water-control tasks. The most important of these officials was the subprefect

Grand Canal–Grain Transport Management 95

(*tongzhi, tongpan*), who managed water-control problems for a separate governmental unit called a functional subprefecture. In carrying out his job, he relied on assistant department magistrates and assistant district magistrates and their staffs of registrars, police, and sluice-gate keepers, who were all low-level functionaries in charge of on-site tasks in market towns (*zhen*) and guard posts (*xun*).[26]

This complement of field and specialist officials supervised the management and funding of smaller works connected to the canal system as well. Because these smaller works benefited agriculture, the peasants, landlords, and traders from contiguous communities were expected to contribute labor, funds, and materials to their repair and maintenance. The subprefect and assistant department and district magistrates were charged with mobilizing that support. Because their authority and funds were limited and their responsibilities great, these grassroots canal officials were often unable to achieve the level of maintenance required for the efficient operation of these works. Such was also the case for water-control projects outside the canal zone.

However, those subprefectures and guard posts located directly on the Yellow River, the Grand Canal, and other major facilities in the canal system fared better because special military units of canal-river troops (*hebiao*) guarded and maintained these larger works. The circuit intendant had authority over these troops, who were stationed in special garrisons along the Grand Canal. Like their grain-transport counterparts (*caobiao*), the canal-river troops were hereditary military men who were left over from the old Ming garrison (*weiso*) system and supported themselves on special state lands (*tuntian*). Although the Qing had gradually demobilized such forces during the early reigns, those in the canal zone were retained for use as guards and laborers and as grain-transport officers and crewmen.[27] Stationed at key points, these troops policed the canal and Yellow River, watching for signs of danger to its facilities (see fig. 14). They manned the guard posts along the river and canal banks, operated flash locks and lateral sluice gates, and provided skilled labor for repair and reconstruction work. Some of the descendants of these grassroots workers and guards continue to work on the Grand Canal today in the People's Republic.[28]

Fig. 14 Guard post on the Grand Canal (K. Leonard after Wm. Alexander).

Early in the dynasty, because of the year-round demand for laborers who were skilled in water conservancy, the Qing leadership established a permanent group of wage laborers called canal-river workers (*hefu*) to supplement the canal troops. Additional laborers also were recruited when manpower was needed urgently. These workers were divided into special categories according to skill: dike workers, dike tampers, dredgers, dam operators, bridge workers, and those that watched and read the water-level markers. Nonskilled workers were recruited from the peasantry and from disaster refugees for the simple but arduous work of digging canals and drainage ditches and building earthen mounds to reinforce dikes.[29] The need for water-control laborers increased over the course of the dynasty, due to the expansion and growing complexity of the canal-riverine hydraulic system and to the mounting ecological threats. This need was particularly great during the late eighteenth century when the ranks of the regular canal troops were depleted by commercialization in the canal zone and by the attractions of alternative, and more lucrative, occupations. This was precisely the time when the government's need for skilled labor was the greatest, but its ability to pay for it was reduced by inflation and growing instability in the monetary and market systems.

Even in the 1820s, when field and specialist administration was floundering due to economic pressures, the emperor and top regional leadership regarded low-level functionaries of the canal-river administration as crucial to its continued operation. The Daoguang Emperor made a practice of reviewing the performance of these specialist officers.[30] During the 1824 disaster, while the governor-general of Liangjiang was pardoned for his failure to avert catastrophe, the ground-level managers—subprefectual officers and military watchmen—were fired and their "ribbons and buttons seized" for their failure to keep the overflow gates on the southeast edge of Hongze Lake repaired, an oversight that was seen as one of the principal causes of the floods. These officers were mentioned by name and rank in the emperor's court letters, demonstrating that direct imperial scrutiny continued to be brought to bear on the lowest levels of the system in the early nineteenth century.[31]

This brief review of regional administration of the canal-river system shows the interconnectedness of field and specialist operations from the directors and mid-level officials to the lowliest of hired wage laborers on the construction sites. On the surface, the specialist canal directorates and regular provincial, or field, governments appear to be discrete organizations with separate, parallel ties to the central government. Yet in the day-to-day performance of their jobs, the canal-river agencies, their officials and military personnel worked closely with and depended on all levels of the regular provincial government to operate the canal system and expedite the yearly shipments of grain tax. Although the canal directors reported regularly to the emperor, the provincial governors and governors-general, to whom they were, in practice, subordinate, also articulated their technical needs and planning initiatives. It fell to these provincial field officials to develop a consensus on planning strategies and to articulate the regional point of view for this small group of specialist officials who managed the three main sectors of the Grand Canal. If the top field official was a skilled administrator and conditions were favorable, he could reconcile imperial goals with the bureaucratic and technical imperatives affecting local canal operations. If not, neither central nor regional interests were served, and the emperor would replace him with someone who could.

The Grain Transport Directorate

The Grain Transport Directorate was a specialist agency charged with the shipment of tribute grain, or grain tax, to the capital to provide a secure supply of food grains for the court and the civil and military establishment in Peking. This charge involved two functionally different responsibilities. As an arm of the fiscal administration, the directorate undertook the transfer of grain tax from district to military authorities at the Grand Canal anchorages. In so doing, it interacted with local field officials and performed similar tax-collection functions. As a shipping agency, the directorate guaranteed the safe conduct of imperial grain supplies on government fleets to the imperial capital, a task connected to the military security of the empire. The performance of both these functions made the transport directorate more clearly definable as a specialist organization at the lower levels of regional government than was the case with the canal-river directorates.

Grain tribute was a special category of the land tax collected in kind from specific districts in the canal zone provinces and was one of the principal taxes levied in the Qing period, along with the regular land tax, salt tax, native customs, and miscellaneous indirect taxes. The total annual value of grain tribute plus surcharges in the mid-eighteenth century was approximately 16.7 million *taels*, which constituted about 23 percent of the Qing state's yearly tax revenue.[32] In the early nineteenth century, approximately 6.2 million *shi* of tribute grains were collected each year, of which 2.8 million *shi*, or roughly 45 percent, were used to pay the costs of collection, transport, and storage. The amount of grain that actually reached the granaries in the capital totalled approximately 3.4 million *shi*, a decline of about 1 million *shi* from the early Qing period.

Grain tribute was divided into two tax categories: direct tribute (*zhengdui*) and indirect tribute (*gaidui*). The former, comprising 88 percent of the total grain-tribute quota, was sent to the thirteen granaries at Peking. The indirect tribute was stored at the two granaries at Tongzhou, 30 kilometers east of Peking. The inspection, storage, and allocation of grain tribute in the capital was the responsibility of two granary superintendents from the Finance Ministry, one Manchu and one Chinese, who oversaw the work of the eighteen inspectors who managed the Peking and Tongzhou granaries.[33]

These granary stores were allotted as salary in kind to the court, the nobility, and the civilian and military bureaucracy, whose numbers, including servants and family dependents, totalled approximately 400,000 in the early nineteenth century. The lion's share of the 3.4 million *shi* that arrived in the capital each year, or about 2.4 million *shi*, was allocated to soldiers of the metropolitan garrison on active duty. Of the remainder, some was used by the Imperial Household for sacrificial purposes, some for gruel stations, and some was sold on the open market in Peking to lower and stabilize food prices.[34]

Tribute-grain quotas were levied on eight provinces each year: Shandong, Henan, Anhui, Jiangsu, Zhejiang, Jiangxi, Hubei, and Hunan. After 1827, a small annual tribute of millet and beans was sent from Fengtian. Tribute grain included ordinary husked rice (5,027,590 *shi*), which constituted 90 percent of the total quota; polished white rice intended for court use (164,180 *shi*); millet (69,562 *shi*); and beans (265,401 *shi*). Jiangsu, Anhui, and Zhejiang contributed 70 percent of the regular husked rice and therefore had the largest grain fleets. The highly prized polished rice came from the Hangjiahu circuit in northern Zhejiang (56,502 *shi*) and the Susong circuit in southern Jiangsu (107,678 *shi*). Additionally, some provinces were required to send tribute in other goods that facilitated the grain transport and storage processes, such as reed mats to protect the grain in the holds of vessels, timber for the construction of junks, and bamboo.[35]

The grain-tribute levies exacted from taxpayers consisted of the basic tax quota, the legal surcharges added to cover the costs of spoilage, transport, and storage, and extra surcharges. The last were technically illegal, but were essential to fund administrative and shipping operations not covered in the existing budgetary scheme. These extra surcharges were determined by a myriad of local factors and the prices of monetary metals and rice.[36] Adding further to this picture of regional diversity was the practice of commuting the grain tax to a currency payment, either on a temporary or permanent basis.[37]

In sum, diversity marked the local grain-tax collection process, and much of that diversity—extra surcharges and extra-legal tax agents—was not reported in the public record because it was technically illegal. Yet, in spite of the cries of corruption and exploitation raised by contemporary observers and the Qing emperors themselves, and reiterated by many modern scholars, the tax system overall, and the grain tax in particular, appears to have been characterized generally by equity and stability until the end of the dynasty.[38]

The Grain-Transport Directorate had to cope with these fiscal intricacies, as well as with security problems and the physical obstacles to canal transport posed by a worsening ecological and hydraulic crisis in northern Jiangsu and Shandong. The director of grain transport was in charge of this agency, which was headquartered in the center of vexing riverine conditions, at Qingjiangpu in Huaiyin on the Grand Canal–Yellow River junction. His rank made him a subordinate of the Liangjiang governor-general (with whom he had the closest dealings when working out the knotty problems of transport through the canal–Yellow River junction), but it theoretically placed him above the canal-zone governors in those provinces not subject to a governor-general. In both cases, he addressed policy and planning strategies with top field officials and the canal directors, while carrying out his practical tasks in the field. He was assisted in the latter by a cadre of seven grain intendants and the military personnel attached to the grain-transport garrisons located close to the anchorages on the Grand Canal.

Like the canal-river intendants, the grain-transport intendants were middle-level supervisory officials, whose responsibilities straddled both field and specialist tasks. As fiscal agents they had broad powers over the transfer of grain tax from district officials, who were the primary collectors, to military authorities at the anchorages on the Grand Canal; they also handled the income and expenditures for the entire military system charged with grain transport. The most important intendancies were the two located in Liangjiang: 1) the Jiang'an intendancy included the Jiangsu prefectures of Jiangning, Huai'an, Yangzhou, Xuzhou, and certain Anhui prefectures; 2) the Susong intendancy included Suzhou, Songjiang, Zhenjiang, and Changzhou prefectures and Taicang independent department. A single grain intendant was assigned to each of the other five tribute-bearing provinces: Zhejiang, Jiangxi, Hubei, Hunan, and Shandong, the last of which carried the responsibility for Henan as well.

The intendants assigned to these jurisdictions took delivery of grain tribute from district officials and—with the assistance of deputies, loading inspectors, and escort officers—loaded the grain on government grain junks and completed all the paper work in preparation for departure. From then on, responsibility for the grain was assumed by fleet escort officials, military and civilian, who accompanied the vessels to the capital, where the cargo was turned over to granary officials.[39] Military personnel from the home anchorages bore responsibility for the actual shipment. They commanded both the fleets and the individual grain vessels whose crews were composed of regular troops and, increasingly, as the dynasty wore on, of hired laborers.[40]

The transport corps, like the canal corps, had little in common with the rest of the Qing military system, either the Green Standard or Banner armies. The transport director had nine battalions assigned to him, three for grain shipping duties, and the rest for policing the canal zone, including surveillance of subsidiary canals that were often used by salt smugglers. They also carried out fleet inspections at Huai'an and patrolled the Guazhou-Yizheng ports on the Yangzi (map 7) to inspect returning grain boats for contraband. The transport garrisons were divided up into approximately seventy stations on the Grand Canal and adjacent waterways. These stations were located in the heart of the grain districts and provided the home anchorages for approximately 120 fleets and about 70,000 officers and transport troops. The largest concentrations of vessels and troops were, of course, in Jiangsu, Zhejiang, Anhui, and Jiangxi. These personnel made the yearly preparations for the transport cycle, selecting officers and crews and building and repairing grain junks.[41]

Fig. 15 Grain junk (*Tiangong Kaiwu*, 1637).

By the nineteenth century, the number of grain junks had declined to about six thousand from the original ten thousand of the early Qing period. They were of varied size but the average was about 18 to 26 meters in length and from 3 to 3.4 meters in width.[42] The junks were keelless, flat-bottomed craft of shallow draft (from .76 to 1.3 meters) to

Grand Canal–Grain Transport Management 103

facilitate canal navigation (fig. 15). Their decks were characteristically wide and squarish from the bow to the stern, which swept up at the back behind the cabin compartments for crews. Sculling oars (*yaolu*) were mounted on the bow-to-stern axis to propel the craft; and two masts, set in the forward half, and two bollards, strong posts mounted on either side of the bow, were both used to fasten ropes and cables that were pulled by gangs of trackers. The trackers walked on the canal banks and towed the vessels through the shallows.

Each junk contained two water-tight grain holds and had a carrying capacity of about 2,000 *shi*. They rarely carried more than 300 to 400 *shi*, however, because of the space needed for the crews' private trade goods. The goods were increased in the early nineteenth century to help supplement the crews' declining incomes. Some craft were larger and sturdier, such as those from the central Yangzi provinces that had to stand up to the rough waters of the Yangzi. These towed smaller, 300-*shi*-capacity lighters behind them, so they could reduce their loads in shallow sections of the Grand Canal. Equally signif-icant on the northbound journey were hundreds of private lighters (*bochuan*, fig. 16) hired to ship the grain cargoes through the shallow sections of the canal north of the Yangzi.[43]

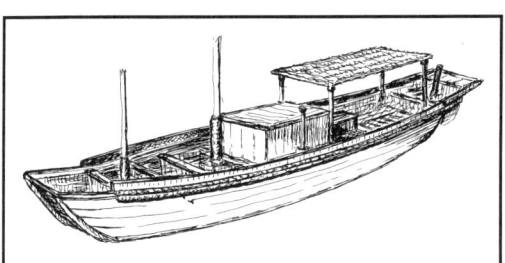

Fig. 16 Grand Canal lighter

Officers from the transport garrisons commanded the grain boats. A transport officer, called a flagman, headed each individual junk and carried the necessary inventory and official documents for the trip.

Individual vessels were organized into groups of ten, commanded by a supervising officer, and each ten-craft group was attached to one large fleet under the overall command of the fleet head and his official assistant. Additional official personnel from their home regions also accompanied the fleets. These officials were generally subprefects who helped the grain intendant with supervisory and inspection tasks. The most important official traveling with each fleet, however, was the escort lieutenant who kept the books, maintained order and discipline among the crews, and interacted with inspection and local officials as the fleet proceeded up the canal through the inspection and checkpoint posts. He knew the fleet, its officers, and crewmen intimately because he generally served with one fleet for many years. When private labor replaced the soldiers as crewmen, the lieutenants were vital mediators between the government and the new labor organizations formed around the Luo sect.

The junks were loaded each year during the twelfth lunar month. By the end of the month, they moved away from their home anchorages and on to regional depots where each took its assigned place in its ten-junk group and fleet. These depots were located in Nanjing (for the central Yangzi boats), Huai'an, Fengyang, Xuzhou, Dezhou, and Linqing (map 1). All the fleets—except for Shandong's, which were close to the capital—commenced their journey on one of three established departure dates to avoid congestion on the canal as they passed through commercial centers, inspection stations, and checkpoints.

Originally, the Jiang'an circuit fleets from anchorages north of the Yangzi went first, leaving Huai'an by the end of the twelfth lunar month and arriving at Tongzhou by the early fourth month. The southern Jiangsu fleets and parts of the Zhejiang and southern Anhui fleets were scheduled to pass Huai'an by the end of the first lunar month, arriving at Tongzhou at the beginning of the fifth month, while the more distant fleets from Zhejiang, Jiangxi, and Huguang were required to pass Huai'an by the end of the second lunar month, arriving in Tongzhou by the beginning of the sixth month. In the mid-eighteenth century, this schedule was revised because silting had slowed the movement of fleets up the canal and often required the hiring of smaller private lighters.[44] By the 1820s, the ability to maintain the three-part schedule, or any semblance of order between or within the fleets, was very limited, and the emperor frequently urged regional officials to abandon the prescribed order and move the fleets through the checkpoints, especially the one at Huai'an, on a first-come, first-served basis. Generally, the fleets were lucky if they crossed the Yellow River by the summer solstice (June 22).[45]

Qing administration of the seasonal grain-transport cycle emphasized speed and discipline. The leadership from time to time placed extra officials along the canal route to eliminate bureaucratic and transit bottlenecks and to pressure, or "hasten" (*sucui*), fleet and inspection personnel to expedite the passage of the junks. These functionaries, in a sense, inspected the inspectors. The Qing also reduced the number of inspection stations and combined them with checkpoint stations early in the dynasty, but then added more of the latter to increase the pressure to meet deadlines.

The Qing regime was responsible for many important changes that served to streamline the administrative hierarchy of the transport directorate, rationalize the transport process itself, and intensify discipline at the lowest levels of the organization. From the director at Qingjiangpu at the top, to the junk crews and checkpoint inspectors at the bottom, all were locked into aspects of field administration in the canal zone, just as were specialist functionaries in the canal-river directorate. Their management tasks were, however, different from and more complex than those of the canal administration because of the strange mix of fiscal-logistical issues with which they had to contend. The administrative patterns of this agency, of course, mirrored that complexity.

Qing achievements were impressive in transport management, just as they were in canal-river affairs. In the end, the canal-grain transport system foundered, not for want of imaginative and sound administrative practices, but because of a flawed fiscal system based on inelastic taxes and fixed budgets, which gave regional administration, specialist and field alike, no flexibility to meet changing economic conditions. These weaknesses in the fiscal system were not easily remedied, given the limits of state power at the local level, the strong tradition of subdistrict economic and social autonomy, and, not least, the difficulty of maintaining accurate land registry and tax data due to the Chinese practice of dividing landed property equally among sons each generation. As for the Grain Transport Directorate, it relied on a shrinking income from *tuntian* rents and revenues, and from transport surcharges. This income had been only marginally sufficient in the best of times in the early Qing. It covered the monthly stipends of the military personnel and their food provisions, salaries for non-military crew, casual labor, lighterage, porterage, inspection and transfer charges at Tongzhou, customary fees on route, and deficits from loss of cargo not covered by wastage fees.

The costs rose sharply for both the canal and grain-transport agencies as the economy expanded and changed in the eighteenth century, bringing inflation and higher material and labor costs that far exceeded the established allocations. Further, the increase in inspection personnel in the Qianlong reign added both salary and customary fees to the budget. Finally, the growing ecological degradation of the canal system meant longer journeys, more delays, and greater use of porterage and lightering services. This, in turn, brought higher labor and shipping costs as well as increases in extra customary fees. Kelley's exhaustive study shows how these myriad fiscal problems led to the collapse of the government-controlled system of military labor for grain shipping. Similarly, changes in shipping craft, the use of private shippers, and changes in the funding and organization of canal work continued to challenge canal-transport operations in the nineteenth century.[46]

Grand Canal–Grain Transport Management   107

The Qing leadership tried to work out solutions to the crisis with imperial reforms, such as increasing the private trade allotment assigned to the crews, placing greater reliance on hired shipping, and making outright grants to cover the increased cost of transport. They did not, however, undertake fundamental reform of the fiscal system. The reasons for not doing so were complex and compelling from the Qing point of view; they touched on some of the deepest-held convictions about the appropriate limits of state power at the local level. These convictions were shaped by a long tradition of subdistrict autonomy and early Qing problems with local control that led to a low and "benevolent" land-tax policy, an unwillingness to exploit the possibilities of commercial taxes, and the curtailment of the discretionary fiscal power of local magistrates.

Given the marginal solvency of regional administration, field and specialist, and the Qing regime's adamant refusal to alter the basic structure of the fiscal system, canal–grain transport management was bound to founder if any one of a number of contingencies occurred: expansion and development of the economy, inflation, population increase, perturbations in the monetary and market systems, or ecological deterioration of the canal-riverine system. All of these did occur, with profound consequences for the state's major tax collecting agency—district government—and thus for the integrity of the entire Qing governmental structure, not only in the canal zone, but across the entire face of the empire.

Historians often have faulted the canal–grain transport system for its allegedly costly and inefficient operations, made the worse by tradition-bound, backward-looking emperors and corrupt, venal officials.[47] Indeed, it is customary to identify those low-level functionaries and supernumeraries, assigned to assist in the management of these problems in the late eighteenth and early nineteenth centuries, as the principal cause of, rather than the response to, the deepening ecological and fiscal crises that gripped the canal zone. Yet, the use of such personnel was perfectly consistent with late imperial patterns of relying on patronage networks and advisory assistants in regional administration rather than expanding the formal structure of government at the local level. In many cases, historians' judgments about canal communications are shaped by culturally and historically inappropriate definitions of what is rational, efficient, and functional. Such judgments often fail to appreciate the strategic, geopolitical logic of the canal–grain transport system in the eyes of China's imperial-official leadership, they ignore Qing innovations in its management, and they grossly underestimate the mounting ecological problems and operational costs that undermined the canal-shipping process by the late eighteenth century.[48] What may, in fact, be most noteworthy about the canal–grain transport system in the early nineteenth century is its continued operation in the face of incredible obstacles, right up to the shift of the Yellow River in the early 1850s.

4

The Grand Canal Crisis

Overview of the Unfolding Crisis

The Grand Canal crisis of 1824–26 began as just another in a long series of emergencies that had occurred with distressing frequency since the late eighteenth century, as a thickening blanket of silt clogged the canal arteries. Ominously high autumn flood waters and the unlucky coincidence of storms in late 1824 ruptured the Hongze Lake dikes, unleashing floods throughout the Huaiyang region that destroyed the Southern Canal near its junction with the Yellow River (map 3). Damage to canal facilities was undoubtedly greater than that from other disasters in recent memory. Indeed, the Daoguang Emperor, in a rhetorical flourish, asserted that it was a disaster the likes of which had not been seen before.[1] But the catastrophe was certainly to be expected, given both the current state of the canal system and the storehouse of historical memories that testified to the Huai and Yellow Rivers' capricious destructiveness.

Yet it was only in the first six months of 1825 that the actual dimensions of the disaster were fully understood, and it came to be seen as a major turning point in the Qing operation of the Grand Canal–grain transport system. The initial stages of canal reconstruction and the tortured process of grain shipment in early 1825 revealed with startling clarity that the adaptive tactics—used since Qianlong days to muddle through each successive canal-transport cycle—would no longer serve to save the canal nor secure the yearly shipment of strategic grain supplies. The flood damage had intensified siltation and crippled the already weakened canal so that far more work was required to restore it than the customary pattern of seasonal and emergency repairs. Furthermore, the geophysical barriers to canal transport, the diminished usefulness of the regular grain junks on the silted canal, and the increased dependence on, but severe shortage of, smaller vessels, or lighters—all cast doubt on the state's ability to continue the normal pattern of imperial grain shipments.

The Daoguang Emperor understood the significance of these realities by mid-1825, when he initiated a major review of canal–grain transport strategies and called for an investigation of sea transport for 1826. The resulting decisions mark a watershed in this key sector of Qing administration. They anticipated the impending shift of the Yellow River and the devastation and disorder that were sure to follow in its wake, and they laid the groundwork for grain shipping and canal maintenance for the next twenty-five troubled years. Because future events were bound to disrupt grain shipments and jeopardize imperial control over the Jiangsu sector of the canal zone, the emperor pushed for dramatic changes based on longer-term planning, rather than crisis-driven, seasonal expedients. The strategies under review included the junction crossing procedures, the practice of transfer-shipping, and canal reconstruction schemes that included redredging and rerouting the lower course of the Yellow River. The reassessment of these strategies resulted in greater reliance on transfer-shipping and made broader use of grain tax commutation, and it set the stage for expanded use of sea transport. When the river finally commenced its northward shift beginning in 1848, a sea-transport system—which had been tried and tested successfully in 1826—was ready for use.

These strategies placed even greater managerial initiative into the hands of regional field officials in the canal zone, while responsibility for many lower-level operations was shifted from local officials to private organizations connected with grain marketing and shipping. Although in some respects these changes departed from long-standing Qing practices, they were, for the most part, consistent with the tradition of flexibility in canal-transport management established earlier in the dynasty. They were consistent, too, with the practice of vesting practical responsibility for these matters in the hands of top-level field officials in the canal zone and of working closely and cooperatively with sectors of the private economy to achieve the well-being of the dynasty and provide for the people's livelihood.

Prelude: The Autumn Crossing Emergency

The swollen waters in both Hongze Lake and the Yellow River in the autumn of 1824 presaged the disaster to come. Normally, the river would have receded enough by the end of the ninth lunar month that empty grain boats, returning from the north, could cross the river into the Southern Canal by early in the tenth lunar month. The timely crossing of the fleets insured that no boats were iced in for the winter north of the Yellow River. It was also essential for the completion of a complex schedule of boat repairs, canal-dredging, and all the myriad preparations for loading and shipping the new spring grain cargoes by the first lunar month. Yet this year hundreds of grain boats were stalled in the canal just north of the river at Yangzhuang, waiting to cross to the south but unable to do so because water levels in the river were too high, relative to the lake, to enable the fleets to cross.

The crossing relied on the carefully timed release of water in a fast and focused stream from Hongze Lake through the Clear Passage to Yuhuang Lock gate, which opened onto the Yellow River (map 11). Empty junks, crossing the Yellow River from the north, were then hauled into the passage against this torrent of clear unsilted water, which both scoured out the passage and acted as a shield against the flow of the Yellow River's silted water into the passage and the canal head. This procedure had been used since the late seventeenth century, when Hongze Lake and its great dike, Gaojia *yan*, became the linchpin of the hydraulic engineering network in northern Jiangsu. By the early nineteenth century, its continued use was jeopardized by the silt-upraised bed of the Yellow River.

In the second week of the tenth lunar month, canal officials watched nervously as the water levels of both the river and the lake remained high and fluctuated capriciously. Because the river had maintained dangerously high levels for several weeks, the Xiangfu and

Wushui drainage gates, located on the south bank of the river northwest of the junction, had been opened to draw off the excess river water into the lake.[2] These gates had originally been built to draw clear water *into* the river to help scour it out near the junction.[3] More recently, however, they had been used to channel the silted river into the lake and had become the principal source of silt seepage into the lake, raising the lake bed and compounding the problem of dangerously high water levels. Besides opening the Xiangfu and Wushui gates, officials opened the drainage gates on the north bank of the river in the vicinity of the junction, one after another, without much discernible effect until midmonth, when the river and lake levels were reported to be nearly equal.

Yet troubling fluctuations continued to hold up the crossing, much to the dismay of the emperor and the panic of officials in northern Jiangsu. This prompted the opening of the important Wangying drainage gate during the third week of the tenth lunar month, which carried the Yellow River overflow north into the Salt Canal. Consequently, the river level dropped approximately 30 centimeters below that of the lake. With this achieved, the Hongze lead-channels were opened on the twentieth day and clear water surged out through the junction passage and Yuhuang Lock gate into the Yellow River. The waiting boats, assembled in the canal on the north side of the river, sailed across the river into the Southern Canal in quick "nose-to-tail" succession, completing the crossing by the fourth day of the eleventh lunar month, to the great relief of provincial officials and emperor alike.[4]

Calamity was averted but only narrowly, and management of the crossing was marred by misunderstanding and conflict between the emperor and regional officials. The conflict was sparked by the failure of officials to keep the emperor fully informed as the emergency unfolded and by their unwillingness to take the initiative to manipulate water levels quickly and effectively. This episode reveals some of the problems inherent in imperial direction of regional decision making on canal-transport issues. Important decisions were complicated by the imperative to act quickly to avert or mitigate danger to the canal and by the contradictory need to involve the emperor in the planning process. When the emperor intervened to direct regional management of the canal–grain transport system, he did so through the court letter–secret memorial interchange. These interchanges took time, and time was in short supply during these fast-moving crises. To insure imperial involvement and simultaneously to guarantee a fast, flexible response to canal problems, officials were required to include tactical planning options along with their detailed reports of impending problems, as explained in chapter 3. From the emperor's perspective, contingency plans were useful for two reasons. First, they served to arm regional officials with a range of alternative strategies well in advance of a full-scale emergency and enabled them to avoid mindless reliance on old ways of doing things—the reactive pattern of muddling through each and every crisis with last minute, short-term expedients. More significantly, however, by requiring regional officials to outline tactical plans ahead of time, the emperor and his inner court advisers had the opportunity to evaluate, respond, and suggest. They could direct the practical aspects of regional planning merely by asking for additional facts, making queries about feasibility, raising alternative possibilities, or simply saying no.

The emperor's repeated injunctions in the court letters to make preparations in advance were not empty rhetorical statements. They were serious directives aimed at overcoming the contradictions inherent in a decision-making process that sought both imperial involvement and speedy resolution of regional canal-transport problems. His insistence on the linkage of reporting and planning shows that he considered these two tasks to be the chief responsibilities of regional officials.

The complexities in tactical planning were sharply outlined in the 1824 crossing emergency described above. The emperor was informed that high waters in the river were delaying the return crossing of grain junks at the end of the ninth lunar month, but regional officials neither spelled out the causes of the high waters, nor did they outline a plan to lower them. The emperor was extremely agitated, not just because the next year's grain shipment might be thrown off schedule, but because the temporary anchorage of fleets north of the river was fraught with other dangers. In a secret edict to officials in northern Jiangsu, he expressed his concerns:

> The wind is high and vegetation dry. Fire could break out. The transport soldiers are sitting around eating and wasting time. Money to cover expenses incurred by the delay has not been advanced. The sailors are numerous and disorderly. Their control is not an easy task! They must not be allowed to stir up trouble.[5]

From this point until the return crossing was ultimately completed late in the tenth month, the emperor used the court letter to drive the process, demanding specific details about crossing conditions, commenting on tactical measures, and urging officials to take action to lower the river level. Yet, in northern Jiangsu, there was clearly a lack of unanimity on the causes and therefore the solutions of the crisis. The grain transport director, Wei Yuanyu, memorialized the emperor directly to criticize the tactics used by the canal director, Zhang Wenhao, to drain the river. The emperor agreed that the latter's plan to drain the river in the middle reaches opposite the canal junction probably would fail because the Yellow River was too high to assure control of runoff. This observation, in effect, directed regional officials to look further for suitable ways to drain the river.

But as the emergency unfolded, regional officials continued to fail to report the reasons for delays or present a plan of action. Normally, planning options were forged and articulated by the Liangjiang governor-general, who, in this case, was Sun Yuting, an experienced regional official who had served with distinction since the Qianlong reign.[6] Sun, however, was apparently unable to forge a consensus among canal-transport officials and did not inform the emperor of this fact. From the point of view of the officials in charge, this was probably the safest thing to do, while they remained unclear about what course of action to pursue. Once the situation became clearer, they could act quickly on their own initiative. The emperor responded angrily to this information blackout in a secret edict on the twelfth day of the tenth month to Sun and other officials charged with managing the crossing.

> It has been ten days, and I have still not received a single memorial about the levels of the Yellow River or the crossing of grain boats. I am consumed with worry over this matter. . . . Don't you know this is a matter of the gravest urgency? Everyone must rouse his conscience to manage the situation.[7]

He demanded explanations for the strange, unseasonable fluctuations in the river level and the latest word on its relationship to lake levels. He coupled these queries for vital details with an unequivocal order to proceed with measures for draining the river and allowing the fleets to cross. When regional officials had done so, they were to report immediately by 400-*li* post "to inform me and calm my worries!"

Four days later, he received a memorial from Sun and other regional officials cataloging the gradual decrease in the river level since the beginning of the ninth month. By the early tenth month, the river had dropped to the level of the lake. Regional officials indicated that if the river level dropped another twenty-two centimeters, they planned to open the Yuhuang Lock gate; if it remained equal, they would open the Wangying drainage channel north of the river and wait for the river to drop sufficiently to cross the fleets.[8]

This was not good enough, in the emperor's view. The winter season had already arrived and "still not one ship has crossed the Yellow River." If there were further delays, the canal "would freeze solid and the fleets could not return to their home anchorages and prepare for the next year's grain transport cycle." Again he ordered them to proceed with the crossing.[9]

On the twenty-fifth day of the tenth month, in response to another report that the fleets had still not begun the crossing, the emperor bitterly attacked regional officials for shirking their responsibilities.

Earlier, because the grain boats were delayed north of the river for a long time and because this was a matter of the greatest urgency, I frequently sent down decrees to the governor-general and others to devise a plan jointly to manage the situation. And now after waiting over ten days, their memorial has arrived. Naturally, I thought that the boats would have crossed by now, but today's report reveals that not one boat has crossed the Yellow River. What are those officials doing out there! The long and short of it is, that they are not seizing the initiative ... and looking ahead to next year's spring transport![10]

This court letter underscores the linkage between reporting and planning and the necessary balance between tactical planning and speedy action. In the emperor's eyes, these were primary responsibilities of regional officials on the scene. Yet the emperor charged they had not been on top of things: they had waited, shirked responsibility, delayed, and as a consequence had lost good opportunities for action. He reminded them that he should not be placed in a position to dictate tactical plans and when to implement them from far away in the capital, yet he felt that he was being compelled to do so because "in the blink of an eye, the canal will freeze over." The following day, the twenty-sixth of the tenth month, he received word that regional officials had opened the Wangying drainage gate on the eighteenth day to drain off river water, and by the twentieth day, the river was low enough to begin the crossing. In neither case had there been time to inform the emperor and his inner court advisers of their decision.[11]

This episode is significant because it shows how the demands of canal-transport administration affected the decision-making process. Imperial direction of regional decisions depended utterly on open and detailed communications. This enabled the emperor to drive the process in an informed and responsible way, but it did not and was not intended to give the emperor the authority to dictate solutions. He oversaw, influenced, and sanctioned, but did not mandate. And he could only do the former well if regional officials supplied him with detailed information about local conditions. However, regional officials often had to wait and assess conditions before reporting, then act quickly and rely on their own experience. The unpredictability of changing canal conditions frequently hampered the emperor's ability to guide regional canal management. The special imperatives of canal administration that limited the imperial sphere of action widened the prerogatives and responsibilities of regional officials.

Yet during the crossing emergency, regional officials seemed unwilling to shoulder their part of the decision-making process. Their unwillingness to act had, in fact, nearly forced the emperor to mandate specific actions, or "to control from afar" and step beyond the bounds of his rightful supervisory role in regional problem solving.[12] The phrase "controlling from afar" (*yaozhi*) then, encompasses the basic assumptions on which the *nonroutine* imperial-regional decision-making process operated: that regional officials bore responsibility to report problems and to craft and implement concrete courses of action for their solution, while the emperor's primary tasks were to monitor, supervise and sanction these actions.

Clearly, the decision-making process during the 1824 crossing emergency was not as open, interactive, consensual, or regionally based as the emperor thought it should have been. He expressed his dissatisfaction and his expectations for the future conduct of canal affairs in his public criticisms of Zhang Wenhao, the Southern Canal director. Zhang had not combined the careful performance of routine duties and procedures with an ability to act decisively in the face of difficult local conditions.[13] But the emperor rejoiced, nonetheless, that the danger was over. "The junks were all pulled safely across because of the Yellow River god's (*heshen*) help and protection. I am sending ten sticks of imperial incense so that Sun Yuting and Zhang Wenhao can make sacrifices of thanksgiving to the god on my behalf."[14]

The Disaster at Gaojia Great Dike and the First Response

But even as the emperor rejoiced in the eleventh month, stormy rains in northern Jiangsu pushed water levels in Hongze Lake menacingly upwards, and high winds whipped up waves that pounded the Gaojia Great Dike. In spite of the frantic efforts of dike guards, the dike buckled and the flood waters poured out to the east, tearing out the secondary earthen embankments that lay behind the great dike.[15] The water raced into the lakes and the Grand Canal and ripped through drainage gates in the eastern side of the canal dike between Gaoyou and Shaobo, then spilled into the croplands of the Xiahe region (map 11).[16]

Reports received in Peking from Jiangsu on the twenty-third of the eleventh month revealed the tragic dimensions of the destruction. The floods had destroyed nearly 30 kilometers of lake dikes. Two major breaches had been made in the stone-clad Gaojia dike, one near the middle at Shisanbao and the largest at Xilang Temple near Zhou Bridge, at the southernmost end of the dike. Many other ruptures apparently occurred where overflow gates were fitted into the main dike wall. These openings, or *koumen*, "where the flood waters are pulled through," had failed to arrest and guide the floods into diversion channels because of the sheer force of the waters and because several were in such a state of disrepair that they could not be opened.[17] As a result, the stonework that buttressed these dam gates was torn out in several places.

The floods also destroyed between 60 and 70 percent of the secondary earthen dikes that reinforced Gaojia dike to the east. These embankments were also designed to act as a protective barrier for the canal dikes farther east that extended from the Yellow River junction south to Shaobo. More importantly, they were supposed to shield the intricate and fragile junction facilities northeast of Hongze Lake, including its network of flash locks, feeder channels, weirs, and waiting ponds leading through the canal head west of Huai'an into the Clear Passage and out into the river through the Yuhuang Lock gate (map 11).

The Grand Canal Crisis 119

Besides the destruction of the stone and earthen dikes, the flood waters cast a blanket of mud over the Huaiyang Canal from the junction to Shaobo, clogging its main channel and the overflow gates. At first, it was thought that the most serious silt deposits lay at the northern end of the canal, from Pinghe Bridge to the junction. But it became clear several months later that equally serious siltation filled the canal as far south as Shaobo (map 7) and clogged the five major drainage gates in the eastern dike wall of the canal from Gaoyou southward to Shaobo, with Zhaoguan gate sustaining the worst of it.[18]

The disaster also revealed the deterioration of three important overflow gates (the Xin, Zhi, and Li gates) situated on the southeast perimeter of Hongze Lake below the rock-faced sections of the great dike, south of Zhou Bridge (map 11). As explained earlier, these three were a part of some ten or more overflow gates that played a crucial role in the control of Huai waters contained in Hongze Lake. Normally, they were closed to accumulate clear water for the crossing of grain boats at the junction and opened when waters were high to help prevent dike collapse and random flooding. The Qing state had invested heavily in these structures, repairing and improving them periodically throughout the dynasty.[19] When it was found, in early 1825, that three of the dams had been so silt-clogged that they could not be opened, a major effort was made to relocate and rebuild them. Finally, the floods had inundated large sections of the Xiahe region east of the Grand Canal between Gaoyou and Shaobo. All in all, the floods had exacted a grim toll on the hydraulic network in northern Jiangsu and on the "huts and fields" (*tianlu*) of the people of Xiahe. These calamitous events portended turmoil in the canal zone and jeopardized the impending shipment of strategic grain supplies, due to commence in a month's time.[20]

An urgent memorial from Sun Yuting bore the bad news to the emperor.[21] It set in motion the first stage of imperial management of the Grand Canal crisis, a stage that lasted four days and included the public announcement of the disaster, the appointment of a new slate of regional officials, and the dispatch of the emperor's agents—the imperial commissioners—to northern Jiangsu.[22] The public announcement was a formal acknowledgement of the disaster which, from the leadership's point of view, had both portentous and practical significance for the well-being of the state. The edict detailed the dimensions of the catastrophe, announced the authorization of funds for emergency repairs and urgent human relief, and named and blamed those officials on whose watch the disaster had occurred. Even though the actual causes had yet to be determined, these officials were, by definition, accountable because their positions entailed specific responsibility for the defense of the canal.

While the rains and winds came "from heaven" (*youtian*), the floods were considered to be both a natural and a man-made disaster because it was assumed that they were partly caused by neglect of vital water-control facilities. The officials identified for blame included Sun Yuting himself, because as governor-general he had overall responsibility for the canal in the Jiangsu sector, Zhang Wenhao, the previously condemned Southern Canal director, and the Huaiyang intendant.[23] But blame was also extended to the legions of low-level canal workers who were stationed on the Hongze Lake dikes in Shanxu and Gaoyan subprefectures and whose "unregulated hearts and wandering minds had led to the careless disregard of precautions. Theirs were serious crimes that should not go unpunished."[24]

The dispatch of imperial commissioners and the appointment of new regional officials were considered imperative. The emperor's initial court letters reveal that he considered the appointment of new, untainted officials to be necessary for a reliable evaluation of and effective response to the crisis. Such a response, from the emperor's point of view, must include an honest, thorough assessment of the root causes of the disaster, the rapid implementation of a reconstruction plan that would "assure the shipment of spring grain tribute," and the establishment of open, sustained communications between the emperor and regional officials in northern Jiangsu. If the current officials were retained in office, the emperor felt that they would try to cover up their wrongdoings and interfere with the assessment of damage, the determination of root causes, and the initial planning process.[25] In other words, their involvement in and responsibility for the disaster compromised their ability to work constructively at the outset to craft an effective reconstruction program.

From the start, the imperial commissioners, Wang Tingzhen and Wen Fu, were particularly important for guaranteeing the unrestricted flow of reliable information from the disaster area. As outsiders to Jiangsu, with specific responsibilities and short-term appointments, they could be relied on to assess the situation in the junction area dispassionately and to sketch out the broad outlines of a reconstruction plan, while simultaneously initiating work on the highest priority projects—those essential to the spring grain-shipping cycle.[26] The Daoguang Emperor emphasized their investigative and reporting functions, probably to avoid a repetition of the events of the crossing emergency, when communications had broken down and imperial involvement was limited.

The commissioners' responsibility to initiate the first stage of reconstruction was made clear in their instructions. The emperor directed them to investigate the first reports of the disaster sent from Liangjiang by Sun Yuting. Specifically, they were to determine if he had reported the scope of the disaster honestly, had assessed prudently the need for funds, and had launched effective emergency work and relief measures in the immediate aftermath of the calamity. On the basis of their investigation, the commissioners were to outline a relief and reconstruction program that would quickly restore the canal and grain shipment process.[27]

The emperor also expected the imperial commissioners to weld the new regional appointees together into an effective consensual leadership group. This is seen in his orders to work closely with the newly appointed Southern Canal director, Yan Lang, "to investigate and plan together." Yan had been Shandong Canal director at Jining. The commissioners were to rendezvous with him there and travel with him to Qingjiangpu, beginning their deliberations en route. It was clear, however, that the canal director was the junior partner. He was to contribute his expertise on canal issues, but defer to the commissioners and carry out their plans after their return to Peking.[28]

Yan was expected to use his technical expertise in water-control management to evaluate and respond to circumstances in the canal zone. When conditions warranted, he was to seize the initiative to safeguard the canal system. Practical knowledge, the ability to finesse regulatory guidelines, and an intuitive grasp of changing realities were the leadership qualities most prized in a canal director—qualities that Yan's predecessor, Zhang Wenhao, had sorely lacked.

Zhang Jing, an experienced intendant from Shandong, replaced Yan Lang in the post of Shandong Canal director.[29] Zhang was later to emerge as an important expert on Yellow River–Grand Canal problems affecting the Henan–Shandong–Jiangsu corridor, and he was destined to play a continuing role in canal management throughout the troubled years of the 1830s and 1840s, prior to the shift of the Yellow River.[30]

The emperor had reservations about Zhang Jing's appointment, and he directed the Henan governor, Cheng Zuluo, to evaluate his work carefully to see that he was up to the special demands of the job.[31]

> Zhang Jing has not come up through the ranks of the canal administration. Cheng Zuluo has recommended him because he has been courageous in managing local affairs; his conduct of public matters is sincere; and when meeting problems he does not run away from responsibility. Because of this, I have promoted him in the past from Jining prefect to circuit intendant. Now I am appointing him to the important post of acting director of the [Shandong] Canal. This position carries with it many important responsibilities: to repair, protect, and defend the canal during the autumn flood season, all matters of critical importance. Cheng is an official concurrently responsible for [Hedong] Canal matters. Let him, at all times, carefully observe this official. Is he or is he

The Grand Canal Crisis 123

not able to shoulder the responsibilities of the position of [Shandong] Canal director? Inform me by memorial![32]

The other important officials assigned to northern Jiangsu were Wei Yuanyu, who moved to the acting governor-generalship from the post of Grain-Transport director, and Yan Jian, who then filled the vacated transport post. Interestingly, although Zhang Wenhao was dismissed, Sun Yuting was retained in service and stationed at Qingjiangpu until the sixth month of 1825. As the emperor stated, "He has expertise from long service in Jiangsu and can be of great value assisting the new official [Yan Jian]" in expediting the passage of grain junks through the junction.[33] Sun continued to act as a kind of field manager at the junction even after Qishan took charge in midyear as governor-general.[34]

The emperor's appointment of a new slate of regional officials and the dispatch of imperial commissioners signaled his intention to intervene in and direct the management of the crisis from the outset. He relied most heavily on the imperial commissioners, whom he expected to facilitate the initial flow of information to the capital, while shaping the new regional appointees into a cohesive group, capable of problem solving. As we shall see below, they performed that role in the assessment of root causes and in plotting out the main outlines of the reconstruction program by early in the first month of 1825.

The emperor clearly used the appointment of these new officials to strengthen his control over the first steps of regional crisis management. This response to the Gaojia dike disaster contrasts sharply with his handling of the crossing emergency in late 1824. During this earlier episode, a low-grade emergency, the emperor was content to rely solely on the two-way discourse of the court letter–secret memorial interchange. However, given the scale and greater significance of the Gaojia dike disaster, he could not risk receiving flawed information that could undermine canal reconstruction and the spring shipment of tribute grain. Therefore, he replaced key regional leaders and sent in his own agents to assure the reliability of reports. It was not that the commissioners were expected to know more about local canal issues than the regional field and specialist officials. But the emperor relied on them to open up discourse between the inner court and the new regional leadership and to provide the widest possible accounting of regional conditions and needs quickly.

Root Causes

The imperial commissioners, Wang Tingzhen and Wen Fu, laid the foundations of the reconstruction policy during their six-week assignment in northern Jiangsu, from the first day of the twelfth month of 1824 (4.12.1) until their departure in the middle of the first month of 1825 (5.1.14). During this brief but critical period, the commissioners first investigated the root causes of the disaster; then, on the basis of their assessment, they outlined the principal themes of Grand Canal reconstruction that regional officials would follow for the first six months of 1825.[35]

The investigation probed the practical geophysical and bureaucratic factors that contributed to the Gaojia dike disaster. A clear understanding of the actual causes was considered pivotal to the design of an effective reconstruction program and was, therefore, far more important to the resolution of the crisis than the emperor's ritualized statement of blame in the public edict describing the disaster (4.11.23).

As noted earlier, floods were understood to be man-made as well as natural disasters because they resulted as often from official neglect of water-control tasks as from natural phenomena. The assessment of bureaucratic factors centered on official performance of specialized water-control tasks. It probed canal officials' grasp and application of administrative regulations and the practical lore that guided the management of canal operations in the face of natural obstacles. This focus on human causes reflects the longstanding Qing emphasis on disciplined implementation of administrative regulations that were viewed as an anchor, but one that could be raised or lowered as conditions required. The emphasis on administrative practice suggests a rather optimistic belief that canal officials could sometimes temper the destructive forces of nature if they followed prescribed administrative routines—routines that were themselves shaped by natural cycles.

The imperial commissioners took four sources of information into account when they assessed the root causes: first, the reports of Sun Yuting and other regional officials, written in the immediate aftermath of the disaster; second, their own on-site investigations of damaged facilities; third, the views of other, outside officials whose memorials were sent to them by the emperor and which presumably reflected his own views; and fourth (at the emperor's insistence), the administrative guidelines and practical water-conservancy lore that outlined the dynasty's customary approaches to canal operation. These varied sources contained very different views of short-term regional imperatives and long-term imperial goals. The imperial commissioners began the process of ordering and reconciling these views as soon as they arrived at the scene of the disaster. The regional orientation of the Qing decision-making process and the overwhelming scope and complexity of the technical, natural, and bureaucratic factors at work in northern Jiangsu determined that solutions ultimately would have to bow to regional realities.

Emperor and officials alike recognized that nature and geography created almost insurmountable conditions of instability in the Grand Canal–Yellow River system. Nature and the Yellow River were the unconquerable enemies, and the corpus of regulations and water-management strategies designed over the centuries for their control recognized the impossibility of winning the war. The goal was to control and harness the Huai and Yellow rivers in the autumn flood season, minimizing their destructive force so that the canal remained functional for the next shipping season. Both emperor and officials felt that if canal-river officials understood and applied the timeworn but tried-and-tested regulations and strategies, they could manipulate powerful natural phenomena to their advantage.

Yet the situation in the early nineteenth century was significantly more dangerous and unstable than it had been earlier. The leadership knew the Yellow River was at the end of its cycle, soon to sweep back to the north to find its exit to the sea. There was little room for maneuver. Many officials felt that human efforts availed little at this stage although few were bold enough to say so as openly as the experienced grain-transport official, Wei Yuanyu. In early 1825, he asserted that the Yellow River could no longer be controlled by human agency as could the clear unsilted Huai.[36] Mute acceptance and "muddling through" really appeared to be the only realistic course of action until the Yellow River's shift was complete. Whether or not the emperor was as sanguine as he first appeared about the state's ability to devise a satisfactory solution to the crisis in the interim period before the shift is not entirely clear. This was, after all, his first major canal crisis, and he may not have been as familiar with the facts as he later became. There is also some evidence that his idealistic statements should be interpreted as ritualized pronouncements of the norm that were uttered at the outset to prepare the way for necessary adaptive changes. In any case, as the crisis unfolded in early 1825, he quickly came to terms with the grim realities of the river and the silt.

Given the geophysical problems at hand, what could the state reasonably expect its officials to achieve in northern Jiangsu? How much could they have done to avert the Gaojia dike disaster and floods? Sun Yuting's account of events suggested that very little, in fact, could have been done. In a series of six memorials written in the weeks following the disaster he asserted, "The lake floods were really caused by violent winds. People's efforts were of no avail." The underlying cause was the unlucky combination of decades, indeed centuries, of siltation and of unfortunate weather that defied man's best efforts "to control the river and protect the canal." Silt blockages in the lower reaches of the Yellow River near the sea caused the river to back up into the Hongze-junction area, swelling the river and causing it to flood over its southern bank, north of the lake, where it seeped into the lake through the Xiangfu and Wushui drainage channels.[37] At the same time that the river and lake were rising, heavy rains and strong cyclonic winds from the northwest caused the waves to batter holes in the great dike. "The violent winds and the excess accumulation of clear water in the lake were from heaven."[38] Nature was at fault, not regional officials![39]

Sun's explanations were intended to emphasize the herculean magnitude of the natural problems that faced canal-river officials in northern Jiangsu. Additionally, they were intended to defend the Southern Canal director, Zhang Wenhao, whom many criticized for his performance of technical water-control tasks. Sun argued to the contrary:

> Zhang has always economized in his administration of the canal. He may have blocked up the Yuhuang Lock gate too late [in late 1824], but the clear water accumulated in Hongze just the same until the floods. The question of clear water accumulation is a thorny, complex issue. I think Zhang should be given special consideration because he is a virtuous and capable official.[40]

Sun's defense is important because it asserts that Zhang responded to imperial appeals for fiscal stringency, and if he did, indeed, neglect water-control maintenance, he did so in a loyal attempt to comply with imperial orders to economize. Perhaps imperial pressure for fiscal retrenchment was to blame, not Zhang. Sun also defended Zhang's keeping the Yuhuang Lock gate open longer than usual in the late autumn during the southward crossing of empty grain boats. He suggested that the closure of Yuhuang was unrelated to the later dissipation of lake water that occurred as a consequence of the dike collapse, and he implied that the water levels in the lake were determined by infinitely more complex issues than merely the length of time that Yuhuang was kept open.

The emperor responded to these explanations with skepticism, asserting that naturally Sun would try to put the best face on things. The emperor believed that Zhang's management of water-control tasks was flawed because he had ignored the practical advice and river-control lore meant to guide canal-river management:

> Sun says that violent winds and the accumulation of clear water to excess are from heaven and that Zhang's economizing of ten thousand to seventy thousand *taels* also contributed to the disaster. I don't believe a bit of this! Most likely it was caused by Zhang's own headstrong nature, stubbornness, and his unwillingness to heed the counsel of others. He did not observe earlier customary procedures. I have no sympathy for Sun's words. I say that Zhang's management ruined state affairs. . . . He is an official who undermines the achievement of state goals and neglects the duties of office. I definitely am not going to extend leniency to him.[41]

No more excuses and coverup. The emperor wanted the "real" causes, and the imperial commissioners were ordered to redouble their investigation of Sun's reports. Was his assessment of the causes and dimensions of the catastrophe and the costs of reconstruction reliable?

The discourse on root causes was broadened to include the opinions of outside officials unconnected with the disaster to assure that additional points of view were brought to bear on the question. During the first two weeks of the twelfth month, the emperor forwarded two such memorials to the imperial commissioners and to top regional officials connected with the canal crisis. The fact that the emperor chose these two memorials for circulation, of course, indicated that the issues they raised had merit in his eyes, and he was using them to press forward his own concerns. Yet their circulation highlights a strength of the Qing decision-making process, which was its ability to consider a range of points of view in the heat of a crisis and to develop a consensus. Because the process was most responsive to, and to a certain extent dominated by, short-term regional imperatives, the outside perspectives probably helped to maintain a balance between central goals and regional needs.

Both "outside" memorials argued that the primary cause of the disaster was human error. Their authors asserted that regional officials had failed to undertake specific actions that could have offset the effects of threatening natural conditions. The first memorial, presented by a central ministry vice-president, Zhu Shiyan, looked at the long-term pattern of canal maintenance and asserted that previous regional officials in northern Jiangsu had, over the years, neglected the proper maintenance of stone and earthen dikes on Hongze Lake.[42] They were driven to do so, not by ignorance of the regulations and lack of technical expertise, nor by a corrupt unwillingness to perform regular maintenance tasks, but by fiscal constraints and the political pressure to economize. Rather than repair the Gaojia dike thoroughly with mortared stonework, they merely reinforced it with tamped earth, which they dug away from the secondary earthen embankments behind it. They then failed to replace the earth taken from those dikes. This led to constant ruptures in the great dike, the weakening of the secondary dikes, and the slow leakage of clear water from Hongze into the other lakes.

Zhu asserted that besides failing to reinforce the lake dikes, generations of officials also had neglected to take proper measures to dredge and drain the Yellow River in its lower reaches and to clear out the sandbars at the mouth of the river on the Yellow Sea. These blockages caused backflows upstream in the lake and junction areas and flooding across the south bank of the Yellow River into the lake. The neglect of dike repair and of dredging the river's mouth was a human failure, and had put the whole system at risk and ultimately cost more in the long run, as the dike disaster had shown. Furthermore, it undermined the practice of accumulating clear lake water for the crossing of grain boats. Thus it threatened the entire transport process, which was, after all, the main purpose of the canal system.

Zhu's critique is important because it shows that he was aware of the official tendency to neglect a wide range of discrete, and seemingly insignificant, water-control tasks because of the pressures of fiscal retrenchment. His assertion that systemic fiscal and administrative problems had compromised the state's ability to maintain the Grand Canal infrastructure also suggests that officials were aware that the centrally funded canal directorate was struggling under the weight of spiralling building and labor costs, just as local officials were struggling to fund and manage smaller facilities and people's works. His critique was courageous because it pointed the finger of blame, not at a single official, but at larger systemic problems that only the central leadership had the power and authority to address. In this respect, his assessment was similar to Sun's defense of Zhang for economizing, the implication being that the central government's pressure to economize had forced the cutback of essential water-control work.

The second memorial was a more pointed, personal attack on the management decisions of the Southern Canal director, Zhang Wenhao. It charged him with failure to follow the regulations for draining the Yellow River and protecting the lake and junction facilities. The memorialist was Pan Xi'en, Hanlin expositor, who was so vocal in his criticism that he was appointed probationary Huaiyang intendant in the autumn of 1825, then several months later promoted to a post created especially for him, assistant director of the Southern Canal.[43] Although Pan's attack on Zhang was narrowly focused, it did emphasize an important issue—the necessity of having a thorough grasp of water-control techniques and an understanding of how and when to use them. Pan faulted Zhang for failing to apply effective drainage procedures for reducing the water levels in the lake and river. He claimed that Zhang had made stupid mistakes that could have been avoided if he had applied the precautionary rules with discipline and insight.

Pan linked the disaster to Zhang Wenhao's earlier mismanagement of the autumn 1824 crossing of grain boats. At that time, he asserted, Zhang had kept Yuhuang Lock gate open too long and risked Yellow River backflows into the canal.[44] The river was unusually high in the middle reaches near the junction precisely because the river had not been drained properly, a point also raised by Zhu Shiyan. Instead of draining it in the lower reaches, and presumably dredging the sandbars near the mouth, Zhang had used the Xiangfu and Wushui drainage channels located above the junction. This procedure kept the water levels dangerously high at the junction and also fed highly silted water into Hongze Lake, reducing its holding capacity.

Pan's critique presented a classic restatement of early Qing hydraulic policy. It reaffirmed the pivotal role of Hongze Lake in the shipment of grain tribute through the junction. The lake was imperative, he said, for the accumulation of clear water reserves for the yearly crossing of grain junks, "collecting the clear to oppose the Yellow." This method, he argued, also scoured out the junction and riverbed and, therefore, safeguarded the canal from silting and preserved it for shipping in the long run. It was the "customary way" precisely because it was the best way (fig. 10). Zhang's extended opening of the Yuhuang Lock gate and his misguided drainage techniques threatened the junction, the continued operation of the canal, and the state's strategic shipments of grain tribute.

Pan's critique, with its emphasis on grain transport, hit a responsive chord with the emperor, as it obviously was intended to do, precisely because it related the mundane details of the disaster to the long-term protection and viability of the canal and to the ability to ship grain tribute. He concurred with Zhu about the significance of the clear water strategy for crossing the grain fleets at the junction, and he recapitulated the latter's concern over the failure to drain the river at its mouth or to repair the lake dikes and overflow gates on the southeast perimeter of the lake in Gaoyan and Shanxu subprefectures.[45]

During the discussion of root causes, the emperor concentrated on three issues of which he wanted regional officials to take account: first, the importance of thorough, reliable information-gathering and reporting; second, the accountability of officials for the performance of technical water-control tasks; and third, the completion of those works most intimately connected to grain transport. He pressed these issues by raising questions about the information and assessments contained in memorial reports from regional officials and the imperial commissioners and by circulating the memorials of outsiders, such as Zhu and Pan, that articulated his main concerns. In both cases, by raising these questions, he sharpened the focus of the decision-making discourse.

This use of the court letter to direct discussions is clearly seen in the emperor's orders to the imperial commissioners. In addition to his frequent queries to double-check Sun's reports of the disaster against actual conditions in field, he pointedly asked for specific information about facilities and problems that he considered most important. "Are the flying dikes on the southeast edge of Gaojia dike closed up?" he asked, referring to the temporary blockage of damaged overflow gates, presumably by fascines, because he later referred to the actual rebuilding of these facilities with rock. "Are preparations underway to repair the largest breaches at Xilang Temple and Shisanbao with careful mortared stonework?" These queries underscored the importance of secure dikes for the accumulation of clear water and thus for the spring grain transport. The emperor implied that these works should be given the highest priority in emergency reconstruction work.

"Are the dikes in the lower reaches of the Yellow River being strengthened to assure the constriction of the river so that the current can scour the channel and mouth?" With this question the emperor pointedly reminded officials that the cause of the Gaojia dike disaster, and the principal threat to the canal system, was a series of blockages at the Yellow River's mouth. With the turmoil in the region after the floods, perhaps officials needed to be reminded that the principal danger remained the precipitously high level of the Yellow River bed in its lower reaches. Finally, "are relief measures underway in Xiahe to provide food and shelter for the victims of the floods?" A later edict on the ninth day of the twelfth month, raised even more questions about the leakage of clear water from Hongze that threatened the crossing of grain boats at the junction.[46]

These questions provided the commissioners with an analytical focus and a starting point for assessing root causes and creating an effective program of emergency reconstruction. At the same time, the emperor's inquiries made it clear that this information was to be sent to the capital and that he intended to play an active role in crisis management from the very beginning. He needed information quickly and continuously so that he could be an informed participant in the planning process. The commissioners' reports opened up regional realities to him, enabling him to enter into the process of problem solving with appropriate and flexible responses.

The memorial reports by Sun, Zhu, and Pan and the edicts written in response to them crystallized the discussion of root causes and revealed a consensus on the main natural obstacles that plagued the canal system. They all viewed the canal system in northern Jiangsu holistically, relating the problems of the parts to the breakdown of the whole. While Sun used the coincidence of the backflows with inclement weather to explain the disaster, Zhu and Pan, with the emperor's concurrence, asserted that bureaucratic inaction and ill-considered actions had worsened these problems. They argued that officials had neglected the established methods for countering the effects of backflows: dredging and draining in the lower reaches of the Yellow River, quick opening and closing of Yuhuang Lock gate, and disciplined yearly repairs of the lake dikes and overflow gates. While Pan's critique identified a single official's lack of basic administrative expertise and his laxness in performing specific tasks, Zhu, more interestingly, addressed larger systemic problems in the fiscal-administrative environment that compromised the ability of canal officials to perform their jobs in accordance with established standards. His assessment challenged both the emperor and regional officials to come up with long-term solutions, not simply short-term expedients.

Their analyses, taken together, implied that canal-riverine problems could be solved by obeying the precautionary regulations governing canal-river management. Every official had access to this technical information and the yearly calendar of repair and maintenance tasks. Every official was, or should have been, familiar with the procedures to offset rising water levels. If officials did not avail themselves of these guidelines, disasters were bound to occur. The emperor shared these general views about official accountability, and he also shared their view that the technical-bureaucratic lore entrenched in the administrative regulations was the cornerstone of the system's successful operation.

Identifying natural and bureaucratic causes was the beginning of the planning process. It focused attention on the engineering and reconstruction work that would be necessary to restore the canal and to guarantee the spring shipment of tribute grain, which was to commence its northward journey in a matter of weeks, early in the first month of 1825. These tasks were herculean and included both the emergency work necessitated by the floods and the regular maintenance tasks that had been neglected over the years. Both were essential to the resolution of the crisis. It was the job of the commissioners to determine whether it could be done and where to begin.[47]

5

Racing Against Time: Reconstruction and the 1825 Spring Crossing

The imperial commissioners' investigation of root causes uncovered shocking details about the weakened state of the canal-riverine hydraulic system and produced a daunting reconstruction agenda for regional government in northern Jiangsu at the dawn of the new year, 1825. Flood damage to pivotal water-control facilities was widespread and severe, but equally troubling were the signs of deterioration that stemmed from decades of neglect of yearly maintenance tasks. The reasons for this neglect are complex and go far beyond the conventional explanations made by contemporary observers and modern scholars, who emphasize that the primary reason for failure to maintain the canal system was the diversion of funds by corrupt field, specialist, and supernumerary officials.[1]

During the canal crisis, the testimony of officials suggested—probably correctly—that the pressure for fiscal retrenchment contributed to this pattern of neglect. The Qing emphasis on retrenchment reflected the leadership's concern with mounting fiscal-economic difficulties associated with inflation of food, labor, and materials costs and growing instability in the monetary and market systems since the late eighteenth century. These problems compromised the ability of both the centrally funded canal directorates and local field administration to finance the regular seasonal repairs of the canal system. A second important factor contributing to the neglect of maintenance, especially that scheduled for the autumn season, was the general slowing of the spring grain-transport process due to the system-wide siltation of the canal in northern Jiangsu. This greatly delayed the movement of grain fleets through the Huaiyang Canal. These delays prolonged the spring shipping cycle beyond the summer solstice, sometimes into the seventh and eighth months. During this spill-over period, human and material resources were directed towards completing the spring shipping process and diverted away from the regular autumn repairs. Yet a third problem was that many important small-scale tasks were the charge of assistant officials at the prefectural and district levels, who were supposed to enlist local leaders, resources, and labor to complete them, but who had too little political influence to do so.

As a result of these factors, imperial planners were faced with a staggering list of canal reconstruction projects in early 1825 that included both the emergency repair of flood-damaged facilities and the rebuilding of facilities that had deteriorated slowly over time. Among the emergency tasks were: the reconstruction of Gaojia dike, the earthen dikes that reinforced it, the Huaiyang Canal dikes, the drainage gates on the eastern canal dike near Shaobo, and the dredging of junction channels and the canal from the junction to Pinghe Bridge, north of Baoying (map 11). Among the long-neglected maintenance tasks were the dredging of the mouth of the Yellow River, the repair of deteriorated lake dikes, and the reconstruction of all the overflow gates and drainage channels leading from the lake to the canal and the Yangzi River. These two sets of tasks were added to the regular schedule of repairs for 1825, placing a triple burden on the canal and field agencies. The imperial commissioners' job was to rank these tasks in order of importance and fit them into an overall program of reconstruction.

In general, all Grand Canal–grain transport work was divided up and performed within two broad periods, or cycles, defined by the seasonal pattern of rainfall and the ebb and flow of Yellow and Huai river floods. The spring cycle lasted from the winter solstice to the summer solstice (*dongzhi*, December 22, to *xiazhi*, June 22). During this period, rains were infrequent and the rivers low, enabling the canal-river administration to dredge the lower course of the Yellow River, clear it of sandbars, and strengthen its dikes, to maximize the river's scouring action on the riverbed. At the same time, canal workers repaired and strengthened the Hongze Lake dikes and its overflow gates, not only to withstand the force of the autumn floods from the Huai River drainage basin that accumulated in the lake, but also to store up a supply of clear, unsilted water for use each spring, from the second to the fifth months, to cross the grain junks at the canal–Yellow River junction.

Finally, the Huaiyang Canal bed was dredged each spring to prepare the way for the advancing grain fleets. Simultaneously, the junction facilities were carefully inspected, strengthened, and dredged, especially the five lead channels that drew the lake water into the junction passage and carried the grain boats through Yuhuang Lock gate out into the river (maps 7, 8). Of all these spring tasks, the most significant and the most vexing was the "accumulation of clear water in the lake to attack the Yellow River." The lake waters had to be high enough to use for the junction crossing, but not so high as to burst the dikes.

The summer solstice marked the end of the spring seasonal cycle and the completion of tasks associated with the spring crossing of grain boats. Thereafter, emperor and regional officials turned their attention to the autumn seasonal cycle, the rising flood waters in the Huai and Yellow rivers, and the priorities of "harnessing the river and protecting the canal." During this period, the canal and junction were again dredged and repaired in anticipation of the southward return of empty grain fleets in the tenth month. But more important was the "guarding" work on the river and lake dikes and the careful manipulation of drainage systems to direct dangerously high waters from the lake and river into alternative diversion channels leading to the sea. Canal troops and laborers stood ready to reinforce the dikes in the event of heavy rains and floods. By the tenth month, the river level normally dropped, enabling the returning grain fleets to cross the river and proceed to their home anchorages. By the eleventh month, both lake and river had receded, bringing the autumn cycle to a close.

The ebb and flow of the floods affected canal–grain transport management in a profound way. These natural phenomena shaped the administrative regulations and management practices used to assure the successful operation of the canal and the yearly shipments of grain. The early Qing emperors had bowed to these seasonal imperatives and had expanded bureaucratic supervision and discipline at the lower levels of regional government "to hasten" the performance of essential tasks within the periods marked by the summer and winter solstices. Yet, by the late eighteenth century, the destructive siltation of the canal system caused constant delays in the spring shipping schedule. These delays often disrupted and postponed the autumn cycle and led to the neglect of many seemingly minor maintenance tasks, which slowly weakened the entire water-control network in northern Jiangsu.

The Gaojia dike disaster had occurred just as the new spring cycle was beginning. By the twelfth month of 1824, the imperial commissioners had assessed the damage and plotted the main outlines of a reconstruction scheme. By early in the first month of 1825, they had presented a program that addressed both the need to prepare the way for spring shipping and the need to protect the system from the autumn floods. The first most pressing difficulty, the spring crossing of grain fleets, was only one month away. Would the canal be clear and the junction ready by the second month, when thousands of grain junks would descend on them?

The emperor had helped to shape the reconstruction program, especially its emphasis on rebuilding the lake dikes and accumulating clear water for the spring crossing of the grain fleets. He considered the most urgent tasks to be the closure of the dike breaches and the damaged overflow gates, especially the Zhi, Xin, and Lizi gates south of Zhou Bridge on the southeast perimeter of the lake (map 11). This would halt the leakage of clear water from the lake and facilitate its accumulation in amounts sufficient for carrying the grain boats out

Reconstruction and the 1825 Spring Crossing 139

through the Clear Passage into the river. The emperor did not place as much explicit emphasis on the emergency dredging of the canal because initial reports indicated that the only thickly clogged sections were those that extended from Pinghe Bridge, north of Baoying, to the junction. It was taken for granted that those parts of the canal would have to be dredged immediately to insure the passage of the spring grain fleets, while the regular yearly maintenance dredging would suffice for the rest of the Huaiyang Canal.

Soon after the disaster, the emperor had expressed his fear that clear water reserves in the lake would be insufficient for the crossing. In his first edict to the commissioners after their arrival at Qingjiangpu, dated the third day of the twelfth month in 1824, he gloomily predicted:

> The lake is losing excessive amounts of clear water, and it will be depleted by next spring when the all-important spring shipping goes north. The clear water will not be able to carry the boats though the junction into the river.[2]

Then six days later, on the ninth day of the twelfth month, he reiterated this fear and emphasized the importance of using clear water rather than Yellow River backspills, which did immeasurable harm to the canal junction.[3]

> After so much water has flowed out of Hongze, the lake's water pressure has definitely weakened, jeopardizing the crossing of the grain shipments in the spring. The plan of using the Yellow to aid shipping is a terrible policy. The commissioners and regional officials must plan ahead and act according to circumstances to see that clear water can be released for the crossing. What is needed after all is to accumulate enough clear water so the ships can pass without the slightest obstruction.[4]

The emphasis on the spring shipments in early 1825 appears to indicate that the emperor was primarily concerned with grain transport at the expense of the canal, and this interpretation of his actions has, indeed, been made.⁵ Yet, a careful consideration of the issues shows instead that his adherence to the spring cycle, his desire to return to a clear-water crossing, and his rejection of the use of Yellow River backspills all point to his commitment to long-term canal preservation. His emphasis on shipping in the spring months merely shows his intention of conforming rigorously to the spring cycle so that the autumn cycle could be carried out on schedule too.

The emperor's emphasis on canal preservation is significant. It indicated to all regional officials that he meant to reconstruct the canal in northern Jiangsu so that the clear-water crossing procedure could continue to be used in the future to protect the canal and facilitate the passage of grain fleets until such time as the Yellow River finally shifted course. All things being equal, this had been the method of choice since the early eighteenth century, when it had become the rationale for enlarging and strengthening the Hongze Lake dikes, especially the Gaojia Great Dike.

But all things had not been equal since the Qianlong reign. Increased siltation of the Yellow River bed had made it increasingly difficult to achieve sufficient levels and pressures in Hongze Lake to equal the force of the Yellow River when the junction gates were opened. In response, canal officials had devised makeshift crossing procedures that used Yellow River backspills. With this method, grain junks were pulled through Yuhuang Lock gate as Yellow River water rushed into the Clear Passage. When Yellow River backspills were used, every effort was made to hasten the boats to the junction to cross before the Yellow River rose too high, its silt content increased, and the difficulties at the junction multiplied. Yet, no matter what precautions were taken, the use of backspills left the junction passages clogged with mud.

The "use of Yellow to assist transport" was flawed from the start precisely because it silted up the junction and canal head, intensifying the clogging and deterioration of junction facilities. This procedure was first used in the Qianlong reign and, as the silt crisis intensified in the

Reconstruction and the 1825 Spring Crossing 141

Jiaqing reign, it was used again from time to time. However, no one pretended it was a good idea. It was always described as a "temporary expedient" (*quanyi*), which regional officials had no alternative but to use in the dangerously unstable period before the shift of the Yellow River. The use of this term, and the meanings associated with it, became increasingly important as the crisis wore on, especially when the emperor tried to justify sea transport also as a "temporary expedient."

The Daoguang Emperor's assertion of the need to accumulate clear water in Hongze Lake was his way of reaffirming his adherence to the strategy that preserved the canal and was in the best long-term interests of canal shipping. He called it the "traditional," or "long-established method." Yet, even as the emperor asserted his commitment to the clear-water crossing, reports from the field indicated that the lake water would not accumulate in sufficient quantities to make this possible.[6] Reports from the demoted governor-general of Liangjiang, Sun Yuting, hinted as much when he described the slow progress of blocking the breaches in the lake dikes. He explained that although the work was proceeding well, dike reconstruction was an arduous, time-consuming process during which the holes were blocked initially with fascines, then permanently rebuilt with mortared stonework. The temporary closure had been completed earlier in the twelfth month.[7] But the permanent reconstruction would take considerably longer because the rock materials had to be transported into Gaoyan and Shanxu subprefectures from other regions, and layered masonry work required careful, skilled labor. Leakage had been slowed in the first stage when the gaps were blocked temporarily, but it would not be stopped altogether until the dike was rebuilt permanently.

Even though the emperor realized that it might be impossible to use the preferred clear-water crossing, he nonetheless asked the commissioners to try to accomplish this goal. He also reiterated his strong disapproval of the use of Yellow River backspills, even though Sun's reports had not explicitly suggested it.⁸ He later pressed officials to dredge out the five lead channels from the lake to the Clear Passage, just in case the clear-water method could be used at the last moment.⁹

The acting governor-general of Liangjiang, Wei Yuanyu, took issue with the emperor early in the twelfth month of 1824, and he did not mince words about the futility of trying to accumulate clear water in Hongze Lake for the spring crossing. The winter and early spring months were the periods of the lowest water levels and the least rain in the Huai River drainage basin. There was little prospect that enough water would accumulate in the lake to make up for that lost when the Gaojia dike collapsed. So, even though the breaches were, for the most part, blocked, there was no point in hoping. He suggested instead that regional officials prepare for an early crossing, using the backspills. It was, he stated, "an emergency procedure" which they "had no choice but to accept."[10]

Wei argued reassuringly that it was not such a bad procedure after all, and regional officials could avoid virtually all damage to the canal by making the crossing earlier than usual. He urged that the canal directorate begin intensive dredging of the canal from Pinghe Bridge to the junction. This would enable the southern grain fleets to proceed quickly to the junction before the Yellow River rose to dangerously high levels. To facilitate the movement of the ships, Wei advised that the fleets abandon their regular sailing order.

> Those that enter the canal at Guazhou from the Yangzi first should proceed north first. If, during the crossing, the Yellow River water enters the canal abundantly, we can haul the boats through. If it comes in small amounts, we can take the initiative and transfer the cargoes to lighters near the junction, lighten the military boats and haul them through.[11]

Wei bluntly asserted: "The canal course is different now than it was in the past. *The Yellow River's fluctuations and meandering are uncontrollable* [author's emphasis], not like the clear [Huai–Hongze] water which can be controlled by human power."[12] In his opinion, officials and the emperor had to accept the use of Yellow River backspills and dredge the junction passages extra deep to offset the increased silting.

In an edict responding to Wei's assertions, the emperor expressed deep skepticism about this proposal and was irked by Wei's complacent acceptance of the backspills. He maintained that long-term damage to the canal from backspills was much greater than Wei had stated so glibly. In exasperation, he lashed out at Wei for pretending that "drawing Yellow [water] into the canal would not cause silting" and that these emergency measures could be managed. The emperor sternly reminded regional officials that he could not manage these matters from afar! But he wanted it clearly understood that the safety of the canal and the security of the grain shipments were matters of *equally* grave importance. If officials like Wei were concerned only about transport each spring and looked only at "previous ways" of muddling through this problem, "in the future, the canal's problems will become even worse and the dredging ever more difficult. Then who will come forward to take the blame!" And, finally, in his strongest statement thus far about the dynasty's strategic interest in grain tribute, the emperor declared, "Grain tribute constitutes the imperial granaries' main supply (*caoliang quanxi tianyu zhenggong*). Its shipment absolutely cannot be delayed!"[13] Perhaps the plans for the clear-water crossing would break down, but for the moment the emperor wanted everyone to exert every effort to achieve this goal.

The emperor then turned to the commissioners to evaluate the issue of backspills and to make appropriate plans with all the top regional officials in Jiangsu. His motive may have been to force those officials dealing directly with the canal crisis to achieve a consensus on this "bad" policy, partly to deflect responsibility from himself for what he perceived would be a disastrous outcome, and partly to assure the wholehearted implementation of the plan should it become necessary. But the emperor may have been optimistic at this stage that winter rains and the determined efforts of regional officials would triumph. In any case, he wanted officials to be prepared for various contingencies and to act according to local conditions. Because he himself did not witness these events firsthand, he could not make tactical judgments "from afar."

But whatever the final outcome of that year's junction crossing, the emperor's edict in response to Wei's proposal made clear that he took a long-term view of the protection of the canal: the repairs to the canal should not be subordinated to the short-term needs of the spring shipping cycle because the deterioration of the canal would only intensify and undermine the transport process in the future. In practice, however, in the early months of 1825, regional planners were concentrating men and materials on those projects that would facilitate a speedy clear-water crossing and ignoring, to a certain extent, the dredging of damaged sections of the canal and junction.

Early in the first month of 1825, three weeks after the emperor's sharp critique of Wei Yuanyu, the commissioners confirmed the emperor's worst fears.[14] The clear water in Hongze Lake, they wrote, was "3.6 meters below the river," and there was little prospect that enough would accumulate to make a clear-water crossing possible that spring. In their judgment, canal officials should prepare to use Yellow River backspills as a temporary expedient just as the Daoguang Emperor's father, the Jiaqing Emperor, had done earlier. References to the administrative actions of the emperor's father were always used to justify advice that the emperor did not want to hear. The commissioners outlined a plan they hoped would eliminate, or at least greatly reduce, the risk of the accidents that had accompanied earlier experiences with backspills. They also presented a detailed set of preparations for the crossing, which was scheduled to take place earlier than usual. They hoped to open the Yuhuang Lock gate between the first and ninth days of the second month and cross all the boats by the end of the fourth. The gate was actually opened on the ninth and kept open past the summer solstice, until the twelfth day of the fifth month.[15]

Reconstruction and the 1825 Spring Crossing 145

This crossing schedule meant that regional officials had only one month to complete an enormous number of preparatory tasks, including both labor-intensive construction work on the canal and junction and the organization of manpower and materials to speed the actual crossing process. Attention was to be redirected to dredging the silted sections of the canal north of Pinghe Bridge to the junction. At the same time, canal workers were to reinforce the dikes that had been weakened by the floods. Wooden weir-like structures were to be built within and along the sides of the canal bed to constrict the water flow and thereby scour and deepen the channel. Extensive dredging also was scheduled for the junction itself, where the greatest silt problems could be expected from the inflow of Yellow River backspills during the crossing. Emphasis, of course, was given to dredging and reinforcing the five lead channels connecting Hongze Lake to the Clear Passage (map 8).

Besides dredging, the protective embankments of the junction and canal head leading into the junction needed to be reinforced and tracking roads needed to be built on either side of the junction so that grain vessels could be dragged by gangs of laborers through the silt-filled channels. The commissioners urged the construction of three weir-like structures on the outer west side of the Yuhuang Lock gate, designed to jut out from the embankment and to divert the river's current away from the junction mouth. Tracking roads were to be built on top of the junction causeways both in and outside of Yuhuang, on each side of the Shuqing Lock gate, and on the earthen embankments buttressing Shuqing (map 11).

The commissioners' plan specified in great detail the actual sequence of events for the crossing. As the military grain junks rushed north from the Yangzi ports, men and material would be readied in anticipation of their arrival. Lighters would be recruited in advance to prepare for offloading and shipping the grain cargoes through the junction if the larger grain junks became mired in the mud. Civilian and military officials were assigned to the junction and to the upper end of the canal, to supervise and "hasten" the process of offloading grain to the lighters and to prepare tracking cables and mobilize gangs of porters and trackers for hauling vessels through the junction. All preparations were scheduled for completion prior to the arrival of the grain boats at the junction. As soon as the grain fleets had arrived and assembled in the waiting ponds at the canal head, officials would rush to seal off Shuqing Lock gate to protect its delicate lead channels from silt. Then, the baulks in Yuhuang Lock gate would be lifted, and the ships would be pulled through the Clear Passage and Yuhuang Lock on Yellow River backspills. When all the fleets had cleared the junction, the canal workers would quickly close the lock gate.[16]

On receipt of the commissioners' plan, the emperor reluctantly accepted the need for backspills, and he made the plan public on the twenty-third day of the first month. He exhorted the governors of Jiangsu, Zhejiang, Jiangxi, and Huguang to "demand that military boats sail fast to the junction and that all lower-level officials along the canal exert all their energies to hasten the boats on their journey."[17]

Although the decision to use backspills concentrated scarce bureaucratic, material, and labor resources on the problems of the junction, the commissioners' plan also urged the simultaneous implementation of a comprehensive program of reconstruction designed to restore weakened facilities by the end of the spring cycle to prepare for the autumn floods. Their primary goal (and the emperor's as well) was the speedy repair of breaches in the great dike at Shisanbao and Xilang Temple (map 9). At the end of the first month, permanent reconstruction was to begin in earnest, with ten additional layers of stonework added to the dike before the autumn floods to compensate for the increased silt levels in the lake bed. These extra layers were to be built "according to the specifications laid down in the regulations." After completing the mortared stonework, canal workers would add layers of rock fragments to the dike for reinforcement.

Completion of the stonework on schedule would be difficult because much of the rock had to be imported from the south, up the Grand Canal

Reconstruction and the 1825 Spring Crossing   147

across the Gao-Bao lakes westward to the great dike in Gaoyan and Shanxu subprefectures. To augment this scarce and costly material, local officials were told to order work crews to pull old rocks out of the lake for reuse.[18] Moreover, as reconstruction of the lake dikes proceeded, it was found that the earthen core had crumbled and eroded in many places and needed to be repaired if the stonework was to be rebuilt securely. Thus, new problems were uncovered as the work proceeded, slowing reconstruction.[19]

Additionally, the commissioners urged the completion of reconstruction on the Hongze Lake overflow gates before the Huai floods began, so that high lake waters could be controlled and, if necessary, drained towards the canal and Yangzi outlets, thus avoiding another rupture of the lake dikes in the autumn. The failure of these gates to function properly was considered one of the principal reasons for the dike collapse in late 1824, and the commissioners hoped to insure that it did not happen again. In addition to the repair of the Xin, Zhi, and Li gates, they decided to build additional new stone-clad "boiling" floodgates near the old Ren, Yi, and Li gates, which were no longer positioned to draw off flood waters effectively (maps 7, 9).[20] Similarly, the commissioners underscored the importance of reconstructing the protective gates and embankments north and west of the lake, especially the Xiangfu and Wushui lead channels, for the purpose of "halting the flow of the Yellow into lake."[21] Lastly, the plan addressed serious problems on the Yellow River: its dikes, drainage channels, and blockages in the lower reaches.

The decision to use backspills for the Yellow River crossing had created a three-track reconstruction program. The first track included the priority tasks associated with preparing the canal and junction for the use of Yellow River backspills during the spring crossing, which officials predicted would last for three months, from early in the second month until the end of the fourth. The second included emergency repairs of flood-damaged parts of the canal and lake facilities. The third and largest program included reconstruction work crucial to resisting the autumn floods and preserving the canal during the autumn cycle. It appears that the first two programs compromised the latter to a certain extent. Just as Zhu Shiyan and Sun Yuting had hinted, scarce resources were spread too thinly, and the result was neglect of vital repairs and maintenance.

The submission of reconstruction plans early in the first month of 1825 signaled the completion of the imperial commissioners' work in northern Jiangsu. In consultation with regional officials, they had made a definitive assessment of the root causes of the Gaojia dike disaster; they had concurred with the necessity of using backspills and outlined the spring crossing schedule; and they had devised the main agenda for the entire reconstruction program. After their departure, the Southern Canal director was slated to take over the management of reconstruction work.

Looming ominously ahead was the spring crossing. The emperor feared problems might arise, and he apparently felt he needed a high-ranking official with sufficient standing and experience in canal-transport issues to oversee the crossing, particularly because the recently appointed grain-transport director, Yan Jian, was new to his job. Thus, even though memorial reports blamed Sun Yuting for some of the causes of the disaster, the emperor decided to keep him at the junction after the commissioners had left because the crossing was, he asserted, a crucial matter for the dynasty, and Sun had been in Liangjiang a long time—nine years in fact. "Therefore, he is ordered to delay his return to Peking; and with Yan Jian, he is to rouse his conscience and work out suitable arrangements for the crossing and manage it with care."[22] The emperor described this decision as "showing Sun exceptional grace by allowing him to participate in the shipment of new grain." In view of the problems he was later to face, Sun might have preferred less grace and an early retirement.[23]

The Gaojia dike disaster had brought to a head the myriad problems that faced the whole canal-riverine network in the early nineteenth century. The emperor and leading officials in the canal zone responded to this crisis with a practical-minded, technical approach to canal reconstruction that emphasized the interconnectedness of the parts to the whole system. Regional managers of the canal–grain transport system were, on the whole, more responsive to short-term seasonal imperatives that affected grain shipping in 1825, while the emperor was more concerned with the long-term preservation of the canal, seeing it as the best way to insure grain shipments in this highly unstable period. In the eyes of the emperor, the silting of the whole, the blockage of the Yellow River, backflows, seepage into Hongze Lake, and damage to drainage facilities, all threatened the very existence of the canal, not to mention internal security in the canal zone. Even in the heat of the spring crossing, the emperor never lost sight of the interconnectedness of the system and the need for preserving the canal. As the crossing situation worsened, the system as a whole, with its economic and strategic implications, continued to dominate the emperor's concern and shape his management of the crisis.

The Yuhuang Lock gate was opened early in the second month, and as the days and weeks passed, problems mounted. First, the crossing went poorly and the emperor was irked that Sun had failed to keep him informed about the opening of the Yuhuang Lock and the crossing of the first fleets.[24] Then ominous reports from the dredging sites on the canal suggested that silt clogging was far greater than originally thought and extended from the junction all the way south to the Shaobo area. The first grain fleets, entering the Huaiyang Canal, were soon stranded in the canal near Shaobo. They had to transfer their cargoes to lighters sooner, and in far greater numbers, than expected; and even the lighters were having problems reaching the junction.[25] To make matters worse, beginning late in the second month, reports from Zhejiang revealed dangerous outbreaks of violence among Zhejiang transport crews associated with the Luo sect over the assignment of new vessels. These disturbances threatened to slow down the Zhejiang fleets and to spark further incidents of violence as they proceeded northward and their crews mobilized canal laborers, haulers, and porters along the way who also were affiliated with the Luo sect.[26]

By the beginning of the fourth month, the need for lighters was critical. More and more grain junks were entering the Southern Canal and becoming mired in silt, especially the larger craft from the middle Yangzi region. Smaller craft were needed urgently, not just to ship the grain to the junction, but to carry it from the junction all the way to Peking. To mobilize the necessary craft, the emperor mounted a three-province drive to recruit lighters, both government and private, which were to converge on the junction by the end of the fourth month to "transfer and forward" the grain to the capital.

With this development, the canal emergency entered a new stage, one in which the emperor played a far greater managerial role than he had thus far. He supervised and coordinated the mobilization of canal lighters from Shandong, Henan, and Jiangsu provinces, demonstrating the organizational flexibility of the late Qing leadership and its willingness to work with private, nonbureaucratic groups to resolve the grain-transport impasse. This episode was to reveal that, with open communications between himself and top regional officials, the emperor need not control, or mandate, specific actions from afar. His trusted field officials would do so for him from the canal zone itself.

6

Muddling Through: Transfer-Shipping

Silt Barriers and Lighterage

The Daoguang Emperor's predictions about the problems of using Yellow River backspills were born out in the second and third months as the grain fleets began the crossing. His ridicule of Wei Yuanyu for saying things could "all be easily managed" had been justified. In spite of elaborate preparations at the junction, the southern grain fleets were so delayed that the Yuhuang Lock gate was kept open until the twelfth day of the fifth month, for a total of nearly three and a half months.[1] By this time, the Clear Passage and canal entrance were an oozing mass of mud. The Yellow River no longer flowed into the passage in sufficient quantities to float the junks through, and it became impossible, Sun Yuting reported, to pull either the large grain junks or the smaller lighters through it.

As it turned out, the prolonged opening of Yuhuang was necessitated by delays in the passage of grain fleets up the Huaiyang Canal. In addition to their delayed entrance into the canal at Guazhou, once the ships began to navigate the Huaiyang Canal, they were slowed, mired, and stranded in impenetrable silt shallows. It became clear that silt damage to the canal extended south beyond Pinghe Bridge to Shaobo (map 7), and that the dredging work, done in the weeks following the flood, had failed to clear this part of the canal channel.

At the beginning of the canal crisis, central and regional leadership had identified the stretch of canal from Pinghe Bridge, just north of Baoying (maps 7, 8), to the junction as the most damaged section of the canal, so emergency dredging was concentrated there. Although memorial reports indicated that the subprefectures on the southern part of the Huaiyang Canal had undertaken dredging work, it appears that work had proceeded more slowly than anticipated and that the quantity of silt was too great to dredge out in time for the passage of grain fleets. Perhaps lower-level subprefects and canal guards had minimized the extent of silting, not wanting to be the bearers of bad news. Perhaps their efforts were limited by an inability to cover the costs of labor and materials. In any case, shipping slowly and inexorably ground to a halt during the third and fourth months.

Silt obstructions were well known on the Huaiyang Canal. Since late Qianlong days, the increased siltation of the canal had often caused shipping problems, especially for the larger junks from the distant Yangzi provinces, whose fleets were the last to enter the canal and the last to clear the Yellow River junction. To meet these emergencies, canal and transport officials had developed an arsenal of techniques to facilitate the passage of fleets up the canal. First, gangs of trackers, using tow ropes, pulled the vessels from tracking roads on the causeways atop the canal dikes (fig. 9). If the trackers failed to budge the heavy junks, porters offloaded the grain and transferred it to lighters (fig. 16). Jiangsu province kept fleets of official lighters (*guanbo*) on hand for just this purpose. When these were insufficient to handle the cargoes, the state turned to private shippers (*minchuan*) to move the grain up the canal, through the junction to the south bank of the river or across the river to Yangzhuang to await the arrival of empty grain junks. The government grain boats, now weighing much less, followed the lighters through the junction and reloaded their cargoes for the remainder of the trip to Tongzhou.

If the fleets were delayed until after the Yuhuang Lock gate was closed around the fifth month, their cargoes were offloaded and "transferred across the junction embankments" (*panba*) by porters or haulers to the south bank of the Yellow River.[2] There the grain was loaded either on government lighters, other regular grain junks from provinces north of the river, or private lighters for the remainder of the trip north, while the original fleets returned to their home anchorages. This was called "transfer-shipping," or "forwarding." If the lighters were recruited from areas north of the river, the cargoes were sometimes transferred again to lighters at Yangzhuang on the north side of the river, or at Jining further north in Shandong, as was the case in 1825 (map 1).

By the nineteenth century, the silting of the canal and growing problems with the Yellow River increased the delays and raised the cost of shipping. It became a common practice to tow the fleets or transfer the grain to smaller craft which often, if the Yuhuang Lock gate was closed, made the entire trip north. Regulations were changed to meet this new situation, and the government became increasingly reliant on private shippers, just as the Northern Canal authorities in Zhili had done since the early Qing period.[3]

After the disaster, in the early spring of 1825 Jiangsu officials had predicted that lighterage would be necessary because of silt damage to the canal. They were not prepared, however, for the severity of the siltation as far south as Shaobo, for the extent of the delays, nor for the fact that grain boats—even with cargoes offloaded—could not make it to the junction before the closure of the Yuhuang Lock gate. Jiangsu officials were confronted with hundreds of grain vessels stranded in the canal and with an urgent need for lighters to ship the cargoes from the mired grain boats to the junction, and, when it became clear that the lightened grain boats could not be towed to and through the junction, plans had to be made for lighterage all the way to Tongzhou.

In the first stages of the crisis, late in the first month, Wei Yuanyu, acting Liangjiang governor-general, always the bearer of bad news, had alerted the emperor to the probable need for a great many lighters. Suggesting that the number of available Jiangsu official lighters and private lighters for hire might be insufficient, he requested that a fleet of 467 newly built lighters, which was en route to Zhili province from shipyards in Hunan and Jiangxi, be detained for use in Jiangsu during the spring crossing. Wei predicted that the regular Hunan grain fleets would be late as they had been the previous year and that they would not reach the junction before Yuhuang Lock gate was closed. That being the case, their grain cargoes could be offloaded and transferred across the junction embankments, to be reloaded onto the Zhili lighters, and shipped to Tongzhou.[4]

Early in the fourth month, the dimensions of the problem were outlined by Sun Yuting, who was stationed at the junction to manage the spring crossing. Sun reported that the Clear Passage and canal head were clogged with more and more mud each day, and the southern grain boats were not able to get through the upper end of the canal at all, even with their cargoes offloaded to lighters. Lighters would have to carry the grain all the way north to Tongzhou. In other words, transferring to lighters for transport to the junction had to be replaced by transfer-shipping to the capital.[5] He estimated that nearly 400,000 *shi* would have to be shipped by lighter, an amount that comprised from 12 to 15 percent of the yearly grain shipments. Well over a thousand vessels were needed to carry the cargoes from the mired junks to the junction, and then on to the capital. And they were needed urgently, before the end of the fourth month. Less than a month remained to mobilize and dispatch the boats, public and private, to the junction.

Sun urged that five types of lighters be drafted for service: 1) all the official lighters owned by Jiangsu province; 2) private lighters from Jiangsu; 3) the so-called West River boats (*Xihe chuan*), which had a holding capacity from 400 to 500 *shi* of grain and were widely used for grain transport in both Henan and Shandong; 4) the official lighters destined for Zhili province; 5) and a class of private boats used extensively on the rivers and lakes of Shandong, adjacent to the canal, for transporting beans and wheat.[6]

The emperor's response to Sun's proposal was immediate and decisive. He authorized a three-province initiative to recruit the needed craft, and he delegated sweeping authority to top regional officials in Henan and Shandong to organize and implement it. He explained the reasons for the plan to regional officials in northern Jiangsu:

Sun and others have reported that the area from Li[xia]he to the canal junction is clogged up more and more each day. To haul [literally, to grind] the grain boats along the shallow channel has become twice as difficult as it was before, so it is necessary to proceed with plans for offloading and forwarding grain cargoes immediately. It has been more than forty days since the Yuhuang Lock gate was opened and Yellow backspills used to aid shipping through the junction. Yet there are still many grain boats that have not crossed the river. Now the area from Li[xia]he to the junction is clogged. In the blink of an eye, the Yellow River will rise. For these military boats which have not yet crossed the river and which cannot take the sea route, plans to transfer and forward the shipments [on other smaller vessels to the capital] must be drawn up.[7]

The Transfer-Shipping Initiative

Launching the transfer-shipping program marked an important new stage in the Grand Canal crisis, one in which the emperor, with strong official support, directed and coordinated a three-province initiative to save the faltering 1825 grain tribute shipments. It also set in motion a process of government interaction with private shipping interests to augment the state's shipping fleet on the canal in northern Jiangsu and Shandong. This initiative drew on earlier patterns of state-private enterprise that vested broad authority in top regional officials to "recruit" (*zhaoshang*) nongovernmental organizations and resources to assist the state.

The emperor delegated wide-ranging powers to both Qishan, acting governor of Shandong, and Cheng Zuluo, governor of Henan, to investigate the availability of small craft in their provinces and to hire as many as 1,200 to 1,500 such craft for dispatch to the junction before the end of the fourth month.[8] Apart from hundreds of official and private lighters in Jiangsu, this plan included the recruitment of the 467 Zhili-owned boats that were passing through Jiangsu; 400 to 500 West River boats, and several hundred wheat and bean boats. These numbers give some indication of the level of private commercial traffic on this sector of the canal in the early nineteenth century. Government awareness of these numbers and of the different categories of craft suggests a vast network of ties between the state and private shippers that was well-established and capable of being mobilized quickly to assist in government grain shipping.

The authority vested in Cheng and Qishan gave them virtually a free hand to alter existing regulations and redefine the terms of work and pay for both government and private lighters.[9] They were empowered to negotiate the hiring price of private craft and the salaries and rations for boat crews and porters, and to offer special exemptions from ship tolls and duties on private cargo. In exercising these powers, both officials were expected to respond to market conditions and develop terms that were beneficial to the state and profitable to private shippers. The emperor cautioned them to arrange fair and satisfactory terms that would persuade private shippers to cooperate willingly. While the greatest responsibility for hiring lighters was vested in Cheng and Qishan, Sun Yuting was designated to work out the special issues relating to Jiangsu vessels and the treatment of government junk crews stranded in northern Jiangsu. The income and expense monies for the latter would be cut as a consequence of their failure to make the entire trip to the capital. The emperor urged both officials to use extreme care in order to avoid a violent confrontation with the regular fleet personnel.[10]

After authorizing the transfer-shipping plan, the emperor immediately dispatched a detailed court letter to all regional officials in northern Jiangsu, informing them that Sun's urgent request for lighters had been authorized and that Cheng and Qishan had been given broad authority to mobilize craft from Henan and Shandong. These craft would descend on the junction and pick up the grain cargoes early in the fifth month (5.5.7) when Yuhuang Lock gate was scheduled for closure. This meant that Jiangsu officials had little more than one month to prepare for transferring the cargoes across the junction embankments. As it turned out, Yuhuang was closed later than this date and, even after it was closed, the transfer and porterage of grain to lighters waiting on the south bank of the Yellow River continued until the early autumn. But at the outset, Jiangsu officials were exhorted to move the vessels to the junction and prepare for transferring the cargoes "no matter how shallow the canal may be nor how hard the pulling work."[11]

The edict authorizing lighterage gave the emperor an opportunity to raise some longer-term questions for official consideration—important questions that concerned the future of the canal and canal-based grain transport. He underscored the fragility of the canal in northern Jiangsu and the danger posed by repeated use of Yellow River backspills, which, he asserted, had already taken a heavy toll on the canal. The Gaojia dike disaster bore tragic testimony to the fact that the use of backspills, decades of siltation, and an entrenched pattern of neglect had irrevocably altered the canal system and, by extension, the grain-shipment process. Nothing showed this more clearly than the massive program of transfer-shipping that he had just authorized. It was symptomatic, he pointed out, of how fundamentally altered grain transport had become. What had formerly been an adjunct to shipping by government grain junk had become a necessary mainstay of the process. The emperor seemed to be asking indirectly what alternatives remained for the future of grain transport. He explicitly referred to "taking the sea route" in the opening passages of the same edict without any discussion or explanation. Did he expect regional officials to take this option seriously and begin planning for it?

The emperor launched the transfer-shipping plan on the second day of the fourth month. His quick response to the transfer-shipping proposal was due both to the seriousness of the crisis and the need for a speedy crossing before the Yellow River reached flood levels. He was able to move quickly was for a number of reasons. Most notably, precedents for transfer-shipping were quite well established. That it was already a well-accepted procedure is shown by instructions to provincial officials to work out many of the details regarding hiring price and labor costs "according to earlier practices"—practices that had developed since the mid-eighteenth century in response to worsening conditions in the Huaiyang Canal. These procedures had been recorded in the Finance Ministry's special collection on grain transport, the *Hubu caoyun quanshu*, as early as 1766 and were elaborated in later editions.[12]

A second factor that contributed to the speedy adoption of transfer-shipping was the tradition of reliance on regional officials to respond to changing local realities. This tradition was born of the secret decision-making process and reinforced by the use of *zhaoshang* recruitment, which empowered top regional officials to work directly with private organizations, bypassing the notoriously corrupt and inefficient lower levels of regional government.[13] In the course of the Qing period, the leadership had slowly and incrementally abandoned anachronistic arrangements governing the grain-transport system and devised new methods that relied increasingly on private labor, grain merchants, and private lighterage. By the 1820s, the state's willingness to work with such private groups and its growing dependence on them in canal communications had fundamentally changed the character of its grain-transport system, resulting in a close integration of state strategic goals and private economic interests.

The emperor's quick action on transfer-shipping must also have been facilitated by his confidence in the two officials who held the Henan and Shandong governorships, Cheng Zuluo and Qishan. Both positions encompassed important responsibilities in canal-transport management; both incumbents had exercised this responsibility with decisiveness and integrity. Cheng, for example, was known for his outspoken insistence on water-control expertise in the appointment of Henan field and river officials, and the emperor had sought and acted on his advice in the case of Zhang Jing's appointment to the Shandong Canal directorship in early 1825. Cheng was also unafraid of taking responsibility in an age when many were hesitant to do so, and he showed great flexibility and invention when he undertook problems of river control and water conservancy.¹⁴ Qishan equally had distinguished himself as an energetic and effective provincial administrator.

More important, Cheng and Qishan understood the tradition of cooperative action required of Henan, Shandong, and northern Jiangsu officials who faced common problems stemming from their location "near the great river."¹⁵ These three provinces were, for purposes of "harnessing the river and protecting the canal," all a part of one single disaster zone—a calamity in one province generally affected the other two. When crises did occur, regional officials were expected "to look beyond provincial borders," to aid one another, and work together to solve these difficulties. Both Cheng and Qishan had shown themselves responsive to regional needs in the immediate aftermath of the Gaojia dike disaster. To help cover the costs of reconstruction of the canal-lake works in northern Jiangsu, Cheng had offered aid from Henan, which included 100,000 *shi* of rice, 3 million *jin* of hemp, and 400 thousand *taels* of silver. The emperor praised this generous act and highlighted the larger sense of unity and purpose that it expressed— one that "transcended" the narrow focus on provincial borders to encompass the problems of the empire as a whole. Cheng "exhausts himself in the interests of the state and does not limit his thinking to separate provincial boundaries. This makes it possible to achieve great things." The same was true of Qishan. In the first days after the disaster, he had offered funds from the Shandong treasury to help fund reconstruction in Jiangsu.¹⁶ Although the offer was not taken up until several months later, the emperor went to great lengths to praise Qishan for his ability to see things from a broad perspective.

These expressions of the emperor's gratitude and admiration in the edicts to Cheng Zuluo and Qishan show how secret edicts were used to praise and exhort officials to strengthen their commitment to empire-wide goals. This function was performed in the early reigns by rescripts on palace memorials, but now it was more routinely expressed in court letters. These letters also draw our attention to the various ways that

Qing monarchs responded to and directed different kinds of regional administrative problems. In the case of a multi-province issue, such as the organization of transfer-shipping, the emperor stepped in to take a more direct administrative role, coordinating and directing the efforts of high provincial officials, because none of them had sufficient authority over the others to draw them together to work out joint, consensual decisions. In these cases, the emperor acted much as a governor-general would have done, and his role contrasts with that in emergencies that were confined to one province alone.

Qishan already had his plan underway by the middle of the fourth month, and the emperor reviewed and sanctioned his regulations governing the hiring of private West River boats and bean and wheat boats.[17] First, Qishan advised that rice rations be given to the hired boats before they left Shandong, instead of waiting until they arrived at Jiangsu. This advance payment was undoubtedly essential to achieve cooperation from private shippers. If the shippers arrived in Jiangsu and were not needed after all, they could keep the rations allotted in Shandong for their trouble. Second, the amount of rations for each craft was to be determined by its size, its cargo capacity, and the size of the crew. Third, Shandong boats were exempted from all Jiangsu taxes and tolls if they were used for transfer-shipping. However, if they were not needed when they arrived, they would be required to pay the taxes. Fourth, each boat would be accompanied by a government escort official who had the authority to negotiate any problems with official personnel on the canal. Each craft would be issued a government certificate, which served as a form of clearance, to insure that it would not be stopped and subjected to bureaucratic red tape on the trip. Fifth, all hired vessels would be outfitted at government expense with hauling ropes and cables in the event that they had to be hauled through shallow parts of the canal on the journey north. Sixth, the officers and staff of the government grain boats mired in the silt in Jiangsu were required to pay the expenses of offloading and transferring the tribute grain to lighters from their own travel allowances and, as soon as the transfer was completed, they were to return south to their home ports.

The emperor approved these regulations, but referred two questions to Sun, whose expertise and position as grain-transport supervisor at the junction gave him special knowledge of and jurisdiction over these issues. First, the emperor was inclined to allow private shippers the right to carry private, tax-free trade goods as an added incentive to participate, but not if they would substantially reduce cargo space for grain or slow the transfer process at the junction. Second, he felt that the unused portion of the rations originally allotted to the crews on the government grain junks for their trip north should be handed over to the lighter crews as an added "incentive," yet he hesitated to do so for fear it would be needed by the grain boat crews "to alleviate their distress." This was another way of saying that if forfeiture of the travel rations would cause unrest or rebellion among the transport workers, the rations should not be taken from them.

These two questions were left up to Sun to decide because he was considered by the emperor to be the best judge of how these policies would affect the speed and efficiency of the offloading and transfer process at the junction. Sun was to communicate his decisions directly to Qishan. The emperor's referral of these issues to Sun shows explicitly how reluctant the emperor was to make tactical, concrete decisions about issues that required on-the-spot judgments. While his direction of a multi-provincial project like transfer-shipping clearly forced him to take more initiative for specific courses of action and greater supervisory authority, he nonetheless generally preferred to defer to top regional officials because of their first-hand experience with local issues.

The emperor's comments about arranging fair and generous terms for the private shippers also show clearly that he realized that the state was dependent on them and that they should not be forced to take a loss if they participated in government projects. The ability to recruit private shippers and obtain fast, efficient service depended on their individual profit from the venture, and the emperor acknowledged the need to attract them with material incentives and tax exemptions. When referring to the re-allocation of rations from the regular grain-transport crews to private shippers, he queried:

> Maybe these leftover rations can be used to pay the private shippers. Or perhaps Sun can find funds from other sources to give them extra pay. To employ private boats for shipping grain, we must provide ample food rations in order to engender support for this shipping work and to make the private shippers more manageable.[18]

Yet at the same time, the emperor was reluctant to inflict hardship on the boatmen, which could spark transport slow-downs or unrest. This was a highly charged issue in the spring of 1825 because of the outbreak of violence among Zhejiang transport crews over boat assignments—violence that was likely to spill over into other areas as the Zhejiang fleets moved up the canal.[19] This possibility was described vividly later that summer in a report by the censor Wang Shifu, who outlined the threat that these boatmen posed for other transport troops on board the fleets and for the communities along the canal:

> Sailors on every southern grain fleet belong to one of three subgroups of the Luo sect, and their numbers total from 40,000 to 50,000 members, not including trackers and porters along the canal who also belong to the sect. Each fleet has a head teacher who is also a boss [*laoguan*] to whom the members kneel as disciples. Every fleet has a special shrine boat that carries a statue of Luozu [Luo Qing, founder of Luo sect].[20] In recent years, each boss extorts money from the transport troops, and if they don't pay, he will stop the fleet. If any sailor causes trouble, the boss will try and punish him, with sentences ranging from trifles to being put to death and tossed overboard into the canal.[21]

Wang specifically pointed out the connection between crewmen on the grain junks and local trackers and porters that the fleet used as it proceeded up the canal. He asserted that sect members were involved in criminal activities and, because of their links to affiliate groups on the shore, the sect leaders on the grain boats had the power to incite mob violence in the communities along the canal. Wang deemed it an outrage that sailors "dared to extort money on the government grain fleets and to instigate an uprising over the assignment of boats. . . . These bandits will continue to wink at the law unless regional officials in Zhejiang and Jiangsu act with courage and dispatch to isolate the sect leaders from their followers on shore." He further predicted that if sea transport were used in the coming year (1826), "hundreds of these men will surely cause trouble."[22]

These problems among the grain junk crews heightened the need for fast mobilization of lighters and disciplined transfer of grain cargoes at the junction. As the number of stalled junks increased, so did the potential for trouble and lawlessness around Huai'an. The fear of trouble prompted the emperor to call for discussion memorials from all the canal-zone officials on methods for regulating the hiring and "guaranteeing" (*baozheng*) of private labor on the grain junks. The official response is interesting because it shows that Luo sect activity was limited to Zhejiang and Jiangsu crews, and apparently did not extend to the crews hired in the other southern provinces.[23]

While the recruitment of lighters was underway in Shandong and Henan, the censor Zhang Ming proposed an alternative plan that would provide more government craft for the northbound shipments. He urged that 800 boats from the regular Shandong-Henan grain fleets, anchored at Dezhou and Jining, be used to pick up the southern grain at the junction in the interval between their two regularly scheduled shipments to Peking (map 1). The first, he explained, already had been completed, and the boats had returned to their home ports. Their next shipment was not due to begin until the ninth and tenth months . Why not use these boats to ship the southern grain during the interim? Zhang argued that there were precedents for such a move, and furthermore the ships' officers and crews were "well controlled so there is no risk of unrest."[24] This was a reference to the fact that these fleets were primarily manned by regular transport personnel, who were considered more compliant than the hired crews of the southern provinces.

The emperor's response to this shipping option was again prompt and focused. He ordered Qishan and Cheng Zuluo to evaluate the feasibility of using these craft, and demanded answers to a number of questions. Had all the Hedong grain fleets really returned to Dezhou and Jining? Were the boats in need of repair during the slack season before their next authorized grain shipment in the autumn? If these junks were used, would the additional trip place too much pressure on transport personnel and possibly lead to unrest and violence? How quickly could these fleets be dispatched? Could they realistically make the trip from the junction to Tongzhou and back to their home anchorages in time to load and ship their autumn cargoes? If the plan looked feasible, Qishan and Cheng were to draw up regulations for summoning the military boats and issuing food rations. Again, broad powers were given to both officials to alter the regular schedule of government fleets and move ahead quickly with the arrangements. There was no need, the emperor asserted, to refer the regulations back to him for approval; time was of the essence. His court letter, sent by 400-*li* post, ordered them to proceed quickly on their own.[25]

By the beginning of the fifth month, it was clear to Qishan and Cheng Zuluo that the scheme for using the regular Hedong grain junks would help a great deal in the transfer-shipment process, but these boats could not do it all. In a report received by the emperor on the second day of the fifth month, Qishan explained that only 540 junks were fit for making the additional trip to the capital. The rest were in serious need of repair. The available junks could only carry about 300,000 *shi*; the remaining 100,000 *shi* would have to be shipped on private vessels. To insure that the government boats returned to their home anchorages in time to ship their autumn tribute cargoes, Qishan proposed that the southern grain be transferred to the Hedong boats at Jining, not at the junction. This meant that Jiangsu lighterage would be required to haul the grain all the way to Jining.[26]

Muddling Through: Transfer-Shipping 165

Qishan worked out a set of seventeen regulations for implementing this process, but because so much of this new plan depended on Sun Yuting's ability to move the grain out of the junction to Jining on Jiangsu-based lighters, the emperor referred many of these regulations to Sun and asked him to decide on a number of issues regarding compensation for the Hedong and Jiangsu boats. How much should be paid to the Hedong boats for travel expenses, monthly rations, and salary rice? As for the private boats from Shandong that were still needed to ship the remaining 100,000 *shi*, how much "squeeze" (*jintie*) should be paid in addition to the hiring price? How much should they be allotted for tolls at the numerous flash-lock gates on the Shandong Canal? How, the emperor asked, could all these monies be paid to the junk officers and crews *without interference from officials* (author's emphasis)? This was a clear reference to the unreliability of local officials. Finally, did Sun have any suggestions as to how to expedite the transfer at Jining so that Hedong's autumn tribute shipments would not be delayed and the crews given no excuse for asking for more allowance?[27]

This edict, addressing the special problem of transferring grain at Jining, shows again the important role of the emperor as coordinator of the inter-provincial plan for transfer-shipping. It also reveals his impressive grasp of the technical detail required for sound supervision of canal zone affairs. Most revealing of the degree of power sharing between central and regional government were the broad powers given to regional officials for devising tactical plans to meet emergencies. Sun was asked to comment on the grain transfer at Jining (Shandong) only because he bore extra responsibility for moving the grain there from the junction. It was a complex and difficult problem, made more so by the need to meet the closure deadline for the Yuhuang Lock gate—the summer solstice (5.5.7).

The transfer-shipping program, proceeding smoothly in Shandong and Henan, began to falter in northern Jiangsu early in the fifth month. Reports from Sun Yuting on the state of the canal, the mushrooming expenses of transfer-shipping, the inability of grain junks to reach the junction, and finally, the prospect of having to store the grain in Yangzhou and Huai'an granaries until 1826, showed that the plan was collapsing.[28] These reports, although not entirely unexpected, shocked the emperor and provided just the opportunity he had been waiting for to initiate a critical review of canal-transport problems and to press forward with a bold plan for canal restoration and sea transport in 1826. The terms of this review, with its stinging critique of regional problem-solving, are considered in chapters 7, 8, and 9. However, the most pressing priority in the fifth month was to confront the immediate crises in northern Jiangsu and to salvage the transfer-shipping operation at the junction. The emperor felt betrayed by Jiangsu officials, who he thought had misled him about actual canal conditions. He now realized that their plans, and the information they were based on, were fundamentally flawed. He needed an executive-level official in Liangjiang whom he could trust for honest reporting and vigorous action.

Qishan to the Rescue

Qishan was ordered to turn over his seal of office in Shandong to Na'erjing'e and leave Jinan for northern Jiangsu "to go everywhere on patrol and supervise all the myriad canal–grain transport tasks." He was assigned the rank of governor-general to head up this three-province region, but his tasks in the junction area more closely resembled those given to the imperial commissioners immediately after the Gaojia dike disaster. He was an outsider, an imperial agent whose primary loyalty was to the emperor alone.[29] His appointment signaled an important new stage in the canal crisis—one in which central planning initiatives and agents of the emperor were to dominate regional canal–grain transport management, at least for a time. The emperor's ultimate aim was to impose central, long-term goals on a regional administration that he believed was driven solely by local, short-term interests.

Muddling Through: Transfer-Shipping 167

When Qishan arrived in northern Jiangsu late in the fifth month, conditions were explosive at the junction. Even though the Yuhuang Lock gate had been closed since the twelfth, transfer-shipping really had not begun because many grain junks and lighters had not yet arrived at the junction. Water levels in the canal were too low to counteract the silt, and even the opening of two new feeder channels from the lakes into the upper end of the Huaiyang Canal had improved navigation only a little. Only 80,000 to 90,000 *shi* actually had been shipped across the Yellow River and that had been accomplished earlier in the spring before Yellow River backspills had clogged the junction and forced the closure of Yuhuang.

As canal officials waited anxiously at the junction for the stragglers to arrive, hundreds of ships crowded into the upper end of the canal, the waiting ponds at the canal head, and along the south bank of the Yellow River, waiting to pick up their cargoes. Nearly 10,000 sailors, transport troopers, private shippers, porters, haulers, and trackers filled the area, creating dangerously volatile conditions. The censor Wang Lin pleaded that security measures be taken to impose order on this seething mass of people:

> At least ten fleets of transport junks and their sailors are waiting south of Qingjiangpu. Additionally, transport men and the sailors from the assembled lighters total upwards of 10,000 men. It will be difficult to guard against the occurrence of drinking, gambling, and theft. Regional officials, civil and military, must take action to suppress disorder. Moreover, fleet officers and local officials along the canal must take defensive measures to prevent trouble.[30]

In response to Wang's report, the emperor directed civil and military authorities at the junction and local officials along the canal to work closely with the fleet officials to quell any signs of unrest. At the same time, he ordered Qishan, who had just arrived, to revive and complete the stalled transfer-shipping plan, so that regional officials could get on with the regular autumn tasks of repairing and "guarding the canal." The emperor wanted Qishan to survey the junction in person:

Have the two new feeder channels opened up from the lake raised water levels in the upper end of the canal enough to expedite the movement of the fleets up to the junction? If so, when will the transporting and hauling across the junction embankment begin, and when will the loading and departure of lighters be completed?[31]

The crossing was, the emperor grimly noted, over a month behind schedule already, and he was determined to move ahead with the autumn seasonal tasks. He asked if the Yellow River backspills had done irreparable harm to the junction and canal head and whether enough clear water would accumulate in Hongze Lake to cross the returning empty grain boats in the eleventh month.[32]

Qishan moved quickly to expedite the movement of grain and ships out of the junction. The grain junks and lighters in the northern end of the Huaiyang Canal were towed to the junction, their cargoes offloaded and portered over the embankments to waiting lighters. Aided by a special deputy, he dispatched the majority of these grain-laden craft northward to Jining, clearing the junction by the end of the sixth month. The main group of ships left the junction by the twenty-first and carried 315,000 *shi* designated for transfer to Hedong military boats at Jining for the final trip to Tongzhou. The remaining craft, whose cargo of 80,000 *shi* was marked for transfer to private craft at Jining, left several days later.[33]

This stage of transfer-shipping was completed without major mishap. The junction area around Huai'an was cleared of vessels so that the remaining fleets from Zhejiang and the middle-Yangzi provinces of Jiangxi and Huguang had an easier approach to the junction. However, over a million *shi* from these late-arriving fleets had yet to be transferred and shipped north. These cargoes ultimately were carried out of the junction in the ninth month by returning grain fleets from Jiangnan and Jiangbei, which were stopped at the Yellow River and forced to make another difficult run to the north as winter approached. Adding to their misery, these fleets then were ordered to remain north of the river throughout the winter to prepare for transfer-shipping in 1826.³⁴

Qishan's ability to revive the flagging transfer-shipment program reassured the emperor and gave him confidence that the 1825 transport ordeal might indeed be brought to a satisfactory conclusion. He urged Qishan to maintain the administrative discipline he had achieved in expediting transfer-shipping and to supervise carefully the work of regional officials and weed out all those who were lax, "in order to reform degenerate customs" in regional administration. With great feeling, he expressed his continuing confidence in Qishan.

> In assigning you to the post of Liangjiang governor-general, I knew that you were certainly an official who could share my deep distress and anxiety. You must continue to exert yourself to deserve the trust I have placed in you.³⁵

But more obstacles had to be overcome in Shandong before the 1825 grain shipments were deposited in the capital granaries. Early in the fifth month, problems had arisen over the offloading and transfer process scheduled to take place at Jining. Na'erjing'e, the acting governor of Shandong, was worried about unrest within the Hedong transport fleets forced to make the extra trip to the capital, and he seemed to want all the conditions of the transfer at Jining spelled out precisely.³⁶ Was the delivery to be made at Tongzhou or Tianjin? What if the Jiangsu lighters were delayed? Would the Hedong fleets be forced to make the extra run to the north even if it would jeopardize their ability to return in time to carry their own late autumn shipments?

The emperor shared Na'erjing'e's concerns. If all proceeded according to plan, he stated, the Hedong fleets were to proceed all the way to Tongzhou, but if the Jiangsu lighters arrived late at Jining, the latter would be required to make the entire trip to the capital. He authorized more stringent security measures as well because he too feared unrest among Hedong transport workers. The emperor also ordered low-level military and civilian officials to police the area, and a special official was assigned to expedite the grain transfer and the payment of salary and transport expenses to the Shandong boatmen.

> Don't give soldiers and officials any excuse for making delays. I am afraid that the transfer at Jining will take too long, and Shandong boats will find it difficult to return in time to make their regular shipment. If no special official is placed in charge of the transfer at Jining, there will be shirking of responsibility.[37]

A second set of problems also emerged in the middle of the sixth month that threatened delays and unrest at Jining. Qishan reported that a fleet of lighters carrying Zhejiang grain cargoes for transfer to Hedong military junks at Jining had been filled only to 70 percent capacity. The boat owners had explained that they carried less in order to ease their passage through the numerous flash locks on the Shandong Canal, but the real reason, Qishan asserted, was that both the private shippers and their military escorts were using cargo space to carry goods for private sale.[38]

Although these lighters already had made the transfer at Jining and the Hedong boats had departed for the capital, Qishan feared that word of the size of their private cargoes would circulate among the remaining military and civilian crews from Shandong, who also would demand the right to reduce the size of the grain cargoes and to increase the space allotted for private trade goods. The combined fleet of lighters had the capacity for 500,000 *shi*, and if they shipped the 400,000 *shi* of tribute grain, there was little space left for private goods. The emperor was quick to assert that the priority, in this case, was grain! He dispatched a special official to Jining to supervise the loading of grain and the removal of private goods from the assembled junks. If shippers or military escort officials caused trouble, they were to be punished.[39] The transfer at Jining went slowly, and the deadline for the completion of this stage of the process was extended into the eighth month.[40] What is more, the repeated trips back and forth from the junction had taxed water supplies in the Shandong Canal, especially those of Weishan Lake and the Dawen River that supplied

Muddling Through: Transfer-Shipping 171

the critical summit section of the canal at Nanwang.[41] Moreover, these water and shipping resources, strained to the limit in 1825, were slated for intense use again in 1826 as it became clear that transfer-shipping probably would be used the following year.

Regional officials faced equally severe problems as grain junks and lighters entered Zhili province. The canalized Wei and Bai rivers that comprised the canal in this province were silted and subject to endemic meandering, as their serpentine courses revealed. Even before the fleets arrived, lighters were recruited and ready for the low water and silt obstructions that hampered travel along their courses.[42] The onset of winter further complicated the last stages of the transport process. Zhili officials rushed to devise contingency plans for storing the grain along the canal, especially at Tianjin, in the event that junks and lighters failed to reach Tongzhou before the canal froze over.[43] Additionally, the prospect of a frozen canal necessitated the arrangement of winter anchorages for stranded fleets in Zhili and Shandong because it was feared that many would not make it back to the Yellow River junction.[44] Even if they did, many were under orders to remain at the junction through the winter so as to be ready for another agonizing year of transfer-shipping if the junction remained closed in 1826.[45] These contingencies foreshadowed more unrest among the transport crews. And trouble with transport crews was not a trivial problem in 1825. It was one that stretched through four provinces—the entire length of the canal.

The 1825 grain shipment officially ended in the middle of the eleventh month, when the emperor publicly congratulated the Zhili governor-general for bringing the grain shipping and storage work to a successful conclusion.[46] This marked the end of an arduous and costly ordeal that had taken the entire year to complete. The bottleneck at the canal–Yellow River junction had caused the principal delays. The crossing, using Yellow River backspills, had started at the beginning of the second month,[47] with that plan replaced in the fifth month by an elaborate scheme for transfer-shipping that dragged on until the middle of the ninth month. The delays at the junction complicated the shipping process through Shandong and Zhili, prompting frantic efforts to conserve water resources, organize the storage of grain, and arrange for the anchorage of fleets caught in the winter freeze.

An Assessment: The Limits of Muddling Through

In spite of prodigious problems, the emperor and regional officials had completed successfully a spectacularly ambitious program of transfer-shipping to save the 1825 grain shipments. It had included the active intervention of the emperor to direct and coordinate the scheme, as well as dogged efforts by regional officials to overcome what turned out to be almost insurmountable geophysical problems. It should not have worked, but it did! Yet it had come so close to failure and had so undermined the autumn cycle of canal maintenance that the emperor was determined to avoid the future use of the tired strategies that had caused so many problems in 1825 and in the past.

In view of the scale of the ecological and fiscal problems that the Qing state faced in northern Jiangsu, the organization and success of the 1825 transfer-shipping program is quite significant. It reveals the state's organizational capacity in the early nineteenth century—a period of fiscal strain and bureaucratic uncertainty—and demonstrates that the state was capable of moving quickly and flexibly at the emperor's direction to manage a problem of great fiscal-strategic importance.

The transfer-shipping program also highlights the special managerial tasks that fell to the emperor in directing and coordinating programs of multi-provincial scope. In this case, the emperor took direct responsibility for coordinating the planning of top provincial leaders in Henan, Shandong, and Jiangsu and for developing a consensual, uniform approach to implementing these plans. This stands in marked contrast to the emperor's role in a low-grade emergency, such as the 1824 return crossing of grain fleets. The latter was confined to one province and was resolved by the joint decisions of a group of officials around the Liangjiang governor-general, the initiative lying with regional officials. The 1825 impasse also differed from an acute emergency, like the Gaojia dike disaster, in which imperial commissioners quickly drew together the newly appointed team of regional officials to craft emergency plans. In this last case, central imperial interests, open communications between center and region, and consensual regional problem solving were all emphasized, as well as speed in emergency planning.

This range of responses highlights the fact that regionally specific conditions and a host of discrete circumstances mandated different imperial managerial actions. It also reveals the consensual nature of decision making and the variety and complexity of patterns of power-sharing between center and region. These examples remind scholars of the need for caution in making generalizations about the decision-making process in the Qing period. They also evoke familiar parallels with some aspects of central-regional politics in the People's Republic of China, where power sharing and consensus also characterize (and often hinder) decision making. Policy formulation and concrete planning initiatives result from complex, drawn-out negotiations between center and region. Multipurpose water control projects, such as the Three Gorges project on the middle reaches of the Yangzi River, tend to bog down in the planning process for years because they are fraught with technical and political problems that pit the central government against the provinces and the provinces against one another.[48] It appears that Qing government resolved such issues more expeditiously, if the canal crisis of the 1820s is used as an example.

The transfer-shipping plan also draws attention to the repertoire of practical options available to the emperor and regional officials when disasters struck the yearly grain shipments. The recruitment of private lighterage was an important component of that repertoire in the 1820s, and represents a mutually beneficial state-private venture, with state supervision of and cooperative ties with private organizations. The imperial state had a long tradition of availing itself of private resources, and these continue to play a vital role in economic development in the modern period.[49] What is unusual in this case is their use for strategic tasks that had generally been undertaken by government agencies in the pre-Qing period and in the early reigns of the Manchu dynasty as well. Moreover, given the Qing regime's jealous control of strategic issues and decision making, it seems out of character for the leadership to turn over this responsibility to private lighterage networks on the canal and, later, to ocean shippers for sea transport. It is not enough to say that these decisions in the 1820s resulted from fiscal weakness and dynastic decline, because lighterage was introduced and used in the early and middle Qing periods, and there are similar examples of using private organizations for the supply and shipment of strategic grain reserves for military campaigns and famine relief, as well as for the transport of monetary copper. It seems clear that such low-level logistical tasks were increasingly shifted to private groups during the Qing period.

Clearly, in terms of canal shipping in the eighteenth century, the Qing regime could have expanded its fleets of lighters and thereby retained total control of the shipping process, yet it chose not to do so. Instead, it turned to and institutionalized, through years of practice, the hire of private shippers. By the time of the 1825 transfer-shipping venture, procedures for working with private shippers were well established so that the initiation of the program occurred quickly, without weeks of haggling over the concept, much less the regulations and procedures. The speed of mobilization (within a month's time) seems to indicate that the ties between regional authorities and private shippers were close and strong, presumably built on arrangements that were perceived as beneficial to both. Certainly, the emperor's statements suggest that the state was willing to approach shippers with fair and equitable terms and was prepared to accommodate their operational and economic needs in the interests of maintaining strategic grain shipments to the capital. Because of the general satisfaction with this cooperative state-private approach to canal shipping, the state turned immediately to private coastal shipping when the canal broke down in 1825.

Much more research needs to be done to determine the reasons for the Qing retreat from these logistical functions, particularly because this regime had so jealously guarded its power and had expanded its administrative role in key strategic sectors of government. One can only speculate that this pattern was shaped by Qing views about the appropriate boundaries of state power at the local level, subdistrict autonomy, and the economic and operational benefits of private, profit-driven organizations, as well as deep scepticism about the efficacy of the government at the district level.[50] All played a part in shaping the retreat from bureaucratic handling of these low-level logistical tasks. It appears that the Qing leadership's deep distrust of Chinese local officials since the beginning of the dynasty played a role in their exploration of new approaches to such problems, as will be apparent below in the discussion of grain-tax commutation.[51] By the early nineteenth century, the growing crises at the lower levels of provincial government seem to have reinforced this negative view of local government and crystallized it into a broader, more pervasive scepticism about the effectiveness of bureaucracy and bureaucratic solutions to regional problems. Seen in a larger historical perspective, the government retreat from low-level logistical tasks accords with the general trend of reducing state involvement in and control over social and economic issues at the subdistrict level since Song times.

To return to the canal crisis, the transfer-shipping program of 1825 was, from the perspective of long-term logistical grain supply, no solution. The use of transfer-shipping failed to address the fundamental problems of river work and canal restoration on which the smooth, on-going operation of the grain-transport system depended. It took too long and swallowed up valuable human and material resources. Indeed, the whole repertoire of crisis-oriented, stop-gap measures to move the grain through the junction did so at the expense of canal restoration. Even when a program of transfer-shipping was completed successfully, its extension into the autumn season compromised the cycle of tasks designed to maintain and protect the canal. It was, at best, a short-term expedient that was fast becoming obsolete. Even if cooperative ties with shippers were long-standing and fairly permanent, regional officials could no longer count on transfer-shipping to muddle through each yearly crisis.

For these reasons, the emperor emerged from the 1825 ordeal determined to avoid a repetition of this costly, dangerous, and ineffective method of grain shipment. The near collapse of transfer-shipping and the failure to complete pivotal reconstruction work by mid-1825 gave him the opportunity to press for a more effective approach to canal and grain-transport problems during the interim period before the shift of the Yellow River. The emperor initiated a full-scale review of canal-transport management late in the fourth month that lasted until early in the sixth month. The review challenged the methods and goals of regional leadership and demanded major revisions in normative approaches to canal restoration and grain shipping in 1826.

7

The Emperor's Critique of Canal–Grain Transport Management

The Watershed

The near breakdown of transfer-shipping in mid-1825 marked a major turning point in the Grand Canal crisis. The virtual collapse of the plan was reported in five key reports from northern Jiangsu.[1] These memorials bear close analysis because they show why and how the emperor was able to move forward and impose his agenda for canal–grain transport reform on regional officials.

The first memorial arrived on the twenty-seventh day of the fourth month. In it, Sun Yuting requested permission to keep the Yuhuang Lock gate open past the summer solstice to accommodate the last fleets from Huguang that were laboriously inching their way up the Huaiyang Canal. If the lock gate were kept open, the spring crossing would spill over into the autumn, diverting resources away from canal-river defense and reconstruction. The emperor refused to say yes or no to this request, but maintained that regional officials themselves would have to take responsibility for a tactical decision of this kind: "When the moment arrives for closing the lock gate, the governors should act according to the situation." He was not going to be forced into taking responsibility for a decision that flowed from their earlier, ill-advised actions—actions that he had harbored deep misgivings about from the start.[2]

> You governors must reckon with the situation and choose the best thing to do. It certainly is desirable if all the grain junks can cross the river, but if the summer solstice passes, consideration should then be given to the general condition of the canal and river. Opportunities for their defense should never be missed because of the desire to promote shipping.[3]

The emperor reminded them that the summer solstice marked the divide between the spring shipping and maintenance cycle and the autumn cycle, when the defense of the canal-riverine network was the primary goal. He knew that the solstice marked the waxing of riverine floods and seasonal rains, and these rhythms of nature had a logic and practical imperative that shaped canal-transport management. Adherence to the broad outlines of canal management accorded with the dictates of nature and, therefore, assured the successful long-term operation of the Grand Canal and grain-transport system. If regional officials chose to ignore these seasonal imperatives, they would have to take the consequences. If the Yuhuang Lock gate were left open beyond the deadline, the continuing diversion of the river into the canal would silt the junction and "slow the current of the Yellow," causing silt barriers at the river mouth. These, in turn, would cause deadly backflows and floods near the junction and lake, like those experienced during the Gaojia dike disaster.

The emperor's refusal to order the extended opening of the Yuhuang Lock gate challenged regional officials to exercise their practical governing prerogatives. By taking this stand, he strongly emphasized his own role as overall supervisor of the central-regional decisional process, while, at the same time, he reinforced the distinction between imperial and official prerogatives, the latter of which included concrete courses of action.

A second memorial from Sun arrived two weeks later, on the tenth day of the fifth month, and contained the price tag for transfer-shipping. This report revealed the futility of using the transfer-shipping process in concrete "*tael*-and-cash" terms.[4] Sun requested an additional 1.2 million *tael*s to complete the transfer-shipping process, over an above the 3 million *tael*s that had already been appropriated that year. The total exceeded the amount normally needed to cover the yearly cost of grain shipping. It appears from the emperor's comments that the spiraling expenses cast doubt on the efficacy of the plan. If the cost had remained within the 3 million *tael* limit, it would have been acceptable, but to the emperor, the escalating cost was symptomatic of the ineffectiveness of the transfer-shipping plan itself, as well as regional planning and its failure to address the fundamental problem of canal deterioration.[5]

In his response to Sun, the emperor made a blistering attack on regional officials for their incompetent planning and their excessive demands for funds. All of this, he asserted, stemmed from a narrow, "conservative" outlook that caused them to stumble from one problem to the next without making a holistic assessment of damage to the canal system and its impact on grain shipping. This not only bound them to anachronistic strategies from the past but also blinded them to new possibilities. As a result, they "suppressed good [alternative] policies," like sea transport, only to be left with festering problems and enough fiscal waste "to fill a bottomless gorge."

> Why can't [you] officials manage such a vital area of government where the yearly pattern of administration is so clearcut? Search deeply within yourselves and find a way to devise workable and fiscally sound plans. You must not wait for recurrent crises to occur and then use them to call for endless sums of money.[6]

Here, the Daoguang Emperor showed that he was keenly aware of the fiscal constraints facing government in his reign. Indeed, historians have criticized him for what is viewed, in retrospect, as mindless pennypinching. Yet his admonitions "to economize" should not be interpreted solely as a demand for frugality, but instead as a critique of the faltering regional leadership for its unwillingness to confront serious long-term problems.

For their part, regional officials rationalized their lack of initiative by crying that changes would be more costly than adhering to conventional approaches. Yet, the emperor was quick to point out that the very tactics that they continued to espouse were all costly and ineffective. Indeed, they paid a high price in mushrooming expenses, but they paid an even higher price in the deepening deterioration of the canal itself.[7] Now, in the fifth month, it was clear that muddling through with transfer-shipping was not working and the price for its completion was astronomical as well. And for all the added costs, the southern grain cargoes still were not moving through the junction. By underscoring this parade of bureaucratic failures and exorbitant costs, the emperor was forcing regional officials to face up to the need for drastic action to save the canal. Canal restoration and sea transport, in the emperor's eyes, seemed the only sensible ways to reverse the almost complete breakdown of the grain-transport process. Officials must not, he insisted, suppress good policies like these.

Nine days later, two reports from Sun and Wei Yuanyu painted an even bleaker picture, which cast doubt on the state's ability to complete the transfer-shipping program and also promised flood disasters in the autumn.[8] One of the reports announced that Yuhuang Lock gate had been closed on the twelfth day of the fifth month because banks of silt had built up on both the inner and outer sides of the lock that deflected the Yellow River away from the junction, making backspills impossible.[9] The closure of the Yuhuang Lock gate signaled the actual beginning of transfer-shipping and the laborious task of hauling the grain cargoes across the junction embankments to craft waiting on the south bank of the river. Yet, although officials at the junction were poised to begin, hundreds of vessels were still mired in the canal far south of Huai'an, and hauling these craft to the junction for offloading was bound to be enormously difficult, time consuming, and expensive. To speed their movement up the canal, regional officials had opened up two additional channels from the lakes to raise water levels in the canal, as was noted above, but the movement of junks was still agonizingly slow.

The emperor responded to this memorial with disgust. The spring shipping tasks had already spilled over into the autumn season. The fact that vessels were still mired in the canal far south of the junction meant that it would take weeks, perhaps months, to complete transfer-shipping, and this, in turn, would divert human and material resources away from the crucial tasks of reinforcement and protection of the canal, lake, and river dikes. With the prospect of more floods, the loss of clear water reserves for next year's grain shipments, and a repeat performance of the old, ineffective approaches to crossing and transfer, the emperor had had enough. There was no need, he petulantly admonished, to report on the transfer of each fleet's cargo at the junction (reports were normally made when each fleet cleared the junction). The deadline had not been met and so officials should proceed with the plans for transfer-shipping. "Don't bother to notify me until the last of the lighters has picked up its cargo and departed from Jiangsu!"[10]

But there was more news that day, and it was also bad.[11] In spite of earlier reports to the contrary, Wei Yuanyu and others reported that the repairs on the Hongze Lake dikes lagged far behind schedule, as did those on the lower Yellow River dikes. The reconstruction of Gaojia Great Dike was only 5 percent finished on the very eve of the autumn floods. Not only, it appeared, had spring shipping broken down, but so had those spring seasonal repairs that were essential for resisting the floods and protecting the canal in the autumn.[12]

Finally, on the tenth day of the sixth month, Sun Yuting recommended the abandonment of transfer-shipping altogether. He reported that water in the canal was insufficient to track the fleets to the junction, a revelation that seemed to indicate that the two new water channels from the lakes were not having any appreciable effect on water levels in the canal. As a result, ten fleets, roughly a thousand junks, had yet to arrive at the junction. Worse yet, only 80,000 to 90,000 *shi* actually had been transferred and shipped in the two weeks since the closure of the Yuhuang Lock gate. Although approximately one million *shi* had been shipped north prior to closure, an additional one million *shi*, or roughly one-third of the 1825 grain shipments, had yet to cross the Yellow River. The remaining fleets were still south of Huai'an, and the cost of transfer-shipping would be even greater than that estimated a month earlier (5.5.10). To avoid more fiscal outlays and delays, Sun urged the discontinuation of transfer-shipping and the immediate storage of nearly one million *shi* in the cities and counties under the jurisdiction of Huai'an and Yangzhou prefectures, from which the grain could either be shipped the following year, loaded on returning empty grain fleets in the fall, or sold on the open market. In other words, the original plan could not be salvaged.[13]

These failures appear to have shaken deeply the emperor's confidence in those regional officials managing the post-disaster reconstruction program in northern Jiangsu. He felt he had been deceived on many issues. The stream of incoming memorials during the spring months—reports on which plans and appropriations had been based—had been inaccurate. At this juncture, as noted above, the emperor called in Qishan to manage the transfer-shipping crisis at the junction.[14] Three days later (5.5.22), the emperor ordered all the top regional officials in the canal zone to draw up feasibility plans in response to proposals for sea transport and the financing of canal restoration.[15]

Prior to this point, as the crisis deepened, the emperor had played his hand carefully, giving only hints of his disenchantment with regional officials and with their plans for the spring grain transport, while, at the same time, acquiescing and deferring to regional initiatives. Now, after six months, their plans were collapsing, as was their credibility. This was the moment for imperial action, and the emperor moved ahead with three initiatives. First, he ordered Qishan to mastermind a new, comprehensive plan for canal restoration in 1826 that would rebuild weakened parts of the canal system and control Yellow River flooding. The goal was to dredge out the river mouth and river drainage facilities so that, in the years remaining before the Yellow River shift, the clear-water strategy could be used to cross the grain junks and scour out the river bed.

The emperor's second initiative was a plan to finance canal restoration in 1826, based on a proposal put forward by Yinghe, a central government official and adviser to the emperor. The heart of this plan was a scheme for commuting nearly all the 1826 southern

The Emperor's Critique

grain-tax quotas to currency to fund the repair work. While repairs were underway, the Huaiyang Canal would be closed to all traffic.[16] The third initiative was an experimental plan for sea transport in 1826, also based on Yinghe's proposal. This plan sought to maintain capital granary reserves at safe levels in the immediate future, but, more importantly, it aimed to test the feasibilty of sea transport for later use when the anticipated shift of the Yellow River would destroy the canal for an extended period. If such an experiment were successful, it would become a part of the administrative record—a precedent for a new method for grain transport. With such a precedent "on the books," the dynasty could respond quickly and effectively to the difficulties that lay ahead.

The time was right, in the emperor's view, to move ahead with these new options. They would start with Yinghe's proposal because his was the only one that had surfaced in response to the emperor's call for official discussion of sea transport early in the second month. Yinghe's first memorial (5.4.10) he reminded them, had outlined the main features of his canal reconstruction and sea-transport plans. The second (5.5.22) contained concrete measures for its implementation. Because regional officials had hitherto failed to respond to his call for discussions of sea transport, the emperor alone was forced to take the initiative. The officials were all ordered to investigate the plan's provisions carefully and determine how it could be implemented in their particular areas of jurisdiction.

Raising the Issues

The debate on the canal–grain transport reforms was argued on two levels. The first addressed concrete aspects of the reforms. The second, superimposed on the first and more obliquely stated, explored the wisdom of undertaking major administrative changes that departed from established canal–grain transport practice. The argument in favor of change was led by the emperor and his allies and consisted of a scathing critique of regional management strategies and of the failure of regional officials to exercise their prerogatives in ways that coincided with and complemented the dynasty's empire-wide strategic goals. The debate began in the immediate aftermath of the Gaojia dike disaster, which suggests that central officials had already begun to work out some of these issues; it gained momentum in mid-1825 when transfer-shipping hovered on the brink of collapse and the credibility of regional officials was low; and it persisted until the emperor laid to rest the last argument against sea transport late in the eleventh month. The debate provides important insights into imperial views about the special nature and significance of administrative change and the contrasting roles and responsibilities of the emperor and regional officials in solving urgent regional problems, such as those plaguing the canal–grain transport system.

Soon after the Gaojia dike disaster, the emperor began to pave the way for his reform program by interjecting key elements of his critique into the political-administrative dialogue that accompanied the first steps of disaster-related reconstruction and the spring transport cycle. At first, the emperor raised these issues unobtrusively because the practical, on-site management of the canal and grain transport were prerogatives of regional leadership. As the crisis deepened and regional management faltered, however, his critique was articulated with increasing force and clarity. He expressed deep skepticism about the utility of short-term expedients, like the use of Yellow River backspills, and he charged that regional officials always looked to the past for previous methods, regardless of their merit, instead of considering the big picture and innovating new plans and strategies that benefited both the canal and grain shipping. Both tasks were equally important, and grain shipping should not take precedence over the canal, as had been the case in recent decades. To continue to emphasize grain transport, the emperor warned, would hasten the collapse of the canal and leave no alternative method of shipping grain taxes in this dangerous period prior to the shift of the Yellow River.

The Emperor's Critique

During the early weeks of the crisis, the emperor made a special effort to identify his priorities respecting canal restoration. In response to Sun Yuting's reports on conditions at the canal–Yellow River junction, he asserted that emergency reconstruction should center on rebuilding the lake dikes, so that regional authorities could return to the strategy of using clear water for the crossing of the grain fleets.[17] This priority revived the early Qing hydraulic policy that centered on the dual use of Hongze Lake to supply water for the crossing and to scour the junction and river channel. This position was reaffirmed in response to Pan Xi'en's evaluation of the causes of the dike disaster,[18] and again three days later, in response to Wei Yuanyu's advocacy of backspills.[19] It will be remembered that Wei had argued that "using backspills to make the crossing was an emergency procedure which they had no choice but to use."

The emperor rejected Wei's argument that silt could be "managed" and retorted that backspills would only hasten the collapse of junction facilities. The real problem in this instance, the emperor asserted, was backward-looking officials, like Wei, who relied on "old planning tactics," instead of developing effective long-range plans. As emperor, he was tied to the capital. He could not and should not be forced to do concrete planning of this kind.

> I am not able to control from afar! The canal and grain transport are both issues of the greatest importance. If officials only look at previously used plans, canal deterioration will worsen in the future.[20]

On one level, the emperor's advocacy of the "clear water" approach sought to avoid, if possible, "the dangerous strategy of using Yellow River backspills." But, on another level, it reminded officials that this early Hongze policy was, in fact, the foundation of Qing hydraulic practice, and regional officials had been departing from it for decades in response to worsening canal conditions. Now it was clear that their earlier revisions of this policy no longer worked. Was it not time to find new, workable options—like sea transport?

The imperial reference to the Hongze strategy could only have been aimed at setting the stage for further revisions of canal-grain transport practice. The Qing emperors had always been well informed about the complexities of canal-riverine management, and the Daoguang Emperor undoubtedly would have known that a return to this inherited policy was out of the question, given the impossibility of reversing over a century of siltation. Surely, this emphasis on Hongze was the opening salvo in a campaign to show that regional officials had a long tradition of altering early Qing policy in response to changing conditions in the canal zone. Now, further changes were needed to benefit the canal and grain transport.

The emperor's first references to sea transport built on the notion that the time was right for change. He initially raised the issue in an imperial decree, without reference to specific official authorship, early in the second month, before the crossing had even begun. He argued that the Gaojia dike disaster had brought a deteriorated canal system to the point of collapse. It was now nearly impossible to fit the seasonal shipping cycle into the ebb and flow of the Huai–Yellow River floods. He reminded officials that although the idea of sea transport had been raised in the Jiaqing reign, no decision had been made at that time. Now, circumstances were such that the leadership, emperor and regional officials alike, could no longer avoid decisions that would entail significant changes in current administrative practice.

Yet, sensitive to their reluctance to lead in these matters, the emperor conceded that these decisions were difficult because they departed from long-standing regulations. He asserted that "if conditions for inland, canal shipping are favorable, then it will be carried out." If not, they would have to face the difficulties and "relax and alter the old regulations." Officials must not, he insisted, be "biased" in favor of old ways of doing things, and they must not be swayed by what they perceived as the perils of ocean sailing, which, after all, must be safe enough if merchants routinely sailed to the north twice a year. Officials had to face up to the difficult job of altering the regulations or face the even worse prospect of undermining the dynasty's strategic grain supplies (and the disloyalty that this implied).

> To give up the inland waterway, to take the great risk of ocean sailing, and to alter the old rules and regulations! These courses of action seem like matters that cannot be done. Yet tribute is the imperial granaries' main supply! If the shipping route is clogged and grain ships are delayed, how can you regional officials sit back without a plan for transporting grain tribute to the capital? You must definitely, in these circumstances, plan in advance and find a solution to the breakdown of canal shipping.

To those who argued that the seas were dangerous because of high winds, pirates, and foreigners, the emperor countered:

> Merchant ships transport cargoes by sea to the north and unload and sell their goods at ports in Shandong, Zhili, and Fengtian. These merchant ships make the trip several times a year when the wind blows in the right direction. It is obvious that the sea route is not impractical. I believe that if grain tribute is levied and collected in the regular way, but is shipped by merchant boats, those experienced sailors, who steer the boats and know the nature of the sea, will certainly be able to handle the dangers [of ocean sailing] and any encounters with foreigners. There is no need to worry about the risks of the high seas or pirates.[21]

At the outset, the emperor called sea transport the first step in an "experiment" (*chuangshi*), which seemed to imply that the plan was intended for wider application than merely the canal crisis in 1825. He understood official reluctance: the venture was new, untried, and difficult; but, he asserted, it should not be feared. Instead, it should be investigated thoroughly, and if it looked feasible, a small experiment should be tried in the circuits and prefectures of Jiangsu and Zhejiang closest to the sea and most accessible to Shanghai (Susongchangzhen and Hangjiahu). First, regional officials should determine whether or not there were sufficient vessels available in Shanghai to carry the regular grain tribute quotas. If the plan could be applied successfully in these two provinces, then later it could be expanded to the middle Yangzi provinces.

The intention of expanding beyond Jiangsu and Zhejiang after successful trials reveals that the emperor considered the sea-transport plan to be more than a limited one-year experiment for 1826. He was prepared, at this early stage, to apply the plan to the middle Yangzi provinces in subsequent years, when and if it was needed. For the moment, however, he wanted regional officials to explore its use for these two provinces alone and consider the following questions. How much should private shippers be paid so that they would not suffer financial loss? Should escort officials be used to supervise the grain cargoes? Which ports at the mouth of the Yangzi were best suited for loading the southern grain? Which northern ports would serve best for unloading the grain? Additionally, the emperor wanted officials to assess the impact of sea transport on the livelihoods of the regular grain-transport corps and boat crews.

The emperor's opening of the sea-transport debate so early in the spring of 1825 served notice to regional officials that he intended to make changes in the grain-transport system. He outlined in a serious and measured way the conditions that mandated decisive action, and he took the lead in arguing the need to break with practices that dated back to the Yuan and Ming periods. Now the question was, given the social-political environment of the times, did he have the political clout to carry out this innovation?[22]

Early in the fourth month, as the southern grain fleets bogged down in the Huaiyang Canal, the emperor showed again that sea transport was very much on his mind and that he saw it as an effective alternative to canal shipping. He regretted that these fleets had already entered the canal from the Yangzi; but because they had, the leadership had no alternative but to press on with the transfer-shipping scheme. It was, in his words, "too late to take the sea route," and soldiers and boatmen would have to haul the boats through the canal in the usual way.[23] The implication is very clear that had these fleets not entered the canal, the emperor would have been prepared to ship the 1825 grain quotas by sea.

In his first allusions to the topic, the emperor very shrewdly treated sea transport not as a major departure from Qing and pre-Qing tradition but merely as a low-level temporary solution to a temporary problem, just like backspills and transfer-shipping. He discussed these alternatives one after another in parallel fashion and used terms like "temporary expedient" (*quanyi banli*) and "current makeshift plan" (*quanyi zhiji*) to describe them all.[24] Not only were they treated as comparable in purpose and scope, but, he pointed out, they were roughly comparable in cost as well. The vital difference among them was that backspills and transfer-shipping no longer worked to benefit either the canal or shipping. For this reason, the emperor insisted that regional officials consider the merits of sea transport to see if it would "contribute to canal restoration and benefit grain transport." He asserted that practical planning of this sort was their responsibility, not his. He refused to usurp their planning authority and, instead, insisted that they do their jobs.

By treating sea transport as a low-level tactical alternative to backspills and transfer-shipping, the emperor down-played its significance as a radical departure from canal-transport practice and simultaneously undermined the arguments of those who opposed the plan. The emperor and his supporters cast it merely as another timely and economical alternative to a system of grain transport that was on the brink of collapse.[25] In the end, regional officials resisted the emperor's attempt to relabel what they considered to be a profound change in canal–grain transport practice. But that the emperor tried to do so indicates that the Qing imperial tradition of responding flexibly to nonroutine problems and changing realities was very much alive.

By the tenth day of the fourth month, the emperor had received replies from all the regional officials who had been asked to evaluate the feasibility of sea transport: the Liangjiang governor-general, Wei Yuanyu; Yan Jian, the grain-transport director; and the governors of Jiangsu and Zhejiang, Zhang Shicheng and Cheng Hanzhang. Their responses were not favorable.

> In a previous edict, I ordered Wei Yuanyu and others to deliberate carefully and solicit a wide range of opinions in their respective jurisdictions on the condition of the canal and the possible use of sea transport. The governors have all reported back that they consider the sea-transport plan to be too filled with obstructions and too difficult to carry out.[26]

None of them, the emperor pointed out, had addressed the two problems they faced: the impending collapse of the canal and the need for a longer-term solution to the grain-shipping crisis. Only Yinghe, a central government official and imperial adviser, had come forward with an "overall" plan that was clear and compelling and provided for canal renovation and the continuation of shipping. The inclusion of both issues was important: "The state's grain transport and canal-river defenses are both extremely weighty matters. If attention is paid only to sending the grain boats through the canal junction, and not to the future peril to canal facilities, the results will be disastrous."[27]

The emperor endorsed the concept of Yinghe's plan and then ordered regional officials to take the broad outlines of the scheme and come up with a practical approach to its implementation. It was urgent that they do so because, although they might succeed with transfer-shipping in 1825, such makeshift tactics would not suffice in the future. "What about the return crossing of empty grain boats in the eleventh month? What about the new grain tribute shipments in 1826? Because of the deterioration of the canal, we will be forced to use lighters again and again to ship the grain quotas to Tongzhou."[28]

In the final passages of the edict, the emperor became at once more sympathetic to the deep concerns of his regional administrators and more persuasive. He realized, he stated, that their stand against sea transport was motivated by extreme caution in managing grain shipments and shipping costs, an acknowledgement of the fiscal crisis that gripped them. And furthermore, their opinions were not without insight.

> Yet the present circumstances create two problems, canal deterioration and [obstacles to] grain shipping, both of which must be faced. Although one must not rush in and recklessly alter customary practices, one also must not treat [the canal] as unimportant and be too conservative. Yinghe's proposal aims at finding a way that is beneficial both for grain transport and the longer-term protection of the canal. On receiving this edict, all of you must carry out exhaustive discussions on ways to maintain grain shipping while benefiting the canal. You must not entertain the slightest taint of prejudice and merely carry out *makeshift plans* [author's emphasis].[29]

The emperor's move to open up discourse on this issue reveals the importance of imperial leadership in driving the decision-making process when innovations were required to meet short-term contingencies in the provinces. The Qing decision-making process, of course, was designed precisely to respond to such contingencies. However, when regional authorities met short-term problems with methods that conflicted with or undermined longer-term imperial interests, the emperor became the advocate of empire-wide goals and acted to resolve conflict in favor of these goals. In this case, the situational needs of the seasonal grain-transport cycle had too long overshadowed canal maintenance and restoration.

At this juncture, it is important to review canal–grain transport problems from the vantage point of regional officials. Although the emperor charged that they had failed to respond effectively to the emergence of dangerous canal conditions, regional officials had sound reasons for maintaining the status quo, as they saw canal deterioration accelerate and grain transport move more and more slowly. First, the grain shipment process imposed itself on regional officials each spring in a more direct and immediate way than did the incremental weakening of canal facilities each season. Canal shipping had timetables and deadlines in the spring, while canal-riverine maintenance was meant to protect against floods that might or might not occur in the summer and early autumn. In short, it was easier to leave these latter tasks till last or fail to complete them at all. Added to this tendency to neglect maintenance tasks, local-level officials, field and specialist, were thinly spread, without the manpower or funds to perform many of their assigned tasks. Moreover, they were faced with increasing problems and diminishing resources by the late eighteenth century. It is not surprising that regional and local officials undertook only the most pressing duties and neglected many others.

Second, by the late eighteenth century, the irreversibility of siltation and the impossibility, noted by Wei Yuanyu, of controlling the Yellow River, had made large-scale canal renovation seem pointless to many regional officials. The impending shift of the Yellow River soon would mandate major reconstruction of those parts of the canal in northern Jiangsu and Shandong. Why not wait until the river stabilized in its new northern course, then focus resources on rebuilding the canal? From this perspective, muddling through in the interim did not seem all that bad, especially in view of the fiscal crisis they faced. In fact, the approach had a great deal to recommend it.

Third, from the perspective of regional officials, the abandonment of canal transport was dangerous. It threatened economic and social stability in the canal zone. Throughout the Qing period, regional officials had built up a web of relationships with private shippers, haulers, porters, and laborers that kept canal transportation operating, however imperfectly.[30] These ties comprised an important part of the socio-economic fabric of the canal zone and their disruption might well create unrest and disorder. Given these circumstances, regional officials probably saw little reason to alter the status quo, particularly when nothing lasting could be gained from undertaking canal renovations immediately.[31]

Yet this is precisely what the Daoguang Emperor wanted to do: chart another course. But what? It seems clear that what he really wanted was not a thorough restoration of the canal back to the early Qing levels of operational efficiency. That was clearly impossible given the time, fiscal, and geophysical constraints. What he sought instead was a limited program of canal renovation that would improve the state's ability to cope with the last stages of canal transport before the shift. Such a plan was, of course, only marginally longer term than muddling through. But if it enabled the state to minimize the economic disruption and political trauma in the troubled period ahead, that was sufficient reason to improve the canal from the standpoint of the reigning dynasty. The emperor's argument for a return to the early Qing Hongze Lake strategy, which implied comprehensive renovations, was, as noted above, merely a ploy to highlight the on-going pattern of change in regular canal–grain transport management and to establish the timeliness of the innovations he sought to make.

Over the course of the spring months, the emperor carefully laid the groundwork for reforms. He cautiously articulated his opposition to those strategies routinely used by regional officials without explicitly imposing a course of action on them. He handled the matter in this way in order to preserve the distinctions between the prerogatives of the imperial center and those of regional officials in the provinces. This posture showed a healthy respect for the nitty-gritty problems that lay beyond his firsthand experience, and it was consonant with the longstanding Qing pattern of bowing to local contingencies with regionally sponsored initiatives. At the same time, he exercised his prerogative to guide the decision-making process to take account of new imperatives and to reconcile them with longer-term, empire-wide goals. In this case, he sought to guarantee the continuation of grain shipments, first, on the canal, and, failing that, by sea. By interjecting his agenda in this way, the emperor neither squandered his credibility, nor violated the regionally oriented decision-making process; nor did he jeopardize the fragile ties of trust on which consensual decision making and disciplined administration depended.

If and when regional strategies failed, however, the emperor had prepared the way and was ready to act to reconcile imperial goals with regional needs. That moment occurred late in the fifth month when reports from northern Jiangsu indicated that transfer-shipping was breaking down. The impending collapse of this last-ditch attempt to save the 1825 grain shipments strengthened the emperor's hand. It empowered him to demand that regional officials formulate new strategies to resolve the shipping impasse, and it cleared the way for a serious consideration of canal reconstruction and sea transport for 1826.

Controlling from Afar

The chain of events surrounding the breakdown of transfer-shipping reinforced the emperor's drive to resolve the canal-shipping crisis in favor of longer-term imperial goals. Yet it remained to be seen if he could persuade regional officials to implement the three elements of his scheme based on Yinghe's plan: canal restoration, the commutation of grain tax, and sea transport. He feared that regional officials' minds were closed to all three parts of the plan and that they would be unwilling to subordinate regional issues and interests to central goals. Therefore, after laying out the main features of the plan, the emperor again emphasized regional responsibility for practical planning by outlining his view of the nature and operation of central-regional decision making and the roles and responsibilities that emperor and official each bore in managing issues that were of vital importance to the state.[32]

This edict, and another that followed it in the sixth month, show that the Daoguang Emperor believed it was his responsibility to provide broad, overall direction and coordination of key aspects of regional administration and to sanction new approaches to changing regional problems, even though these approaches departed from normative administrative practice.[33] For their part, regional officials bore responsibility for reporting on emerging problems and for providing the conceptual outlines and practical plans for their solution. Communications through the secret memorial–secret edict interchange enabled both emperor and regional officials to do their jobs. It carried problems and plans to the center, provided a channel for communication leading to consensus, and it conveyed imperial advice and authorization to the provinces after consensus had been achieved. It was the crucial medium by which divergences between central long-term goals and short-term regional imperatives were reconciled. Because of the special technical, bureaucratic, and geophysical problems of the canal-riverine system, the day-to-day management of this system was, by necessity, dominated by local authorities—their definitions of problems, their mastery of local administrative lore, and their ideas for solutions. Now an imperially driven reassessment of those solutions was underway because they had failed to resolve regional problems in ways that accorded with strategic imperial interests. The emperor explained his interventionist role in the revision of policy:

> I manage the country as a whole and search out information from everyone. Then I select a good plan and follow it. Moreover, I do not go into the planning process beforehand with a prejudiced view.[34]

He expected all regional officials in the canal zone to deliberate conscientiously on the provisions of Yinghe's plan and to evaluate it on its own merits. His reference to "a prejudiced view" was clearly intended to discourage bias favoring customary practices. The emperor urged them to complete their deliberations and memorialize their suggestions without further delay. He was not prepared to tolerate empty words and the evasion of their planning responsibilities any longer.

> The planning must be completely perfect in order to benefit public affairs. Besides this plan, there may be even better methods and excellent ideas which can benefit the canal and aid transport. Let

regional officials express their various views. Report according to the facts and let me know.³⁵

Early in the sixth month, the emperor reiterated his stand on regional decision making with even greater force in response to Wei Yuanyu's proposals for grain transport in 1826.³⁶ After the appointment of Qishan to the post of Liangjiang governor-general, Wei had been reassigned to his original post of grain-transport director. In this position, he articulated the needs of the grain-transport directorate and its established practices, especially its reliance on lighterage networks for moving the grain shipments north each year. Over the years, this agency, as previously explained, had adapted to changing canal conditions by developing a network of ties between its civil and military personnel and private organizations of shippers, laborers, and grain traders. The prospect of abandoning canal transport for one year to experiment with a totally new system of sea transport would disrupt ties with the groups on whom the faltering grain shipment process had come to rely. All these suggestions seemed ill-advised in Wei's eyes. Confronted by the order to investigate and apply Yinghe's proposal, Wei responded by painting an overly optimistic scenario for canal transport in 1826; it was nothing more than a replay of his earlier memorial arguing the merits of Yellow River backspills.³⁷

The emperor recounted Wei's glib assurances in detail. Wei asserted that ten extra layers of masonry work had been added to the great dike and already over 2.3 meters of water had accumulated in the lake. At this rate, nearly 4 meters would surely accumulate by the 1826 shipping season. On the basis of these optimistic predictions, Wei urged that they stick with canal shipping, using either clear water from Hongze Lake or Yellow River backspills. "Shipping," he confidently asserted, "can be managed according to the old regulations." However, he acknowledged with feigned deference, "If the emperor himself makes a decision for sea transport, I will go along with it."³⁸

This response was an affront to the emperor and to the long Qing tradition of vesting responsibility for practical governance in the hands of regional officials. To the emperor, this was another example of the bankruptcy of regional leadership, and he did not let this high-handed behavior pass without comment. He responded with savage directness; after being ordered to work out details for Yinghe's plan, Wei Yuanyu arrogantly had refused to do so. What is more, he advocated adherence to the old pattern that had just been discredited. Had Wei learned nothing from recent events? The emperor recounted again the situation that led to the urgent necessity of considering Yinghe's proposals for sea transport and canal reconstruction. Wei's conservative response glaringly exposed just how prejudiced officials were against change, in spite of the emergence of radically changed and dangerous circumstances affecting both the canal and grain shipping.

Wei Yuanyu, the emperor sarcastically declared, claimed that conversion of grain taxes to currency to pay for reconstruction was "too fraught with difficulties" to carry out. He "feared obstructions." Yet, the emperor insisted, it was obvious that "the situation in the various [canal-zone] provinces is not the same as it once was."

> Yinghe understands the changed circumstances and has responded with a plan of action. [Wei Yuanyu clearly has not.] All officials must get down to business and devise a workable plan that is free of corruption and will benefit the state.[39]

Effective decision making depended, he stated, on imperial direction of the deliberative process from the top. But the concrete aspects of planning could only be fashioned by regional officials who knew local conditions.

> The sea-transport experiment was originally proposed because the Grand Canal was shallow and silted. It was conceived as only a one-time, temporary expedient. I consulted far and wide across the empire to search out good ideas. My purpose was to select an excellent plan and follow it. Later, I sent out an order to regional officials to work out the myriad details carefully and satisfactorily. [I did so] *because I do not control from afar* [author's emphasis].[40]

The emperor went on to say that Wei Yuanyu rejected this process.

> [He] wants to rely on and proceed from an imperial decision. His intention is to make excuses and shirk planning responsibility. This is an extreme case of failing to carry out the responsibilities of office![41]

The emperor was not prepared "to tolerate prejudice against new courses of action."[42]

The emperor's assertion of the need for an alternative to canal transport was totally justified just four days later (5.6.10), when reports from northern Jiangsu indicated that transfer-shipping had ground to a halt.[43] Sun Yuting found himself in a situation similar to that of Wei Yuanyu earlier in the spring, when the latter had argued for the use of Yellow River backspills. After putting too rosy a glow on the prospects for his plan, Sun was forced to face up to the grim realities and acknowledge the failure of transfer-shipping. Sun's failure proved that the emperor had been right all spring, and the emperor seemed to take delight in reviewing Sun's mistakes and castigating him for faulty planning. He recalled sarcastically that when the clear water in the canal was too shallow and they were forced to used Yellow River backspills, Sun and others had repeatedly said that all the grain could be shipped north with no problem. When the Yuhuang Lock gate was opened, they had reported that the water ran freely into the canal, and that there was ample time to cross all the ships before the summer solstice. The emperor said he had been continually reassured that if the Yellow River were to rise unexpectedly early, not more than 3 percent of the boats would be left behind, and the transfer-shipment process could easily accommodate the stragglers. When the decision to implement the transfer-shipping plan was made, forty fleets had yet to cross the Yellow River. Even if these forty had all crossed (which they had not), the expense of transfer-shipping was too great; "state money was wasted and the people harmed." Now, Sun reported that plans for transfer-shipping had collapsed and nearly one million *shi* would have to be stored in granaries south of the Yellow River. This was a colossal fiasco, the emperor stormed, and all those regional officials in charge were to blame.

> Sun Yuting and Yan Jian [the former grain-transport director] did not make a broad overall plan for transferring and forwarding tribute grain to the capital, but just took one step at a time. Now, all of a sudden, they are beginning to feel concern about deadlines and the budget implications of their actions. Where is their conscience? This is the height of ingratitude for their appointments! Wei Yuanyu, [then Liangjiang governor-general], participated in joint discussions and preparations, and he went along with their course of action. He has no escape from blame. . . . Even though Qishan has just been appointed governor-general, he is not immune from blame either. [He had only been on the job for three weeks.] If there is no way to turn this situation around, Wei should ask himself what punishment he deserves.[44]

At this point, the emperor's only remaining question was this: could some of the grain be salvaged for shipment north or not?

Sun's report confirmed that the planning process had been flawed from the beginning. From the emperor's point of view, regional officials had failed to grasp the gravity of the flood damage and its probable impact on shipping earlier in the year; or, if they had done so, they certainly had not reported this information to the emperor and his central advisers.

Throughout the early months of 1825, regional officials had resisted the emperor at every turn and had placed him on the defensive for his exploration of new approaches to canal restoration and grain transport. Yet, all those stop-gap measures that they themselves now used had been radical departures in the past. Because canal officials had used these remedies for so long, they now regarded them as permanent institutions that were impossible to change. From the emperor's point of view, these practices—justified in the past as necessary expedients—now violated the only really fundamental institution of early Qing policy: the necessity of responding to changed conditions with timely and effective action.

The emperor, on the thirteenth day of the sixth month, turned the tables on regional officials and forced them to confront the issue of the early Qing Hongze policy by circulating a proposal by a former Southern Canal official, Shen Cheng. This proposal reaffirmed the main principles of sound canal management laid down in the early Qing period—the *authentic* old precedents (*jiugui*).[45] It urged a return to these hydraulic principles: use Hongze Lake to accumulate clear water for the crossing from the Huai and Si rivers only; never drain the Yellow River into the lake; strengthen Gaojia Great Dike by constructing graded or sloped outer walls; use only clear water from the lake for crossing grain boats at the Yellow River junction; and never use Yellow River backspills. Most important of all, Shen's proposal stated that the canal directorate must focus its human and material resources on clearing out the mouth of the Yellow River and reinforcing the river dikes to assure the scouring power of the current. To meet the spiraling costs of labor and materials, the state must levy additional taxes for this purpose in Huai'an and Yangzhou prefectures.

Shen concluded that if the canal directorate adhered to these principles, canal-based shipping would improve dramatically, and there would be no need for lighterage, transfer-shipping, or sea transport. Yet, he charged, regional officials since the late eighteenth century had abandoned these principles and, among other questionable practices, they routinely had used Xiangfu and Wushui drainage gates on the north side of Hongze Lake to drain the Yellow River into the lake. This caused silting and the continual rise of the lake bed, higher lake levels, the need for higher dikes, and more and more devastating floods, such as the recent Gaojia dike disaster.

Shen's proposal, in effect, enabled the emperor to charge regional officials with abandoning the authentic early Qing traditions in canal-transport management. His indictment also was timed perfectly to highlight the commencement of the autumn maintenance cycle and the urgent need to redirect regional resources to the defense of the canal-riverine network. The emperor ordered Qishan to consider Shen's proposal and undertake these "defensive" tasks in new, more effective ways. By so doing, Qishan would, in fact, chart a bold new course in canal restoration that would improve the canal system for the troubled period ahead, leading up to the shift of the Yellow River.

The problems raised by Shen revealed the limitations of regional canal management. The canal crisis had been long in the making and resulted from the intersection of geological processes with complex issues of economic and demographic change and of changing bureaucratic strategies for coping with canal–grain transport problems. In the past, these strategies had bowed to regional needs and expedients. Now, a reassessment was warranted by hopelessly difficult conditions in the Huaiyang Canal zone. But it remained to be seen if the emperor could succeed in imposing his agenda.

The Dynamics of Central-Regional Decision Making

Tracking the parade of disasters in canal–grain transport management in the first six months of 1825 provides an intriguing picture of bureaucracy and decision making in an area of government that had been vitally important to the Qing imperium since the early reigns. The conditions faced were irreversible and the problems constant, and unsolvable, like a cancer. The strains these problems placed on central-regional decision making prompted an imperial review, not just of canal management, but of the very process of central-regional decision making and the roles that the emperor and regional officials each played in successful government. The Daoguang Emperor saw his job as being responsive to local conditions and bending the rules for regional administrators so that they could solve new and difficult problems as they arose. He needed open and reliable communications with regional officials to do so. For their part, regional officials were required to apprise him of the imperatives they faced and the courses of action they recommended. This information instructed the emperor on the need for change, garnered his support for their actions, and provided the measure against which their administrative initiatives were judged.

This is not to say, however, that departures from normative practice were rubber-stamped by imperial authority. Points of disagreement between center and region were ironed out and reconciled in the dialogue carried on by court letter and secret memorial. On the whole, the system worked to address local problems with locally inspired solutions. The emperor expected the system to work this way, as had his imperial forebears. He did not impose the solutions, nor did he want to hover over regional officials, guiding their every move. And as he so often stated, he did not intend "to control from afar." Yet conditions in northern Jiangsu forced him to do so, at least to the extent of demanding that regional officials assess the practicality of the three proposals raised by the central leadership.

The decision-making process placed a heavy burden on regional officials to develop a consensus among themselves and to craft workable plans of action. The system had worked reasonably well when responding to crises. In the eighteenth century, central-regional leadership had created new techniques for coping with canal–grain transport problems that departed from earlier Qing practices. But, what were they to do in the early nineteenth century when these approaches no longer worked and officials had become so deeply entangled in and dependent on private shipping interests that they seemed incapable of responding to imperial goals? In this predicament, where regional planning had essentially broken down, reformist solutions began to emanate from the center—the capital—and from imperial agents appointed to key regional posts. These agents, too, were confronted by the same bleak realities as their predecessors and by a consensus among regional officials to oppose bold changes. What kind of reconciliation was possible between long-term imperial goals and regional realities?

8

Canal Restoration

Yinghe's Plan: Silver for Tribute

Canal restoration emerged as the top priority in the sixth month when regionally inspired plans for transfer-shipping and reconstruction collapsed, and the autumn maintenance cycle began. The centerpiece of the scheme, on which all the other discrete parts depended, was the sweeping plan for financing repairs of the canal–Yellow River network put forward by one of the Daoguang Emperor's closest advisers, Yinghe.[1] As noted above, the plan called for the commutation of grain tax to currency to pay for reconstruction. Without massive funding in this period of escalating costs, the state could never hope to undertake work on the scale required to rebuild the canal system in northern Jiangsu. The funds raised through commutation were to be combined with the labor, material, and bureaucratic resources normally used to perform the regular seasonal repairs in order to carry out an intense one-year reconstruction plan. To insure that these resources were not squandered on shipping problems, it was initially thought prudent to close down the Huaiyang Canal while the work was in progress in late 1825 and 1826.

However, the plan depended on a number of variables that had yet to be worked out. First, it depended on the ability of local officials to carry out complex fiscal and market transactions honestly and efficiently. Second, closure of the canal depended on the ability of regional officials to organize and implement quickly a sea-transport scheme in order to assure minimum shipments of grain to the capital granaries in 1826. Exploratory planning for sea transport was just beginning. The Jiangsu treasurer, He Changling, had only just been sent to Shanghai to investigate the possibility of recruiting (*zhaolai*) private coastal shippers, and was as yet unclear if a sufficient number of ocean-going craft would even be available for hire in 1826. Third, limited use of the canal might be warranted if clear water accumulated in sufficient amounts to use the clear crossing, or if sea transport were to fall through, or if other contingencies arose. These complicating factors troubled the commutation debate from the sixth month to late in the seventh month. By this time, the emperor had reshuffled some trusted officials into key posts to assure that he had effective and loyal support in Jiangsu: Qishan took charge in Liangjiang; Tao Zhu was now governor of Jiangsu; Chen Zhongfa became grain-transport director, while Sun Yuting and Yan Jian had been dismissed.

During the Qing period, there were two kinds of grain-tax commutation: permanent and temporary. Permanent commutation was used in the more distant southern provinces of Jiangxi, Hunan, and Hubei, where transporting grain tax in kind was difficult. In this case, the peasant producer's payment in cash was determined by the market price of a *shi* at the time of conversion.[2] Temporary commutation, in contrast, occurred when the actual grain could not be collected due to the breakdown of shipping, or local sale was needed to stabilize grain prices or to provide funds for other purposes.[3] In these cases, the magistrate normally undertook the conversion. Such handling of grain tax was fairly routine and did not threaten metropolitan granary supplies because extra reserves were kept for just such contingencies. The whole shipment of 3.4 million *shi* could be held back for one year or 2 million *shi* for three consecutive years without depleting the capital granaries.[4] Yet grain-tax commutation was never widespread until the 1850s, when the shift of the Yellow River and the Taiping occupation of the lower Yangzi valley dramatically altered the grain-transport process. It had never been done on such a large scale as proposed in Yinghe's plan, nor had it been associated with the complete closure of the Grand Canal—a highly symbolic and strategically important government operation in the late imperial period.

Deliberations on the commutation plan centered on three approaches to handling the 1826 grain tax.[5] The first was peasant commutation, in which the peasant undertook the market sale of his grain and the delivery of the proceeds to the district magistrate. The second was magisterial sale of tribute grain. In this case, the local magistrate collected the grain tax in kind from peasants, arranged for its sale on the open market for silver, and forwarded the proceeds, in this case, to canal authorities in northern Jiangsu. Third, if there were locales where neither peasant nor magisterial commutation was appropriate, and canal shipping was temporarily stopped, officials were asked to plan for the storage of the 1826 grain tax until 1827, when the canal presumably would be functioning normally again.

From early in the sixth month to the eighth month, regional officials considered these options in light of conditions and practices in their respective provinces. The arguments for and against are discussed in detail elsewhere.[6] In general, however, regional officials were uniformly and adamantly opposed to peasant commutation, and only somewhat more receptive to official commutation. Throughout the Qing period, local officials routinely had been responsible for a wide range of fiscal functions connected with interprovincial grain transfers, the provision of relief grains, and price stabilization. And regional officials seemed to think that official commutation of the 1826 grain tax would be easier than changing the procedures for grain-tax collection.

Another reason for preferring official commutation was financial need at the provincial level. Department and district (*zhouxian*) officials and their provincial superiors depended on manipulating the market to fund the basic operations of provincial government, especially district government. They could manipulate the rate of collection of unhusked to husked rice and husked rice to copper cash when collecting from the peasant, then turn around and sell both at artificially high prices on the market for silver, a golden opportunity to squeeze additional income during a period when they were all strapped for funds and constrained by an inelastic budget. Even so, regional officials still warned that officially managed commutation would unleash a flood of corruption connected to the manipulation of the market prices of silver, copper cash, and grain. Commutation offered local officials a perfect opportunity to make money to cover their own administrative costs and/or private needs rather than raise money for canal restoration. Moreover, the widespread sale of grain would flood the market, drive prices down, and reduce the income derived from its sale.[7] Destabilizing the grain market might further destabilize the copper and silver markets and encourage deflation of rice prices.[8]

The response of top regional officials to the commutation scheme reveals what they perceived as the greatest obstacles to the implementation of any major imperial undertaking that relied on the administrative actions and fiscal integrity of local government. Their comments seem to reflect an awareness that local magistrates were caught in a bind. They had to cope with the effects of economic change and demographic crisis with fiscal-administrative tools crafted in and intended for conditions in the seventeenth century. Times had changed but institutions had not. As a result, local magistrates were viewed, with varying degrees of hostility or sympathy, as either ineffective or corrupt or both. In light of these problems at the *zhouxian* level, top regional officials were reluctant in their support of official sale of grain tribute in 1826, and they stressed the daunting obstacles to its practical implementation—obstacles that they knew would dampen the Daoguang Emperor's enthusiasm for the plan, given the long-standing Qing resistance to magisterial tampering with the fiscal process.

Another unspoken issue, equally important, motivated officials to oppose the plan and to argue for the retention of the usual pattern of grain collection and shipment: unrest and rebellion that might occur as a result of disrupting the normal pattern of canal transport. That pattern depended on private labor, marketing, and shipping organizations for shipbuilding and repair, lighterage, engineering, reconstruction, dredging, and hauling grain cargoes.[9] These private organizations were enmeshed in the yearly canal-transport cycle and formed part of a complex network of ties between the government and private interests. To disrupt this network was to disrupt economic conditions along the canal and invite hardship and perhaps rebellion.[10] Any changes in government grain shipping, therefore, were bound to affect the canal zone profoundly, particularly if those changes were made rapidly, as was proposed in 1825, giving shippers little time to adjust to the economic consequences. Rhetorical arguments about *zhouxian* corruption and "maintaining the old regulations in canal transport" at least partially masked the issues of joint government-private networks, the political-economic power they represented, and the fear of economic turmoil that would result from sweeping changes in 1826.

As noted earlier, these same officials also wanted to maintain the status quo because they had serious misgivings about the wisdom of investing huge sums in canal reconstruction. They doubted that much could be done to reverse the deterioration caused by centuries of siltation. Muddling through until the shift of the Yellow River seemed to be the wisest course in view of the problems of *zhouxian* corruption, the potential for economic disorder, and the impossibility of achieving any significant gains in canal-river reconstruction.

At the outset, the emperor had favored peasant commutation, probably because it seemed less vulnerable to official exploitation than the sale of grain by officials on the open market. When regional officials argued that this was unworkable and would inevitably lead to manipulation of the collection process, the emperor quickly abandoned it. And when they also asserted that official commutation would engender corruption that might very well destabilize regional economic conditions and cause widespread unrest, the emperor began to question the wisdom of the plan. The Qing dynasts had always attached great importance to the integrity of the tax-collection process and to their personal responsibility for maintaining fiscal equity and economic stability. As the Daoguang Emperor weighed the commutation plan, he declared, "The most important thing to keep in mind when considering this plan is that both the government's and the peoples' interests must be served."[11] The plan must benefit "the state's revenues and the people's livelihood."[12]

By the seventh month, the emperor had resigned himself to the fact that commutation was too complicated and too vulnerable to official corruption to carry out, and by early in the eighth month, he scuttled the plan completely.[13] In a public edict summarizing the official response to the commutation plan, he explained that the implementation of such a large-scale project that autumn would disrupt the collection, shipment, and marketing of grain. It was prudent to adhere to the normal process of grain collection.

> Grain tribute is the dynasty's main supply. Levying and collecting grain tribute in kind has been the established way of doing things for a long time. Now, changing the system and receiving commuted silver will give rise to corrupt practices. Therefore, I have sent down an edict to terminate all discussion of this matter in Jiangsu, Anhui, Zhejiang, and Huguang.[14]

The abandonment of grain-tax commutation severely compromised the state's ability to undertake a program of canal restoration, and it reflected long-standing concerns with structural weaknesses in district-level government, the local tax-collection process, and the funding of local government operations. The demographic crisis had exacerbated those weaknesses and created more problems in the late eighteenth and early nineteenth centuries. Moreover, special problems of the early nineteenth century intensified the leadership's sensitivity to economic turmoil. Serious shortages of imperial revenue occurred in the Jiaqing and Daoguang reigns (1796–1850), and instability in the monetary system (caused by a general rise in the price of silver and an oversupply of monetary copper) exacerbated fiscal problems at both the central and local levels of government, and they also unsettled market conditions.[15] At the same time, there appears to have been a market-generated scarcity of silver, which also may have been influenced by the expansion of opium smuggling in the 1820s, at least in the major cities and markets on the coast and the lower Yangzi valley.[16]

Most important was the sharp fall in grain prices from 1815 to 1850 that led to appreciation in the value of silver relative to grain. This placed an enormous burden on the taxpayer when paying his land tax in silver. The general deflationary forces at work also decreased the taxpayer's income from cash crops and off-season employment.[17] Moreover, the instability in the monetary and market systems placed a burden on the local magistrates, who generally raised the rate of collection for both the land and grain taxes to keep pace with the rising price of silver. As a result, taxes in the Daoguang reign were rising, and at the end of the reign they were twice as heavy as in the 1820s and three times as heavy as those in the Qianlong and Jiaqing reigns. Therefore, even though the economic picture was generally positive from 1750 to 1910, according to Wang Yeh-chien, the period from 1820 to 1850—the entire Daoguang reign—was marked by considerable economic turmoil.[18] Even though the causes and effects of this phenomenon were not clear at the time (nor are they altogether clear today), the emperor and the upper levels of the bureaucracy identified the source of the problem as magisterial abuse of fiscal-economic power.

The emperor did not need much persuasion to go along with this view. He felt that fiscal corruption was dangerous and subversive, undermining the imperial alliance with the people, his commitment to their livelihood, and the very foundations of the state. Fear of it mandated the rejection of grain conversion, the only plan that had promised effective, if temporary, funding for reconstruction of the canal system. Problems with local government also seemed to predispose the emperor and his advisers to turn to private, subdistrict organizations to implement at least one of the schemes to alleviate the breakdown of grain transport on the Grand Canal—sea transport of grain tribute in 1826.

The debate on commutation reveals important facets of the central-regional decision-making process. First, it confirms that official consensus and support for a course of action were essential for its implementation. Although the emperor acted to overrule regional strategies for canal-transport management and had ordered regional officials to consider Yinghe's plan, in the end he could not impose a centrally inspired plan without regional support because the plan relied so heavily on local administrative action for implementation. In contrast, he was freer to pursue the alternative sea-transport plan because it bypassed local administration and relied instead on nonbureaucratic organizations—in this case, on ocean shippers.

Second, the debate reveals the emperor's powerlessness to control aspects of the fiscal process. The discourse on official corruption indicates that the imperial center and, to a certain extent, the top levels of regional government, could not assure official diligence and honesty at the district level. They may not have been clear about the extent to which institutional rigidity in the budgetary-fiscal process and the effects of sweeping economic and demographic changes in the eighteenth century had undermined the ability of local government to perform its basic functions. They generally recognized, however, the difficulties facing local officials and apparently felt it was unwise to impose an additional set of fiscal-market operations on this overburdened level of government.

Third, the debate illuminated the Daoguang Emperor's view of the special responsibility of imperial leadership to insure the integrity and operation of the fiscal process. If the commutation plan overburdened *zhouxian* officials, jeopardized the stability of the tax collection process, and caused economic hardship in the canal zone, then it was out of the question. Additionally, imperial statements emphasize the emperor's responsibility for the economic well-being of both the state and the people. It is clear from the discussion of commutation that the Qing leadership interpreted fiscal-economic issues in strategic terms, and they operated from the assumption that economic order and well-being preceded and were necessary for political order and security. Seen in this light, the commutation scheme was a dangerous undertaking, capable of unleashing official corruption, robbing the people of their livelihood and the state of its just revenues, and precipitating turmoil and rebellion.

The abandonment of the fiscal underpinnings of canal reconstruction doomed the restoration plan and imperial prospects for prolonging the life of the Huaiyang Canal. Because of the nature of the geological processes associated with the cyclical change in the course of the Yellow River, these solutions could have been only temporary at best—a fact recognized by emperor and officials alike. The emperor, however, wanted to pursue ameliorative solutions. He was dissuaded from doing so, not by mindless adherence to canal transport traditions, but by what he perceived as the inability of local government to implement the plan and the fearsome possibility that changes in the tax-collection process and official manipulation of fiscal-market transactions would destabilize the economy and spark rebellion in the southern canal zone. The question that remained was this: could any of Yinghe's plan be salvaged?

Taming the River

The plan for canal restoration had two essential pillars. The first, and more important, was clearing blockages at the mouth of the Yellow River, and the second was the solid reconstruction of the Hongze dike system. Each was enormously expensive, and each required massive reconstruction of pivotal water-control facilities. If adequate funding were provided, the emperor and his allies thought that the two goals could be achieved during the eighteen-month period from mid-1825 to the end of 1826. However, as planning progressed in the autumn of 1825, the scale and complexity of reconstruction work on both the Yellow River and Hongze dike projects turned out to be vastly greater than originally thought. Even with the emperor's funding scheme, it was not at all certain that adequate restoration of the system could be accomplished. The rejection of tax commutation in the eighth month and the lack of any other viable funding source diminished further the prospects for canal restoration at the outset. Without adequate funding, the lower levels of regional administration, its field and canal agencies, could hardly make a dent in the long list of required tasks. They were hampered by spiraling costs and severe revenue shortages, which, in turn, meant shortages of necessary labor and materials.

Canal restoration was further complicated by the decision in the seventh month to keep the canal open and to use transfer-shipping for part of the 1826 grain quotas.[19] This decision was made because He Changling's investigation of the feasibility of sea transport revealed that Shanghai shippers had the capacity to ship only one-half of the 1826 Jiangsu grain-tax quota (1.5 million *shi*) to Zhili. Both the emperor and regional officials agreed that the remaining southern grain should be sent by canal in 1826; the former because he feared the depletion of granary reserves in the capital, and the latter because they feared the turmoil that would result from disrupting the private groups connected with canal shipping. The decision to use canal shipping meant that the leadership again faced the prospect of trying to move cargoes through the badly damaged Huaiyang Canal and junction. It would be months before canal officials would know whether or not a clear-water crossing was feasible. If it was not, they would have to struggle again with the expensive, time-consuming process of transfer-shipping. At least the emperor definitely had ruled out use of Yellow River backspills, and this decision would protect the junction from further silt damage. Nevertheless, the use of the canal in 1826, with all its myriad complications, obviously would divert scarce resources into shipping rather than into repairs.

Sea transport was not the panacea that it first had appeared to be. Besides the inability of Shanghai shippers to transport all of the Jiangsu grain quota in 1826, regional officials from Zhejiang and the middle Yangzi provinces asserted that they had access neither to sea ports nor to ocean shippers, so there was no way to send their grain-tax quotas by sea.[20] All these factors complicated canal reconstruction and grain transport in 1826 and forced the Daoguang Emperor to scale back his plans for restoration.

The emperor's scheme for canal restoration sought to achieve the smooth operation of the whole by fixing one of the main parts. His intention was to concentrate human and material resources on removing silt blockages from the lower course and mouth of the Yellow River in order to curb backflows, seepage into Hongze Lake, and silt infiltration of the entire canal-riverine network. If successful, the plan would take pressure off the river, canal, and lake dikes; it would facilitate the timely clear-water crossing of grain fleets before the summer solstice; and it would allow, for a time at least, a return to the normal seasonal cycles of canal shipping and maintenance.

This approach reflected both the imperial and the official views that the silt-upraised bed of the Yellow River and silt blockages at the river's mouth were the main causes of systemic dysfunction in the canal-riverine network. It also seemed to be the most time- and cost-efficient way to restore canal operations in the face of overwhelming physical and fiscal obstacles. It did not make sense to invest heavily in the Hongze dike system or other parts of the network if the levels of the Yellow River were not brought down first. Some repairs to the lake dikes would be made, but even these could not be done quickly. The dike work was also terribly expensive. Therefore, central and regional officials struggled to find a balance between dike repairs to prevent catastrophic floods and resolution of the core problem: blockage of the lower course of the Yellow River. The controversy over these issues is revealed in the memorials of Qishan and Zhang Jing from late 1825 to the end of 1826. Qishan insisted that more preventive maintenance on Hongze dike was required to assure the minimal safety of the Huaiyang region, while Zhang Jing emphasized opening up the lower river course.

The focus on silt in the river's lower course also reflected the fact that few other practical options existed. The river and lake dikes could hardly be raised higher, nor was it possible to dredge out and expand the Xiahe and Yangzi drainage outlets by the end of 1826. The attack on blockages in the Yellow River was all that was left, and it represented a last-ditch attempt to save the canal system. The emperor and his central advisers had greater faith in the plan than regional officials in northern Jiangsu, who cowered beneath the lake dikes and the up-raised Yellow River and knew full well the enormity—indeed, the impossibility—of digging their way out of the silt problem.

Even though the emperor's approach to canal restoration centered more heavily on silt removal from the lower river course than on restoration of the lake dikes, he and his supporters cloaked the scheme in the legitimizing mantle of early Qing policies and practices. They treated it as a program for restoring the authentic Qing model of canal–grain transport management, one that promised a return to the policies and practices of the Kangxi and Yongzheng reigns when the clear-water crossing of grain fleets was regularly used. The restatement of the early Qing model was not a call to return to out-dated policies, but simply a way of giving legitimacy to and garnering support for a very limited and practical plan for keeping the canal system functional until the river shifted. It was far narrower than the broad, multifaceted program of canal reconstruction of the early Qing reigns, when the entire system was rebuilt and expanded. The Daoguang Emperor and regional officials had no illusions; there were few options left in 1825, given the state of the canal–Yellow River system.

The scheme for opening up the Yellow River, included techniques that early Qing engineers had used to remove silt, such as narrow-diking, the use of weirs, and the straightening of river bends, all of which intensified the self-scouring effect of the current (fig. 10). Reinforcing these techniques were regular dredging methods that removed silt from the riverbed, the sandbars at the river's mouth, and the silt build-up at the entrances of important drainage channels leading off the river. Both dry and wet dredging were used: the former temporarily blocked and diverted the river from badly silted sections of its bed during the winter months when the water levels were low so that laborers could dig and carry out the silt. Wet dredging was achieved without diverting the river. This work required legions of unskilled laborers to dig and cart the silt, as well as skilled workers who operated dredging ships, some outfitted with silt scoopers, which were manipulated by pulleys and cables running off the mast (fig. 7). Vessels also were used in pairs to drag large silt scrapers—cylindrical devices with sharp teeth—to dig up and loosen the silt so that it could be scoured out more easily by the current (fig. 8).[21] Besides these standard dredging and scouring techniques, Qing hydraulic engineers turned to larger schemes for permanently rerouting a part or the whole of the Yellow River in its lower course.

Many of these techniques had been discussed during the initial investigation of the disaster and in the emperor's critique of regional canal management during the spring. As the summer solstice passed, and pressure to complete the fall maintenance schedule intensified, officials drew ever more attention to them. Shen Cheng, as noted earlier, reaffirmed the value of early Qing principles and techniques for silt removal. He insisted that regular, seasonal dredging was the only way to remove silt blockages from the river and that resources should be focused on dredging the mouth and lower reaches. Skilled dredgers and dredging machines should be used, and, if necessary, taxes should be raised to do the job thoroughly.[22] Similarly, Finance Ministry officials strongly urged regional canal managers to return to the regular program of seasonal repairs and reconstruction so that pivotal "defensive" (*fangyu*) tasks in the autumn season were not neglected. They warned against delaying and neglecting these tasks, which they claimed were essential to keeping the river's course open and to safeguarding the river dikes. If they were ignored, devastating floods were bound to occur, not sometime in the future but each year.

The Finance Ministry's warning expressed the heightened sense of urgency felt as the autumn floods approached in 1825.[23] The canal-riverine network was extremely vulnerable that year because little headway had been made in reinforcing the river dikes and dredging the lower course of the Yellow River. And both projects had been pushed aside as regional resources were soaked up by the heavy demands of the grain-transport process. As a result, emperor and officials alike braced for what promised to be a dangerous and potentially disastrous autumn flood season. If they survived the floods without major mishap, their task of restoring the canal system in 1826 with a program of emergency silt removal would be slightly less daunting.

Although Qishan was charged with formulating a multifaceted plan for restoring the canal-riverine system, his immediate and most urgent task was to expedite the autumn work cycle that centered on the security of the river and lake dikes against the rising floodwaters of the Huai and Yellow rivers.[24] After surveying conditions in northern Jiangsu for several weeks after his arrival late in the fifth month, Qishan bluntly reported what he saw at the work sites on the eve of the autumn floods:

> Grain boats are blocked by silt in the canal. The water level of the lake is low, while that of the Yellow River increases daily. Canal laborers are working to the point of exhaustion. Because our great emperor is deeply concerned about these issues, I must devote all my heart and wisdom to these tasks.[25]

The emperor replied that he had appointed Qishan precisely because of his ability to manage difficult regional problems, and he observed, "Even before I order you to address [problems], you have already brought them up. This shows we have the same concerns."[26]

In the sixth month, regional canal officials began work on two major projects "to harness the Yellow River" which they believed would enable them to divert dangerously high autumn flood waters in the middle reaches of the river. The first was the Wangying drainage channel, discussed earlier, which lay opposite the junction on the north side of the river and directed the river's flow into the Salt Canal, a major diversion canal (map 7). The officials in charge of this plan argued the acute need for extra laborers, over and above the regular skilled and nonskilled canal-river workers, military and civilian, who normally shouldered the construction and dredging tasks each year. Even though the emperor authorized the appropriations, he noted that the scale of work and the appropriations for this project were far greater than any since 1816 and 1819, late in the Jiaqing reign; he did not contest the need for such flood control projects in 1825. He simply did not want officials to think that large appropriations of this kind would be forthcoming automatically in the future.

> Suddenly, the provinces request more funding than before. The country's revenue is limited; there must be restraint on expenditures. I fear that the assertions of regional officials about economizing at all times are merely empty words. You must be careful to eliminate waste. Don't assume that the approval of your present requests can be taken as a precedent.[27]

The emperor's response is significant because, although it shows that he certainly recognized the special challenges posed by the autumn floods in 1825, it reflects his fears about fiscal problems and highlights his continual demands for economy and retrenchment. Zhu Shiyan and Sun Yuting had been correct to point out this pattern at the time of the disaster. Now, later in 1825, regional officials were again pressured from the top by the emperor for economy while simultaneously facing herculean tasks and the threat of floods.

The second major drainage project sought to divert floodwaters into an outlet that lay further east, midway between the junction and coast. This scheme sought to expand a 540-meter lead channel from the Yellow River to the Chang River and to construct approximately 18 kilometers of new dike embankments on the Chang to prevent floods when the Yellow River waters came surging into its course.[28] By improving both these drainage channels, canal-river managers hoped to avoid draining the river into Hongze Lake through the Xiangfu, Wushui, and Maochengpu channels north and west of the lake. Even though they had to facilitate the flow of clear water from the Huai River basin into the lake for the sake of a clear crossing, they also had to prevent additional spillover from the silted Yellow River because of the danger to the lake dikes.

While these flood control measures proceeded, canal-river engineers simultaneously moved to appraise the condition of the Hongze dike system to determine if it would hold during the autumn floods. It was unclear in the sixth month just what the actual situation was. Reports on the progress of dike reconstruction, especially the great stone-clad Gaojia dike, had varied over the spring and summer months, with some asserting that the work was neither solid nor complete. A report from Wei Yuanyu in the middle of the fifth month, which had thrown the emperor into a panic, asserted that only 5 percent of the work actually had been finished.[29] In contrast, a month later, Yan Lang reported that the work was really 70 to 80 percent complete, although there were fears that the mortar would not set before the autumn floods.[30]

The ugly truth about the weakened condition of the great dike would not be exposed until much later, after the floods had receded in the tenth and eleventh months. At that time, Qishan's inspections showed that vast stretches of the great dike were still at risk—forty kilometers out of its total sixty-kilometer length, or fully two-thirds of the whole. Yan Lang's reconstruction work had proved to be cosmetic and superficial. He had plastered over the breaches and other weakened parts of the dike but had failed to build up its inner earthen core, which had eroded over the years due to pressure and seepage from the lake. In Qishan's blunt opinion, it was necessary to tear down parts of both the old and the newly repaired sections where the inner structure was crumbling. The plans for doing so were incorporated into his master plan for restoring the canal system in late 1825.[31] As it turned out, in spite of continued work on the great dike, parts of it were again swept away during the 1826 flood season.

The junction and Huaiyang Canal also had to be dredged, both to accommodate the returning empty grain fleets in late 1825 and the new spring grain shipments in 1826. Yet, because many ships were likely to be delayed north of the river that winter and transfer-shipping was more likely than a clear-water crossing in the spring of 1826, canal officials emphasized canal dredging alone, assuming that the Yuhuang Lock gates would be kept closed throughout 1826.[32]

Paralleling the seasonal work on river defenses in northern Jiangsu, Zhang Jing, the Shandong Canal director, energetically embarked on a campaign to reinforce the Yellow River dikes in Henan and Shandong. He also worked out drainage schemes to draw water into the Shandong lakes (Weishan, Zhaoyang, Dushan, and Nanyang) that were essential for supplying the Shandong Canal and were being depleted in the autumn by the lighterage of 1825 grain cargoes between Jining and the junction.[33] No matter how small the task, Zhang reported his every accomplishment, as well as every job left undone by his predecessors. By the tenth month, he even began advancing proposals for dredging, straightening, and diverting the course of the Yellow River in its lower reaches in northern Jiangsu, an area that was outside his own jurisdiction.[34] Zhang succeeded in attracting imperial attention to himself and finally secured a permanent appointment to the Shandong Canal directorship in late autumn and then to the Southern Canal directorship the next year, in the third month.[35]

Once regional officials turned their attention to the round of autumn flood-control tasks in 1825, they did so with a renewed sense of purpose and commitment. By forcing the issue of canal restoration, the emperor had shaken them out of their habitual pattern of concentrating on shipping and ignoring water-control maintenance. Whether or not they sincerely believed that the canal could be restored to effective operation, regional officials were all agreed that the Yellow River had reached a new stage of precariousness, and they were unanimous in their assertion that these conditions warranted new standards of vigilance from lower-level canal-river managers, guards, and laborers. As the censor Liu Yinheng had observed:

> Officials in charge of canal-river affairs must now personally supervise the dike defenses. It is said that in the past, canal-river

officials would leave the dike sites and return to their offices when the flood season passed and winter arrived, leaving canal troops to take care of the dikes. This was the usual pattern. Yet, river conditions are now so dangerously unstable that it is necessary to supervise and defend the dikes at all times! How can officials use the frost and the dropping river levels as excuses for ignoring the river [in the winter months when dredging should be done]. The accident at Gaojia Great Dike last year is a prime example of the consequences of such neglect.[36]

The expectation was that major floods, not simply meandering, would occur each season for the foreseeable future until the river shifted course.

In response to the need for greater vigilance at the dike sites, Qishan exerted greater discipline on field and canal officials who managed canal-riverine defenses and reconstruction work. He formulated regulations imposing greater accountability on officials for the quality of reconstruction work carried out under their supervision, and he demanded greater discipline at the lower levels of the canal administration—an initiative that the emperor endorsed:[37]

> From now on, the canal director and others must work together to monitor and discipline the lower-ranking officials responsible for the canal. When the winter comes and the winds are strong, these [high-ranking] officials should go personally to the river and inspect the reconstruction and guarding work. They should order circuit officials to check [on these tasks] carefully and secretly. Anyone who performs canal administration tasks in a loose, perfunctory way must be reported and punished strictly without forgiveness.[38]

After Qishan had completed the immediate tasks of transfer-shipping and flood prevention, he turned his attention to the third and most problematic task. This was the opening up of the lower course of the Yellow River, the pivotal part of the emperor's plan for canal restoration. In the seventh month, he brought forward a plan to reroute the lower course of the Yellow River northward into the bed of the Guan River and channel it to the sea by this new route, avoiding "the last 120 kilometers of the Yellow's silted bed." The emperor liked this plan because he initially thought that it would "reduce river levels near the junction, and obviate the need for such high water levels in the lake to resist the Yellow River's current during the crossing of grain fleets."[39]

Generally, the water level in Hongze Lake had to be 7.2 meters to resist the inflow from the Yellow River. Yet in late 1824, the great dike had collapsed when the water level reached 6.1 meters. Draining the Yellow into the Guan would reduce the need for such high levels in the lake and for correspondingly high dikes. Yet, the emperor was also worried about the enormous price of the scheme:

> Before deciding to proceed with this plan, the governor-general and others must be clear about its cost, both the direct costs of moving the mouth of the Yellow River, building new river dikes, dredging the Guan River bed, and restoring the people's fields and huts as well as the human costs associated with the upheaval. These must be weighed against the long-term advantages. How long will this scheme work? Which measures are expensive and which are easy to implement? Send me a detailed report after you have considered these questions. Since the plan is a comprehensive one that includes the entire canal-riverine system, I will not stint on money. However, the plan must benefit both the canal and grain transport for a long time, and not be just another temporary expedient. Then and only then will it be a truly beneficial plan.[40]

By the end of the ninth month, it was clear that the Guan River scheme would not work because the mouth of the Guan was even higher than the mouth of the Yellow.[41] The emperor commented pessimistically that:

> This discharge of the Yellow River into the sea will be obstructed. The mouth of the Guan is narrow and cannot be dredged deeply. If the Yellow River is diverted into it, the water will spill over the

banks. Compared with the present Yellow River mouth, the Guan mouth is worse and would be more difficult to control. When it was originally used in the Kangxi reign, the river dikes burst repeatedly.[42]

After the failure of the Guan proposal, canal-river officials used three approaches to clearing the blockages in the lower half of the Yellow River, from Yunti dike to the Nijia and Wangjia sandbanks at the river's mouth. In this part, the river passed the ten Marshgrass Bends (*tao*), where reeds trapped the silt and formed protrusions that extended out into the river, slowed its current, and caused more siltation. First, they worked on "straightening the bends"—clearing out the marsh grass outcroppings to increase the velocity and maximize the scouring effect of the current. Second, they dredged the sandbanks near the river's mouth. Third, they dug a drainage, or bore, channel (*yinhe*) through the silt and clay so that the river could exit more quickly than through the original channel alone. None of these measures worked because of the impossibly high levels of silt and problems with clay soils along the coast, north of the river's mouth.

Work on the river between the junction and Yunti dike included strengthening the river dikes to constrict the current and scour the silt. Important among these dikes on the south side of the river were the Taihuang, Jingjia, and Shijia dikes, and on the north, the Yongfeng, Zhujia, and Yunti dikes.[43] In the early Qing, this part of the lower course received much more attention. At that time, river engineers relied more heavily on the release of Hongze water through the junction to scour the river bed and often built temporary dams to divert the river into the Wangying–Salt Canal drainage system (map 7) to enable them to "dry dredge" the river bed near the junction. By the early nineteenth century, the silt levels and backflows were so serious that only the opening of the Yellow River mouth offered any hope of ameliorating conditions at the junction.

It was not until the eleventh month, when the flood season had passed, luckily without incident, that Qishan turned more attention to the vexing problems plaguing reconstruction of the great dike at Gaojia.⁴⁴ Initially, in the seventh month, he had reported that the closure of breaches caused by the floods was 90 percent finished. To reinforce these newly mortared parts, he proposed depositing piles of rock fragments behind them. The emperor was doubtful about the wisdom of the scheme, not just because it was costly, but also because the loose rock fragments were no substitute for solid mortared stonework. In any case, the project could not be finished by the end of 1826. "It is a big project because the dike is 60 kilometers long; the costs will total six million *tael*s, and it will require several years to complete."⁴⁵

However, as noted above, on closer examination Qishan discovered ominous signs of structural deterioration of staggering dimensions. Erosion had weakened the dike's earthen core, leaving a crumbling foundation, caved-in sections, and holes that recent repairs had covered over but not fixed. Qishan urged a comprehensive reconstruction program, lasting probably four to five years, during which both the crumbling older sections and the newer patched parts would be torn down and thoroughly rebuilt, then buttressed by large deposits of stone fragments, as he had suggested earlier.

> Both the old and the new work are substandard and unreliable. The dike will not be able to withstand the force of the wind and waves if it is simply reinforced by rock fragments thrown down behind it and its foundations are not made firm. If the dike does not last, that means that millions of *tael*s will be washed away, leaving untold damage.⁴⁶

These weaknesses in the dike system made the reduction of water levels in the Yellow River even more imperative. Any further seepage from the river into the lake would put the great dike at even greater risk. The clear, unsilted water from the Huai and Si rivers flowing into the lake would also have to be monitored very carefully.

Because of the revelations about the shoddy reconstruction of Gaojia dike, Qishan renewed his campaign to make officials accountable for the work they personally managed. Earlier, in the sixth month, he had attacked the work of subprefectural officials, charging that they often exaggerated the urgency of problems, especially immediately before the autumn floods, so that they could secure large appropriations. Even so, they often failed to complete the required work.[47] Now, in the tenth month, when Qishan uncovered the true extent of the weakness of the great dike, he insisted that the time period during which officials were held accountable for their work should be extended in order to eliminate shoddy workmanship and the use of substandard materials. The emperor concurred:

> The Hongze dike project is essential to save clear water to aid transport and protect the people's livelihood. The former officials in charge of it did their work recklessly, thereby impeding grain transport and injuring the people. I am outraged by their actions.[48]

The need for a new sense of commitment and a stricter standard of accountability also had been raised by the censor Liu Yinheng. In his view, the river situation was so unstable that high-, middle-, and low-level canal and field officials had to be on constant alert for floods. None of the old patterns of neglect "after the river falls and the winter comes," could be tolerated.

Early in the tenth month, Zhang Jing began to propose schemes for controlling the river in northern Jiangsu, an area that was technically outside his jurisdiction. He reiterated that an effective strategy for controlling the Yellow River must contain two elements: dredging the lower course and mouth in the spring and then continual reinforcement of the river dikes in the autumn. In the past, he charged that canal officials had neglected both regular and emergency dredging work and had only built and guarded the dikes.

> After the river drops and the frost comes, officials used to believe that the danger was over and did not try to find a way to dredge the rivers. Gradually, the river bed became higher and higher, and clear water could not flow out through the junction. Instead, the dikes were raised higher and higher. Every year, the people that live below the river level and the canal directors asked for

millions to repair the dikes. Obviously, the state must protect the people's livelihood regardless of the cost, but what if the canal-river work is poorly done?[49]

Besides the regular, seasonal dredging tasks, he offered ideas for the larger canal-restoration program, particularly a plan for straightening the "bends" in the eastern end of the river's lower course.

The emperor's response to Zhang's memorial showed his pessimism about river work and dike reconstruction. He explained that Qishan's scheme to divert water into the Guan River had come to nothing because the mouth of the Guan was even higher than the mouth of the Yellow River.[50] Because Zhang's proposal offered some hope of opening up the lower course of the Yellow River, the emperor forwarded his proposals to Qishan and regional officials in northern Jiangsu for their assessment. A month later, primarily at Zhang's urging, the emperor sent Zhang himself to northern Jiangsu to map out with Yan Lang and other northern Jiangsu officials a joint strategy for clearing the lower course of the river. This assemblage of officials was entreated to work together to devise a multifaceted dredging scheme that would benefit the state in the years to come.

Even though regional officials struggled on through 1826, workable options for the river were not forthcoming. They explored different combinations of dredging options, including self-scouring with the Yellow River's current, scouring with the clear lake water, dry and wet dredging, clearing out the "bends" and sandbanks, and the diversion and rerouting of the last stretch of river. Controversy attended the search for alternatives for "harnessing the river." Similarly, conflict emerged over reconstruction strategies and the scale of investment in the restoration of the Hongze dike system. These controversies were not primarily due to political careerism and factionalism as has been contended, but largely to the fact that officials were entering into a new stage of precariousness with the Yellow River.[51] Old methods were not capable of meeting these new conditions, and the emperor and regional officials alike were unsure if or how to proceed. Those that tended to favor greater investment in the Hongze dike system did so because they doubted the efficacy of new Yellow River schemes and because they thought the state's priority should be flood protection for the Huai-yang region, bound to be hit continually by catastrophic floods in the near future. All their schemes ended in failure because there was neither the time, the money, nor the physical means of conquering the silt.

The central goal of the emperor's canal restoration campaign had been to make marked improvements in canal shipping by opening the Yellow River's lower course. From late 1825 to early 1827, regional officials in northern Jiangsu—those who faced the crisis firsthand—demonstrated by their failed efforts the insurmountable magnitude of the silt build-up. Their reports educated the emperor about what was possible and what was not. What was possible were redoubled efforts to maintain the yearly dredging and maintenance cycles to limit flood damage and enable grain shipments to pass through the junction by means of transfer-shipping and Yellow River backspills. What was not possible was opening up the lower course of the river and returning to a clear crossing and the original early Qing pattern of shipping through the junction. Nor was it possible to expand the Hongze dike system to meet the challenges of the Huai and Yellow river floods, a fact that was tragically confirmed in late 1826, when autumn floods from the Huai River ruptured the Hongze dikes again—two of the breaches were located in precisely the same places in the great dike that had collapsed in late 1824.[52] By the end of the two-year canal crisis, the emperor had accepted the inevitable message from northern Jiangsu officials: muddling through was the most prudent course during the dangerously unstable period before the Yellow River moved northward. Consensus had been established again between the center and the region on the management and reconstruction of the canal-riverine system.

9

The Sea-Transport Experiment

Forcing the Issue

The sea-transport experiment, in contrast to the canal debacle, was a success story. The planning and implementation of the scheme lasted from early in the second month, 1825, to the middle of the eighth month, 1826, when Zhili officials deposited the last of the sea-transported grain in the capital granaries.[1] The entire undertaking should be seen as a process of creating a new administrative strategy, or practical precedent, for grain-tax shipment. When the emperor first proposed it, the sea-transport option was an untried and unaccepted idea (5.2.5–5.6.6). During the period when the concept was debated and a compromise was being worked out between the imperial center and canal-zone officials (5.6.6–5.7.23), it was described as a "one-time expedient." Once concrete plans were worked out and decisions were made by trial-and-error during the actual shipment process (5.7.23–6.8.13), sea transport was discussed as a first-time experiment. Finally, after its successful completion in the eighth month of 1826, sea transport became established as a legitimate option, expanding the current repertoire of practical strategies used to cope with the deepening crisis in the canal. The importance of this new strategy and of the expanded use of transfer-shipping for the future was clearly recognized in the late 1820s, and the imperial order to revise the Finance Ministry's regulations on grain transport in 1829 reflected the widely shared view that changing conditions in the canal zone required new procedures.[2]

The innovation of sea transport shows how the Qing leadership changed administrative practices and established new precedents in response to changing regional conditions. In this particular case, the initiative for change began with the emperor and his central advisers, who forced a largely unwilling corps of regional officials to take the scheme seriously and to discuss its applicability to their provincial jurisdictions in the canal zone. This first stage of the campaign lasted from early in the second month to early in the sixth month and it was, by far, the most difficult part of the process leading to the implementation of the plan. During this period, one might say that the sea-transport option waxed as the spring shipping process waned. The first three imperial orders to discuss sea transport went virtually unheeded until the regular shipping process ground to a halt in mid-1825.[3] The breakdown of grain shipping discredited the management strategies used by regional officials and provided the opportunity for the emperor to force consideration of the sea-transport option.[4]

During the early phase of the debate, the emperor linked sea transport to the state's long-term goals for restoring the canal and reviving grain transport on the Huaiyang Canal. It also was attached to the larger and more difficult issues of canal-riverine reconstruction and grain-tax commutation, both of which comprised the heart of the central leadership's initial plan. The emperor urged the use of sea transport because it guaranteed minimum grain shipments to the capital while providing regional officials the time and resources to plan and execute a canal restoration program. Because it departed from the institution of inland, canal-based transport and from the established strategies used each year to manage the canal–grain transport process, the emperor carefully rationalized the need for change, urging the relaxation of old regulations and arguing for the safety and feasibility of the sea route.[5] In his view, they were faced with three alternatives for grain shipping in 1825: regular shipments on military junks, transfer-shipping on private lighters, or sea transport. The first was best but impossible because of canal-riverine conditions; the second was a fairly workable and well-established alternative, but silt damage to the canal and junction limited its use in 1825.[6] That left sea transport, an option that the emperor described as comparable in usefulness and cost to transfer-shipping. In other words, it was another acceptable *temporary* expedient. Its use did not constitute a violation of a time-honored institution, in his view, but was merely a practical response to difficult realities. All that remained, from the emperor's perspective, was the speedy formulation of new procedures for its execution.

The emperor first explored conditions for its implementation in Jiangsu and Zhejiang. When the Zhejiang governor explained that neither the harbor at Chapu nor that at Ningbo was suitable for transferring grain tribute from junks to sea-going vessels, the emperor turned his attention to the "circuits and districts close to the sea" in Jiangnan: Susongchangzhen and the port facilities at Shanghai.[7] During this early stage, the emperor indicated that had he known how damaged the canal was in the early spring of 1825, he would have used sea transport for the stalled shipments.[8] Moreover, he was prepared to apply the scheme to Jiangxi, Hubei, and Hunan if it proved to be successful in Jiangsu and Zhejiang.[9] Yet, as opposition mounted and he sought to enlist official support for the plan, he moderated his statements and referred to sea transport as a one-time response to the problems of 1826.[10] Both he and his regional opponents knew better. Once sea transport was carried out successfully, it became history—a part of the record, an experiment on which later administrators could build. And this was precisely the emperor's intention. Once implemented, it would be ready for use later when the Yellow River shifted course.

Even though the discussion of sea transport was in its infancy in the spring and early summer of 1825, the emperor raised four major practical issues. These remained the foci of discussion throughout the following year and included the recruitment of merchant shippers, the organization of the transfer of tribute grain from government boats to private sea vessels in Shanghai harbor, the maintenance of government control and protection of the grain ships while at sea, and finally and most difficult, the reorganization of bureaucratic procedures in Zhili for the lighterage of the seaborne grain cargoes from the coast to the Grand Canal at Tianjin.[11]

By late in the fifth month as grain shipping stalled, the emperor lost patience with regional officials for failing to respond to his call for exploratory planning. He ordered them to reply to the two proposals put forward earlier by Yinghe, to which none of them had hitherto responded.[12] On the sixth day of the sixth month, he repeated the order to consider the feasibility of sea transport.[13] Finally, late in the sixth month, the emperor made the decision to move ahead with sea transport after receiving Qishan's assessment of the prospects for the scheme in Jiangsu that suggested that part of Jiangsu's grain-tax quota could be shipped successfully from the port of Shanghai.[14]

Among all the southern canal-zone officials, Qishan was the only one to push ahead with exploratory planning for sea transport from the outset. He reported to the emperor that he had consulted with Tao Zhu, the Jiangsu governor, and had sent the provincial treasurer, He Changling, to Shanghai to make a preliminary investigation of conditions in that port and of the possibility of recruiting merchant shippers for sea transport. On his return, He would discuss his findings with Tao, who would then make a specific recommendation to the emperor. In the event, Tao would bear primary responsibility for working out the details and supervising the implementation of the plan because he was headquartered in Suzhou, in the heart of the Jiangnan grain districts.[15] Qishan, for his part, would continue to oversee the project, but his primary charge would continue to be the reconstruction of the Huaiyang Canal system and the opening of the lower course of the Yellow River.

Because He Changling had not yet returned from Shanghai, Qishan explained that he did not know precisely how much Jiangsu rice could be shipped by sea, but he predicted that it would be limited by the shortage of craft available for hire and by port congestion, which would make the transfer of grain cargoes from lighters and government junks to sea vessels very difficult. For those parts of the canal zone that could not send their grain by sea in 1826, Qishan cautioned that it was very unlikely that a normal clear-water crossing could be made at the junction, and regional officials would have to consider the options of transfer-shipping, commuting grain taxes, or storage.

When Tao Zhu's memorial reporting on He Changling's investigation indicated that merchants could ship 1.5 to 1.6 million *shi* by sea, the die was cast for sea transport. The emperor proceeded to define the final terms for grain transport in 1826.[16] He directed He Changling to travel once again to Shanghai to finalize arrangements with merchant shippers, and when he returned, Qishan, Tao Zhu, and He were ordered to draw up procedures and regulations for hiring sea vessels, for lighterage of grain cargoes to Shanghai, and for transferring the cargoes to the sea vessels in the harbor. The plan was to be sent directly to the emperor for authorization.[17]

The emperor also decided at that time to send the remaining half of the Jiangsu grain quota by the canal, even in its damaged state. It was, at this stage, unclear to him if a clear crossing could be made, but whatever the situation in the spring of 1826, only a clear crossing or transfer-shipping would be used, not Yellow River backspills.[18] The decision about commuting grain tax was postponed for the moment, both because provincial officials in the other Yangzi River provinces had not responded to this issue and because the emperor was unwilling, as yet, to give up this important scheme for funding canal restoration.[19]

Compromise

Plans were, at last, underway. The emperor had forced the issue of sea transport and had authorized its implementation in Jiangsu where he had official support for the scheme. Yet, while he scored this victory in Jiangsu, he lost the initiative to regional officials as the debate gained momentum from early in the sixth month to late in the seventh month. One regional official after another argued that neither sea transport nor commutation was possible or practical. They insisted that the canal remain open and that as much grain as possible be sent by canal. They argued that this course of action would not impede canal restoration. If the clear-water crossing was used, the scouring effect on the riverbed would help lower the Yellow River. If transfer-shipping was used and Yuhuang lock gate remained closed, canal officials could thoroughly dredge the Huaiyang Canal with no interruptions in the winter and spring so that they would be prepared for the return crossing in the autumn.[20] The emperor finally seemed convinced. "The use of both sea and canal transport in 1826 will benefit both grain transport and the canal, and the old system of grain transport can be restored in 1827. Isn't this a better way to control the river," he asked rhetorically, "than halting grain transport on the canal and commuting grain tribute?"[21] But was he really convinced?

In the end, a new consensus was formed around a grain-transport plan for 1826 that included both sea and canal shipping. None of the canal zone provinces besides Jiangsu participated in sea transport, and the latter did so because executive officials in this province were closely aligned with imperial interests and with local interests that supported the plan.[22] Even though the emperor stated that he thought his goals for canal restoration could be realized with this scaled-back plan, the rejection of grain-tax commutation limited the funds and, therefore, the prospects for canal restoration.

The compromise that was worked out in the sixth and seventh months, however, was very valuable for both parties, central and regional, as they faced the future of canal-transport operations. For regional interests, the compromise left important official-private networks in the canal zone intact. It softened the economic impact on those groups that regularly participated in the grain-shipping process and gave them and regional officials the time to adjust to changes that clearly lay on the horizon. It also helped avoid a further deflation of rice prices, which would probably have resulted from large-scale sale of grain tax in 1826. The compromise also resolved tensions between the imperial center, with its long-term strategic goals, and the canal zone provinces, dominated by the short-term imperatives of ever-changing riverine conditions. Realistically, the initiative for canal management belonged with regional officials in the canal zone where the demands of day-to-day administrations were greatest and the decisions about whether or not to adapt and change customary practices were clearest. These local conditions were precisely what the Qing decision-making process was designed to address.

In the end, the central leadership emerged from the experiences of 1825–26 with a more practical understanding of the great obstacles faced by regional canal–grain transport administrators, and they had fewer illusions and lower expectations for the future. Regional officials, who generally had no illusions to start with, could be more open about the crisis they faced. After the canal restoration experiments of 1826 failed and showed the impossibility of countering centuries of silt build-up, the grandiose schemes of central advisers and a few careerist regional administrators gave way to small-scale ameliorative actions.[23]

Finally, both the center and the provinces benefited from the Jiangsu sea-transport experiment. This so-called "one-time expedient" demonstrated that a limited program of sea transport could work, and it established a model and practical regulations for such a plan in the future. Accordingly, the experiment took its place in canal–grain transport administrative history. It was ready and available for use in the future as Yellow River conditions worsened and culminated in the river's inevitable destructive northward shift, which would lay waste to northern Jiangsu, eastern Henan, and Shandong provinces. But all that lay further in the future.

Operational Planning

The initial campaign and the compromise debates extended from the sixth month of 1825 to the end of the eleventh, when the Daoguang Emperor's response to a memorial from the esteemed Songyun opposing radical changes in grain transport effectively marked the end of discussion. The debates had paved the way for Jiangsu officials to work out the practical details for sea transport in 1826, which were finalized by early in the ninth month. The plan provided for the shipment of 1.5 to 1.6 million *shi* of grain from the prefectures of Susongchangzhen and Taicang department, plus some grain delayed from 1825. Over one thousand sea vessels would carry the grain in two trips, one in the early spring and the second in early summer, both to be accompanied by military escort officers. Elaborate efforts were made to facilitate the transfer of grain from lighters and government junks to sea vessels in Shanghai harbor (fig. 17).

Fig. 17 Shanghai sandboat or *shachuan* (He Changling, 1826).

When the ships were ready for departure, circuit and prefectural officials in Shanghai were to check them and take a sample of the rice from each vessel, seal it in a labeled container, and then forward it to a specially appointed imperial commissioner in Tianjin. The commissioner would check the samples against the cargoes of each arriving ship to insure against damage or tampering. Assisted by Zhili provincial officials, he would also supervise the unloading and transfer of cargoes from the coast up the Hai River to the east gate of Tianjin, where Finance Ministry officials would receive the grain and oversee its transfer to canal lighters for its final trip to the capital granaries.[24]

The security of the rice cargoes was a matter of great concern to both the emperor and Jiangsu officials. This concern stemmed from the strategic importance of the cargo, their inexperience in organizing such an unprecedented venture, and nagging worries about piracy. Although recent outbreaks of piracy on the China coast had failed to penetrate the northern coastal waters, memories of its destructive impact on the southeast coast must have caused some apprehension, especially among regional officials who had participated in its suppression.

Security was intensified along the entire route.[25] Locally based military junks from Susongchangzhen were designated to patrol the internal waters along the Huangpu and Wusong rivers that led to Shanghai while the grain was transported from the anchorage granaries to Shanghai's harbor at Wusong. Extra precautions were taken at the mouth of the Wusong River and at Chuansha, east of Shanghai, because of piracy in the off-shore islands of the Chengsi and Dayang chains. The same kinds of measures were taken to safeguard the lighterage of grain from the mouth of the Hai River to Tianjin. Even greater attention was given to protecting the fleets during the sea voyage along the coasts of Jiangsu, Shandong, and Zhili.

The state of military readiness from the Jiangnan coast to Zhili was called into question by the censor Xiong Yutai, late in the seventh month of 1825. Marine coastal defenses existed only in name, he charged. Coast-guard ships had been neither repaired nor replaced when worn out; fortifications and weaponry had deteriorated; and troops on the military rolls had dwindled. None of the marines received training or practical patrolling experience. Military funds were routinely embezzled, leaving the coast and the upcoming sea-transport enterprise exposed and vulnerable. Xiong asserted that although there was little piracy north of Shanghai at the present time, bands of pirates infested the offshore islands of Jiangnan. He urged that battalion commanders from every military district from Jiangnan to Zhili carry out patrolling maneuvers and chase down pirates to give their troops experience. He cautioned that, although conditions along the coast were, for the most part, peaceful, regional officials should be prepared for trouble the following year, when sea transport was scheduled to take place.[26]

The most intriguing part of the sea-transport experiment was the care taken by the emperor and top regional officials to fashion terms acceptable to the merchant shippers in Shanghai. Earlier reference has been made to the emperor's insistence on fair terms in the hiring of canal lighters for the transfer-shipping program in the spring of 1825 and on the importance of formulating equitable terms for merchants in cooperative ventures with the state—terms that would not damage or disrupt the merchants' livelihood. This same concern was expressed in discussions of Shanghai shippers' involvement in sea transport.

Flexible arrangements were made for merchant sale of extra rice allowances, or wastage rice, in the event that they were not needed to cover the replacement cost of rice damaged in transit. These provisions gave merchants the opportunity to make the greatest profit, free from the interference of low-level officials and *yamen* underlings. Merchant shippers were given 240,000 *shi* of wastage rice, or 240 *shi* per ship, to cover the costs and risks of the sea voyage. After arrival at Tianjin, they were allowed to sell the grain on the open market because it was assumed that they would get a better price than if they sold it to Zhili officials. Yet market conditions turned out to be unfavorable in 1826, and Zhili officials were ordered to move quickly to purchase the grain at a fair price so that merchants could recoup their expenses and depart speedily for other northern ports to pick up private cargoes for their return trip.[27]

Merchant liability for the rice cargoes was also designed to protect their interests. The liability terms were clearly spelled out, and merchant responsibility for damage or loss of grain cargoes was limited. If cargoes were damaged or lost, due to pirate attacks, damage to the ships, or theft, merchant shippers were not held accountable for the rice, and if sailors suffered injury in these cases, regional officials were obliged to compensate the families of the victims. Only when there was no clear reason for damage or loss were merchants required to make up the loss from their allotment of wastage rice, or, if this was insufficient, from their own resources.[28] These arrangements are significant when one considers the tradition in Chinese business practice of unlimited liability and of the less-than-generous terms imposed on the regular transport officers for covering lost or damaged cargoes on government grain junks.

The emperor and top regional officials also worked hard to simplify bureaucratic procedures in Tianjin and control those bureaucratic personnel involved in managing sea transport at the Zhili end. Their purpose was mainly to speed the offloading and transfer of grain cargoes from the coast to the canal at Tianjin, so that the Shanghai shippers' continuing journey to the northern ports and their return to Shanghai were not delayed.[29] Similarly, it was deemed important to help them sell their wastage allotments quickly. The interests of the shippers would be served best by speedy and reliable payment, which could be undermined by the corrupt practices of local officials.

There were, of course, other factors that caused emperor and officials alike to place a premium on speed. One was the shortage of lighterage fleets to transfer grain from the coast to the Grand Canal at Tianjin and then on to Tongzhou. These fleets were also needed to transport nearly 700,000 *shi* of delayed grain that had been deposited in Tianjin granaries in late 1825 because the winter freeze had kept grain junks from proceeding northward to Tongzhou. Finally, lighters were needed to assist the regular grain fleets in the spring of 1826 when they entered Zhili from Shandong.[30] Of greater import still was the state's vital interest in seeing the first sea shipments completed quickly so that the ships could return promptly and catch the northward winds of early summer for their second shipment.

The emperor and Jiangsu officials also worked assiduously to streamline procedures for the transfer of grain to sea craft in Shanghai harbor. Their goal was to minimize disturbances and congestion in the harbor and to protect the merchant shippers from the inefficiency and predatory demands of official transport personnel and *yamen* underlings. So concerned was the censor Xiong Yutai that he advocated bypassing the regular transport personnel altogether. Instead, he proposed that Shanghai officials hire private lighters to collect the rice at the canal anchorages and bring it back to Shanghai, where merchants should then be left alone to manage the loading of grain onto sea vessels.

> Don't make trouble for the merchant shippers! Listen to them and let them carry out sea transport according to their own convenience. Don't detain them and lose the benefit [of their experience].[31]

Xiong warned against short-sighted economies like underpaying coolies, using government transport personnel and craft, and skimping on the hire of lighters in Tianjin, because this caused more trouble and expense in the long run.

In order to avoid corruption, interference, and inefficiency, top regional officials were delegated to make the arrangements with private shippers personally, bypassing and usurping the roles and responsibilities of lower-level officials. The three highest Jiangsu officials—the governor-general, the financial commissioner, and the governor—worked out the sea-transport scheme. The latter two undertook direct discussions with merchant shippers and local officials in Shanghai to forge the agreement. When arrangements were clarified in the ninth month, Tao Zhu personally undertook the journey to Shanghai, using his "personal prestige to reinforce" the arrangements.[32] The earlier organization of transfer-shipping on the canal, it will be remembered, showed a similar pattern of bypassing the lower levels of regional government to mobilize lighterage. The only difference was that the earlier joint venture had precedents and the procedures were fairly routinized.

High-ranking officials also were used to impose strict discipline on the regular bureaucracy at the Zhili end of the sea route. A special commissioner was appointed to supervise the entire operation, and oversee the Zhili governor-general's management of canal-grain transport matters and of the lower levels of the bureaucracy at Tianjin. A Finance Ministry vice-president supervised the receipt of grain cargoes in Tianjin and the transfer to canal lighters that would make the last leg of the journey to Tongzhou. A high official from the Grand Council was charged with the supervision of brokers acting on behalf of the shippers and the granary personnel in the capital.[33]

Pressure from the top in joint ventures like sea transport was to protect the operation from destructive interference by officials, and to protect merchants' legitimate interests, and to take advantage of their organizational and managerial expertise. This pattern of dealing with private organizations reflects the Qing leadership's assumptions about the interconnectedness of the people's livelihood and the security of the state. It also reflects their desire to cultivate ties with private shippers so that they would be willing to participate in similar ventures in the future, when the state would desperately need their managerial skills, fleets, and knowledge of coastal shipping. Finally, it seems to reflect the leadership's preference for working with local, nonbureaucratic organizations to manage logistical operations. This preference was partly to take advantage of what was perceived as private organizations' greater expertise and efficiency in the performance of specialized functions. But, as in the case of grain-tax commutation, it also seems to reflect a desire to avoid working with the lower levels of provincial bureaucracy, which were considered overloaded and incapable of performing important functions with efficiency and integrity. The imperial center and top regional officials both had deep reservations about the ability of local-level civil and military functionaries in both Zhili and Shanghai to manage their respective ends of the operation.

Songyun's Memorial

As arrangements for sea transport crystallized in the eleventh month, the last of the arguments against it were finally laid to rest when the Daoguang Emperor responded publicly to the highly esteemed Mongol grandee, Songyun, who voiced his opposition to the plans for sea transport and transfer-shipping in 1826. Songyun was an incorruptible official who had served three emperors with distinction. His career had spanned over five decades and included important posts in the capital and in the new borderland dependencies of Manchuria, Mongolia, Turkestan, and Tibet. He had held the most challenging governor-generalships in the provinces of Huguang, Liangguang, and Liangjiang. In the last post, in 1810–11, he had worked diligently on river conservancy and was well acquainted with the problems afflicting the northern Jiangsu canal system. He had also personally escorted the Macartney mission on the Grand Canal from Tongzhou to Hangzhou in 1793. He was an official of great achievement. He knew the traditions of the Qing imperial state and its problems intimately, and by the 1820s commanded great respect for his accomplishments and his integrity.

Songyun stated in his memorial that he was deeply troubled about grain shipping plans for 1826, both sea transport and transfer-shipping on the canal, which required the closure of the Yuhuang Lock gate. The canal alone should be used for state grain shipments, he asserted, as was the practice in former times, and only the clear-water strategy should be used for the junction crossing. He objected to the fact that both transfer-shipping and sea transport placed responsibility for the state's strategic grain shipments in the hands of private interests instead of governmental agencies. He urged the emperor to rely exclusively on the boatmen and sailors of the regular grain fleets and to increase their profits by allowing them to bring more private goods to sell at Tongzhou. "Only if this course is followed will the state's resources and the people's livelihood be benefited."³⁴ For Songyun, who knew the strategic importance of the state's grain supplies, the abandonment of regular canal transport and of government control of the shipping process spelled trouble.

The emperor responded to Songyun's admonitions very skillfully to articulate, once and for all, the state's position on the grain-transport crisis and to attack factionalism on these issues. Showing great respect for this seventy-three-year-old official, who had served both his father and grandfather before him, the emperor began the edict by asserting that Songyun's memorial was solely motivated by his concern for the public interest (*gong*), thus distinguishing it from factional and careerist arguments. Yet, he continued:

> Conditions with the lake and river are not the same as they were in Jiaqing 16 [1811] when Songyun was Liangjiang governor-general. Now the bed of the canal is piled high with silt. The clear water from Hongze Lake is not high enough to scour out the Yellow River. If we were to open the Yuhuang Lock gate at this time, the Yellow River would pour in again, and the river, the lake, and the canal would all be damaged. How, then, can we [follow Songyun's proposed course of action] without making the same mistake twice?³⁵

The emperor explained that Qishan, the current governor-general of Liangjiang, had argued insistently that the Yuhuang Lock gate be kept closed in 1826 to avoid further damage to the canal and that any grain tribute sent by canal be transferred across the junction embankments and shipped by lighter to the north. In response to Qishan's advice, "I sent down an edict authorizing this plan."

The emperor summed up his views by explaining that the decision about sea transport and transfer-shipping did not mean that the canal would be abandoned permanently as the primary means of shipping strategic grain supplies. Nor did it mean that these temporary expedients would be used *regularly in the immediate future* (author's emphasis). Both were responses to temporary conditions on the canal, and, because these conditions might crop up again, the plans were also intended to prepare for future crises when they might be used again as temporary expedients. He assured Songyun of the safety of the sea option. "Merchant shippers all say that the route is safe for making two trips to Tianjin, and they will guarantee it." Even though the leadership had discussed these issues for months, no one had come forward with convincing evidence that the sea route was vulnerable to dangerous weather or piracy. "After all," the emperor pointed out, "merchant shipping goes on throughout the whole year. Really! The sea route and the canal route are like following a single track (*ruchu yiche*)." After due consideration of all these issues, the emperor affirmed:

> At this time, we are going to ship 1.5 million *shi* by sea, and by so doing, prepare an alternative method. It is not a case of using only sea transport from now on and of setting aside the canal. Therefore, let there be no further discussion of the issues raised by Songyun.[36]

The Daoguang Emperor's public response to Songyun clarified his position and placed his leadership on the line in this crucial area of administration. It is also important for historians concerned with innovation in the Qing administrative process because it shows how new precedents were created to cope with changing historical conditions. Because of historical imperatives born of centuries of experiments with the logistical aspects of imperial security, the principle and the institution of canal-based transport of grain taxes were firmly established. In 1825, the Daoguang Emperor and officials were not attempting to change this principle but were concerned primarily with questions of operational necessity that required the temporary discontinuation of canal transport. They were prepared to countenance change or adjustments in the procedures and expand the range of practical options in grain shipping as had been done so often in the past.

Regional officials had devised a fairly stable system built on bureaucratic organizations, specialist and field, and on nonbureaucratic organizations in the canal zone. On the whole, they were not prepared for radical departures from the practices of the recent past because they did not feel much could be done to reverse canal conditions.[37] Changes might, in fact, destroy what little they were able to achieve. They were prepared, however, to undertake transfer-shipping because it was built on preexisting bureaucratic and nonbureaucratic networks in the canal zone, and they thought that the closure of the Yuhuang lock gate might be enough to provide for small-scale ameliorative reconstruction of the lake, river, and canal dike systems.

At the outset, the emperor was not content with the yearly operation of the crisis-ridden system and hoped that more substantial improvements could be made during the dangerously unstable period in which they worked. His schemes for funding canal restoration and sea transport represented his attempt to expand the repertoire of practical strategies for canal reconstruction and grain transport further than had been done before. Even if he did not succeed in improving the canal, his decision to implement sea transport in 1826 represented the first step in establishing a new option that would prove useful in the future as river conditions worsened. He did not intend to use it regularly in the immediate future, and he resisted factional and careerist pressure to do so.[38] But, as his edicts make clear in 1825–26, he was keenly aware that this experiment constituted an important alternative for the threatening time that lay ahead.

By the end of 1825, a memorial sent by Qishan captured the emperor's point of view perfectly, as it must have done for other officials as well: "Sea transport is by no means a perfect plan and was never intended to be carried out for a long time." The real goal was to create conditions in which "the rivers are controlled, grain transport continues, people are at peace, and officials do their jobs."[39] And that state of affairs, everyone knew, would not occur until after the river's shift of course. Sea transport was designed to help out for a short period of time. The Grand Canal as an institution and as an operational system was fundamental for longer stretches of time.

Riding the Black Ocean Waves

Although it was something of an anticlimax after the crises and controversies of 1825, the execution of the sea-transport experiment in 1826 was a resounding success that bore out the emperor's predictions. The first shipment of 1.2 million *shi* left Shanghai during the first eight days of the second month, with the first vessels arriving in Tianjin on the twenty-first. As soon as word reached the capital that the first ships had arrived, Special Commissioner Muchang'a and Granary Vice-President Bai Chun left for Tianjin to supervise the unloading and transfer of grain from Shanghai craft to lighters that carried the grain from the coast to Tianjin. And because of silting on the Hai, they also organized the mobilization of legions of trackers to pull the lighters through the shallows. They made special efforts to expedite the transfer process so the Shanghai merchants could proceed to the other northern ports, pick up their cargoes there, and return to Shanghai.[40]

The second shipment left Shanghai like clockwork in the middle of the sixth month and began arriving in Zhili early in the seventh. By the middle of the eighth month, Muchang'a reported that all the ships had arrived and their cargoes safely transported to Tongzhou. A total of 1,633,000 *shi* had been transported on 1,562 vessels. Although it was later found that one ship was lost at sea, and three others met with accidents that damaged their rice cargoes, the emperor's pleasure at the time was complete: "Not one life nor one bit of grain was lost!"[41] These gratifying reports had been preceded in the fifth month by Qishan's proud announcement that Jiangsu officials had finished transfer-shipping on the Grand Canal, sending 100,000 more *shi* of grain across the junction embankments and completing the job faster than in 1825.[42] Both grain-transport experiments had worked, demonstrating the wisdom of the emperor's decisions and the soundness of his judgments. The emperor was "deeply moved" and lavished rewards on officials, high and low, for their efforts, especially those connected with the sea transport experiment.

The Sea-Transport Experiment 245

But gratitude to the gods came first. The experiments had been in harmony with nature, and the gods had responded by "extending their power and protection." Tao Zhu had reported that:

> The sea vessels survived and returned from the great black ocean where they had encountered storms. Yet when danger arose, the gods aided the ships. . . . Grain transport was benefited and the waves quieted.[43]

Tao Zhu had already visited the temples of the gods of wind and sea in the coastal city of Baoshan, outside Shanghai, near the mouth of the Wusong River, and he had also traveled to the Temple of Seamen on the banks of the Huangpu River to give thanks. On receiving this report, the emperor sent ten sticks of imperial incense to Tao and asked him to return to the temples and reverently give thanks to the gods on the emperor's behalf for using their power to aid the sea-transport venture. "In this year's sea transport, the gods have truly changed danger to peace."[44] He vowed to send special imperial tablets to be placed at the entrances of each temple.

Yinghe was singled out for praise as the innovator of the sea-transport experiment and as an exemplar of "one who sincerely manages affairs."[45] Equally outstanding was Qishan, who had taken the initiative to organize the venture in Jiangsu, had coordinated it with the canal restoration and transfer-shipping schemes, and had supervised the overall plan. Tao Zhu was praised as one who had distinguished himself by personally attending to the arrangements in Shanghai and "grasping every opportunity" to make the plan work.[46] Nayancheng, governor-general of Zhili, deserved commendation because he had worked out the thorny issue of revising the regulations for grain transport in Zhili and had mobilized the energies of the lower-levels of the bureaucracy around Tianjin.[47] Responding to the examples set by these top-level officials, all manner of lower level civil and military officials had "exerted themselves" to make sea transport a success, right down to the merchants and shippers at

Shanghai and Tianjin who had helped to recruit the shippers and hire the necessary craft.[48]

Complete success for sea transport in 1826! The emperor must have been cautiously optimistic. Although campaigns against Jahanger in the northwest were going poorly, reports from Zhang Jing suggested that the lake dikes in northern Jiangsu were holding, at least so far.[49] Perhaps 1826 would be a good year!

Conclusion

The events of 1825–26 marked a watershed in canal–grain transport management. The geophysical crisis in the canal-riverine system in northern Jiangsu, exacerbated by economic change and fiscal rigidity during the early nineteenth century, had come to a head during the early years of the Daoguang reign. Aware of the mounting problems in the canal system and the failure of regional agencies to cope with the breakdown of canal shipping and maintenance, the new emperor used the central-regional decision-making process to mount a critical review of management practices and force a thorough exploration of what appeared to be the last remaining strategy for ameliorating canal dysfunction—opening up the lower course of the Yellow River. He used talented regional officials to investigate ecological conditions in the lower reaches of the river and to devise a multi-faceted program for canal restoration. The conclusions, after two years of toil, were sobering but realistic. The best plan was no plan at all, just flexible year-to-year muddling through, using a slightly broadened repertoire of shipping and maintenance practices and applying it with more rigor and discipline. Thereafter, neither the emperor nor the regional officials harbored any illusions, or any great expectations. In view of the fiscal-monetary instability which they confronted, their greatest hope was to limit losses.

But an important addition had been made to the standard repertoire. Sea transport had proved itself in 1826; its procedures and regulations now lay embedded in administrative experience. Thereafter, it could be used to continue strategic grain shipments to the capital if and when the canal broke down completely. The scheme provided a way to cope successfully with the logistical and symbolic crisis that loomed ahead and for which the emperor would be held personally accountable. The capital could be supplied. The vast, empire-wide logistical network that bound together the parts of Greater China could be maintained intact. In the meantime, the leadership could devote its energies and scarce resources to undertaking small-scale, ameliorative projects to protect the Huai–Yellow River basin from flood devastation and economic upheaval as best they could.

The narrative of the 1820s canal crisis shows how the central-regional decision-making process worked, not in general, but specifically in Grand Canal–grain transport management—a select, high-priority sector of the Qing imperium's strategic sphere of responsibilities. Two key events in mid-1825 shaped the resolution of the crisis. First, the breakdown of transfer-shipping in the fifth month enabled the emperor to force regional officials to make decisions about canal restoration and sea transport that took into account empire-wide goals. Second, the rejection of grain-tax commutation by regional officials in the eighth month quashed plans for a major program of canal restoration and, consequently, helped create a new and more realistic consensus for small-scale ameliorative approaches to canal reconstruction. This consensus taught the emperor and his central advisers about regional realities and enabled them to make the most of limited administrative and material resources during a period dominated by hopelessly irreversible riverine conditions, economic instability, and fiscal crisis.

The phrase "controlling from afar" expressed the tensions inherent in the decision-making process and the dilemma posed by imperial involvement in concrete regional problems. The tensions sprang from key attributes of the nonroutine decision-making process in canal-transport administration: its regionally specific orientation; its complex, technical, and practical operations; its vulnerability to rapidly changing natural conditions; and, importantly, its direction by the emperor and his central advisers, who were far away from the daily and seasonal challenges to its operation.

The Daoguang Emperor recognized the dilemma and tried to overcome it in his approach to decision making, affirming the consensual nature of the process and the necessity of sharing power with regional officials. While he retained the imperial prerogative to

Conclusion 249

define and scrutinize the handling of nonroutine problems, he was ready to approve new strategies devised by regional officials to cope with changing conditions. He encouraged and cajoled these officials to come up with effective plans. When conflict arose, it did so because regionally inspired courses of action failed to work or else they undermined empire-wide strategic goals. Practical governance at the regional level had to serve both the region and the empire. When it did not, as in the case of canal–grain transport strategies, imperial leadership played a vital role in reconciling central and regional differences. It played an even more crucial role when conditions mandated major changes in administrative practice. An innovation in practical governance required strong imperial support in order to gain acceptance. Even then, it was an uphill battle, as the 1825 campaign for sea transport demonstrates.

Yet, when all was said and done, the emperor admitted the inability of the central leadership to design and implement practical courses of action. Only regional officials with a firsthand grasp of regional realities could identify emerging problems and craft effective solutions to them. The practical logic of this approach shaped the Qing leadership's view that there were limits to central imperial power and that dictating solutions to regional problems was dangerously reckless. The emperor's phrase "controlling from afar" captures his particular struggle to find the correct balance between central leadership and regional initiative, and it expresses his deep personal concern with operational practicality. It encapsulates the concept of imperial direction of, but regional dominance over, the management of the canal crisis of the mid-1820s, but it also epitomizes the legacy of flexible leadership that the Daoguang Emperor inherited from and shared with his imperial forebears.

The drama of the canal crisis, with all its complex, frustrating, and mundane detail, reveals the unrelenting practicality of canal–grain transport management at both the central-imperial and regional levels.[1] Imperial-regional dialogue on these issues focused invariably on practical regulations, practical strategies, and practical innovations, each of which was measured in terms of its workability and its appropriateness to circumstances in different parts of the canal zone. Flexibility was a necessity if these conditions were to be addressed. There was little concern for the specifics of earlier Qing approaches to canal problems, and little reference was made to the particularities of the so-called traditions of the imperial ancestors. Even Songyun's memorial was more concerned with the long-term strategic implications than with the particular approaches sanctioned by the early Qing emperors.

The practicality of the Daoguang Emperor and his regional officials during the canal crisis highlights a strength of the Qing administrative system: its ability to sustain an incremental pattern of ameliorative change in the operation of a high-priority sector of government. This practical orientation was consonant with and undoubtedly was influenced by longstanding approaches to statecraft (*jingshi*) that had developed and matured since Song times and that were experiencing a revival in the early nineteenth century.[2] This tradition sought operational rationality in the political-administrative process, and its practitioners, some of whom were involved in the canal crisis, championed small-scale, piecemeal reforms to adjust to changing times. They were prepared to tinker with the machinery of government to enhance "the state's resources and the people's livelihood," both of which were thought to contribute to the achievement of a more perfect moral order. The pursuit of these broad, idealistic goals with practical, narrowly focused reforms was characteristic of Confucian statecraft in the late imperial period. It may be that this orientation limited the leadership's ability to conceptualize and implement a broad program of transformative change, capable of addressing the larger structural problems that lay at the heart of governmental dysfunction in the early nineteenth century. It also may be that the commitment to subdistrict autonomy,

Conclusion 251

embedded in some aspects of the Statecraft approach to practical governance, contributed to the neglect of these structural problems.

The reasons for the Qing government's inability to confront these intractable problems are not entirely clear, but if the Grand Canal crisis is any measure, they seem to lie in the Qing imperium's definition of the boundaries between the imperial state and the subdistrict community, the practical limits of state power at the local level, and the leadership's unwillingness to expand the functions of government into the local societal and economic sphere at the subdistrict level. But in broad historical perspective, perhaps their practical approach to institutional change and reluctance to intervene in subdistrict affairs may prove to have been a strength—one that allowed private interests and institutions to grow and evolve in response to the complexities and challenges of social-economic change at the local level.

This preoccupation with practical, low-level management questions was set against the backdrop of the enduring and unchallenged significance of the Grand Canal as a strategically vital institution, capable of transferring grain supplies from the provinces along its north-south and east-west axes, not just to the capital, but to grain-deficient provinces in the interior as well. Peking alone might be served by sea transport, but what about famine relief and military campaigns in the interior? From the Qing perspective, the strategic value of canal communications was obvious and remained unquestioned during the canal crisis; it was only the policies regarding its troubled seasonal operation that were the subject of review and revision. This practical orientation and the flexibility that it implied were the canal-transport administration's greatest strengths and remained the Qing imperial ancestors' greatest legacy to canal–grain transport management.

The study of the Grand Canal crisis of the 1820s shows that the central-regional management process worked effectively during a period of acute crisis to build a consensus for the sea-transport experiment and for the expanded use of transfer-shipping. It also reestablished regional control over practical aspects of canal–grain transport management. As a result, this consensus enabled the imperial center to direct from afar, but also moderated its demands, so that regional officials could continue to control the government's response to dangerous events from the banks and causeways of the canal-riverine network.

These conclusions should not surprise us, for they are fully consistent with the pattern of imperial direction of the canal-transport process in the earlier reigns. The Daoguang Emperor went about his work in much the same way as his imperial forebears. He responded to the same strategic imperatives and geological processes, and he directed the decision-making process with similar discipline and flexibility. The difference was that he had the bad luck to face more challenges with fewer options. We need to be reminded of the continuity with the earlier Qing pattern and the effectiveness of early nineteenth-century Qing administrative actions in select areas of government, such as canal communications, because there is a seemingly irresistible tendency among Qing scholars to treat 1800 as a great divide after which one finds only intractable problems of imperial decline and administrative breakdown. When seen in broad historical perspective, however, the logistical and strategic issues associated with the canal crisis did not exist in isolation, nor are they necessarily representative of decline, but rather of complex growth and change, especially in subdistrict institutions, that affected canal and sea transportation. The canal crisis shows that imperial leadership responded to these conditions by rejecting bureaucratic solutions and by moving beyond local government to work with private shipping organizations to manage one of the state's most sensitive tasks. This represents a readiness to change and an ability to devise new solutions to old problems.

These conclusions bear out the interpretations of scholars who have measured Qing institutional performance against the dynasty's political-institutional goals and who have highlighted the organizational capacity and creativity of imperial-official leader-ship, not just in the

Conclusion

early and high Qing, but in the early nineteenth century as well.[3] Furthermore, they suggest the need to revise interpretations that seek to explain the complex issues and events surrounding the canal crisis with social-scientific speculation about elite behavior, careerist officials, and factional politics.[4] Finally, these findings challenge the Eurocentric and retrospective judgments of modern scholars who see the troubled Grand Canal–grain transport system as a symbol of Qing decline and a prime example of the Qing state's bureaucratic inefficiency, corruption, irrational use of resources, and backward authoritarian rule.[5] These approaches fail to appreciate the internal logic of the system, its strategic goals, its institutional limits, and its considerable achievements.

Epilogue

Angry storm clouds descended on the Huai–Yellow River basin in the autumn of 1826, and flood waters again assaulted the great dike on Hongze Lake, rupturing it in precisely the same places that had burst in 1824. In the advisory circle around the Daoguang Emperor, the euphoria only recently created by the successful sea transport experiment evaporated, and the emperor, his central advisers, and regional allies grimly returned to their appointed roles in the sisyphean drama that dated from the dawn of the imperial age.

The Qing leadership followed the 1820s script in the 1830s and 1840s. All the experiences and lessons of 1825 and 1826 were incorporated into the corpus of lore that canal managers applied to get through each year's faltering cycle of shipping and maintenance. This up-dated information adjusted past practice; it contained more realistic goals and a more manageable agenda for regional officials, the emperor, and his central advisers; and its rapid incorporation into the Finance Ministry's guide to grain transport established its legitimacy and sanctioned its use until the 1860s. Meanwhile, canal-river directors and low-level specialists stoically continued to repair and guard the dikes that protected their homes and communities, and developed their own devices for strengthening the water-control system on the Yellow River by marshalling human and material resources in new and creative ways.

By the late forties, the river began to spill northward, with the main branch cutting to the sea through northern Shandong in 1852. Westerners were organizing their trading enclaves in the first treaty ports; the Taipings were poised for their advance into the lower Yangzi valley; and soon, sea shipment by junk and steamship would largely replace canal transport of what was left of the grain-tax quotas. Sporadic attempts were made to rebuild the canal around a northward-flowing Yellow River, some grain continued to be shipped by canal where possible with a combination of lighterage and haulage, and local efforts in northern Jiangsu into the twentieth-century attempted to deepen the Huai River channel across the silt flats to the sea. But it was not until the construction of the Huai River project a century later, in the 1950s, that a new, unified Chinese state provided the leadership and resources to resume the state's age-old responsibilities for flood control, irrigation, and canal shipping in northern Jiangsu.

Notes

Abbreviations

Abbreviations for Qing documents refer to archival materials held in the Qing Archives, National Palace Museum, Taibei. They consist of secret edicts, or "court letters," court letter drafts, public edicts, and palace memorials. In addition to an abbreviation indicating the type of document, the citations also include the reign year, lunar month, and day. If there are two edicts issued on the same day, they are listed in a-b-c order, according to their order of appearance in the *Da Qing lichao shilu*. *Shilu* citations include a page number as well as the date.

P	Public edict. Shangyudang fangben (Record books of ordinary Grand Council affairs).
PM	Palace memorial. Waijidang (Record book of palace memorials)/Junjidang (Grand Council Archives).
S	Secret edict. Shangyudang fangben.
TJ	Court letter draft. Jiaobu tingjidang (Record books of court letter drafts).

* * *

Full citations for the following works are found in the Reference List, with the exception of readily available periodicals.

BH	Brunnert and Hagelstrom. *Present day political organization of China*. 1912.
BLOC	British Library Oriental Collection documents.
CAT	Sun. *Ch'ing Administrative Terms*. 1961.
CHC	*Cambridge History of China*, Vols. 1, 3, 7, 10, 11.

CSWT	*Ch'ing-shih wen-t'i.*
DHL	Wang and Jiang. *Shi'er chao donghualu.* Nd.
DMB	Goodrich and Fang, eds. *Dictionary of Ming Biography.* 1976.
DOT	Hucker. *Dictionary of Official Titles.* 1985.
ECCP	Hummel. *Eminent Chinese of the Ch'ing Period.* 1943-44.
FEQ	*Far Eastern Quarterly.*
FYBKZL	*Fuyin baokan ziliao.* 1985-89.
GGJK	*Gugong jikan* (Taibei).
HJAS	*Harvard Journal of Asiatic Studies.*
JAOS	*Journal of the American Oriental Society.*
JAS	*Journal of Asian Studies.*
JRAS	*Journal of the Royal Asiatic Society* (North China Branch, Shanghai).
LIC	*Late Imperial China.*
LSYJ	*Lishi yanjiu* (Beijing).
MAS	*Modern Asian Studies.*
QDCJCK	*Qingdai chuanji congkan.* 1985.
QHXZ	Lu and Wu. *Qinghe xianzhi.* 1855.
QS	*Qingshi.* 1961.

Notes   259

SL   *Da Qing lichao shilu*. 1937.

XXSJJ   Li, et al. *Xuxingshui jinjian*. 1832.

Notes to Chapter 1

1 Buchanan 1970, 73–93; Cressey 1934, 183–201; Czaya 1981, 52–63, 173–96; Sinclair 1987, 11; Tregear 1980, 266–74; Zheng 1966, 65–92. See also *Huanghe shuili shi shuyao* 1982.

2 Czaya 1981, 173–96; Sinclair 1987, 112–25.

3 Cressey 1934, 158–82; Needham 1971, 217–27; Tregear 1980, 266–82.

4 Chang K.C. 1986, 71–74; Tregear 1980, 271–74, 282.

5 Lowdermilk 1924, 11–18; 1925, 379–90; Needham 1971, 217–27, 237–40; Tregear 1980, 271–74.

6 Buchanan 1970, 81–93; Cressey 1934, 43–49; Needham 1971, 232; Tregear 1980, 271–74; Zheng 1966, 65–92.

7 Buchanan 1970, 73–81; Cressey 1934, 60–79; Lowdermilk 1926, 127–35; Needham 1971, 218–19; Tregear 1980, 14–24; 271–74.

8 Cressey 1934, 43–48; Needham 1971, 208–209, 221–27, 237–41, 242: fig. 69; Tregear 1980, 271-74.

9 Needham 1971, 217–32.

10 Tregear 1980, 279–81.

11 Gandar [1894], 2–50; *XXSJJ* 1832, 1:1–23; Lowdermilk 1925, 379ff.; Van Slyke 1988, 7–14; Wu Tongju [1928], 683–746; Zheng 1966, 136–59; Zhu 1962, 67–181.

12 Needham 1971, 211–17.

13 Needham 1971, 211–17, 227–47.

14 A detailed layout of the Qing hydraulic scheme in the middle and lower reaches of the Yellow River, as well as other pivotal parts of the Grand Canal–Yellow River network, can be seen in a magnificently illustrated 10-meter

scroll, dating from the early eighteenth century, held in the Oriental Collection of the British Library. BLOC: 2362.

15 *CHC* 1, 44–46, 65, 297, 419, 487, 554, 573; *CHC* 3, 114–15, 134–38, 209–10, 277–79, 355–57, 399–400, 416–20, 695–700; Needham 1971, 269–72, 284–306.

16 Needham 1971, 272–73, 285–87.

17 The two canals were extensions of the Honggou Canal, originally built around the fifth to sixth centuries B.C. One of the canals (Lang Tang Qu) extended to the Huai headwaters and the other (Bian Canal), destined to become a part of the Grand Canal in the Sui dynasty (A.D. 581–618), reached east and south to the lower Huai region. The Hangou Canal connected the Huai with the Yangzi, and some canal construction began around Lake Tai that was completed in the Sui-Tang period and became the Jiangnanhe section of the Grand Canal that linked the Yangzi with Hangzhou (maps 4, 5). Needham 1971, 272, 309–10.

18 Needham 1971, 269–73, 306–20.

19 Needham 1971, 273–81.

20 Alexander n.d., Drawings taken in China, 194–95; 1792–94, Journal of voyage to China with drawings, Add. Ms., 35, 174: 27v–28, 31–31v.

21 Czaya 1981, 216–17; Needham 1971, 209–17.

22 Dodgen 1989, 41–65; Needham 1971, 217–47. Needham shows a 1935 photo of a rectangular fascine with a cross section measuring six by fifteen meters, p. 917.

23 Illustrations and explanations of these devices are contained in an important nineteenth-century text on water conservancy techniques. Lin Qing [1836], *juan* 1–4; Needham 1971, 211–31.

24 Needham 1971, 362; Shen Bing, 1960, 171–76; Zhang Jinqi and Wang Qiaonian 1918, 14–20.

25 Needham 1971, 247–69; Toyama 1938, 202–4; Zheng 1966, 1–23, 132–35, 187–200; Zhu 1962, 1–31.

26 *CHC* 3, 48–149, 150–635; Elvin 1973, 54–68; Twitchett 1957, 23–79; 1961, 175–94; 1963, 84–96, 193.

27 Gandar [1894], 7–23; Needham 1971, 306–320.

28 Lo 1953, 262–85.

Notes 261

29 Elvin 1973, 54–68.

30 Work on this section of the canal included the alteration of the course of the old Honggou, or Bian, Canal (map 4), and additionally, the junction gates at the Yellow River end, the earlier Metal Dike of Han, were improved and equipped with flash locks and a double slipway. In the Tang, from 734–37, a bypass canal, called the Guangji Qu, was built from Xuzhou to Chuzhou to avoid the Huai rapids. Needham 1971, 307–309.

31 Earlier canal beds which it utilized were straightened dramatically, and flash locks and double slipways were employed at both the Huai and Yangzi river junctions. A complex system of lateral canals intersected this part of the canal from both the east and the west. Those on the western side of the canal functioned as feeder channels, drawing water from the adjacent lakes region to the west, or Shanghe (literally, "above the canal"), to maintain water levels sufficient for barge traffic, with excess drained off eastward to the sea. Those drainage channels on the eastern side of the canal diverted flood waters eastward across Xiahe ("below the canal").

32 Reischauer 1955a, 16–30; 1955b, 72–78, 153.

33 Wang Gungwu 1958, 1–135.

34 *CHC* 3, 137.

35 *CHC* 3, 48–149, 150–635; Elvin 1973, 54–68; Twitchett 1963, 84–96, 193; Wechsler 1974, 79-105; Wang Gungwu 1973, 193–235; Wright 1978, 82–107.

36 Gandar [1894], 15–23; Lo 1953, 262–85; 1955, 489–503; Needham 1971, 306–20; Rossabi 1988, 76–114, 119–27, 131–41, 188–90; Sung 1956, 75–87, 108–30; Wu Jihua 1971, 1:125–37; Wu Tongju [1928], 638–53, 946–69; Zheng 1966, 42–92.

37 Lo 1953, 262–85; Rossabi 1988, 188–90, 213–24.

38 The progress and achievements of the Directorate can be measured by the increasing amounts of grain shipped to the capital each year, from 42,172 *shi* in 1283; 433,950 in 1286; 919,934 in 1289; 1,361,513 in 1292; 2,500,000 in 1309; 3,500,000 in 1329. One *shi*, a dry measure for grain, is equivalent to about 60.5 kilograms.

39 Lo 1953, 262–85; Zou 1981, 80–98.

40 *CHC* 7, 107–304; Dreyer 1982, 12–64, 221–36.

41 Huang, Ray 1964, 14–19, 102–25; Needham 1971, 317–20.

42 Wolters 1967, 33–36, 42–43, 153–68, 230–35; 1970, 44–61, 155–87.

43 Farmer 1976, 28–70; Lo 1955, 489–503; Wang Gungwu 1964, 87–104; 1968, 34–62; 1970, 375–40; Wu Jihua 1971, 1:125–37; Wu Han 1936, 137–86.

44 See Chen Wenshi 1966 for a thorough coverage of the Ming prohibition of the coastal trade. Farmer 1976, 98–133; Lo 1958, 149–68.

45 Elvin 1973, 91–110; 1975b, 96–98; Farmer 1976, 148–72; Lo 1958, 149–68; Wu Jihua 1971, 1:138–54, 175–236.

46 *CHC* 7, 39–40, 61–62, 252–54, 310–12; Chuan 1981, 536–49; Huang, Ray 1964, 102–25; Gandar [1894], 24–31; Wu Jihua 1971, 363–400; Zheng 1966, 217–24; Zhu 1962, 67–91. See also Yang Zhengtai 1986, 104–129.

47 *DMB*, 1:157–59.

48 Huang, Ray 1964, 261, n.18; Liao 1987, 115–16.

49 Dodgen 1989, 32–33; Liao 1987, 115–16.

50 Huang, Ray 1964, 21–37; Zhu 1962, 67–91.

51 *DMB*, 2:1107–1111; Dodgen 1989, 28–41.

52 *DMB*, 1:825; Huang, Ray 1964, 21–37.

53 Huang, Ray 1964, 38–63; Hucker 1958, 1–66; 1966, 1–46; 1975, 307–15.

54 Huang, Ray 1964, 81–102, 175–90.

55 Huang, Ray 1964, 64–81; 1969, 73–128; 1974, 51–55, 252–53, 317–18.

56 Hoshi 1938, 183–85; 1970, 29–40; 1980; Huang, Ray 1964, 39–43, 81–102; Yang Yafei 1968, 162–68.

57 Fitzpatrick 1979, 1–50; Masato 1969, 97–109; So 1975, 41–79, 122–40.

58 Chang Te-ch'ang 1933, 264–82; Chen Wenshi 1966; Elvin 1975b, 96–98; Leonard 1984, 63–77; So 1975, 41–79, 122–40.

59 Cushman 1975, 160–87; Ng 1983, 184–212. See above chap. 2, 68–71.

60 Leonard 1984, 63–77; Murray 1987, 99–136; Pritchard 1936; Struve 1984, 1–14, 167–95; Wills 1974, 105–93.

Notes

61 He 1826b, *juan* 1–4; 1826a, 48:1–4b; Lin 1991a, 14–15; Wei Yuan [1878], 7:31–37.

62 S/TJ 5.2.5; Elvin 1975b, 96–98; Tregear 1980, 198–202; Wiens 1955, 248–50.

63 Gandar [1894], 33–43; Wu Tongju [1928], 2:535–786; Zheng 1966, 65–92; Zhu 1962, 192–47.

64 For contemporary maps of the confluence of the Yellow-Huai rivers and the Huaiyang canal, see Feng Daoli 1840, 1:1b–2; Lin Qing 1841, "Tushuo" 1–25b; "Fushuo" 1–7b; *QHXZ* 1855, "Tushuo," *juan* 1; *XXSJJ, juanshou*.

65 A scroll map of the Grand Canal illustrates and explains that the function of these two drainage gates was to draw clear water into the Yellow River to scour its bed. BLOC 2362.

66 Feng 1840, 1:5b–6, 7b–8; Guo Shu 1982, 47–60; Tong 1861, 31:1–33; Wu Tongju [1928], 535–753, 946–69.

67 *QHXZ* 1855, "Tushuo," *juan* 1; *Gongbu celi* 1815, 51:4–5, 6.

68 The Hongze strategy (fig. 10) is illustrated and described on a scroll map of the Grand Canal held in the Oriental Collection of the British Library (BLOC 2362.

69 These changes are illustrated in two important nineteenth-century texts by Feng Daoli and Lin Qing.Feng 1840, 1:3b–4; Lin Qing 1841, maps 2–9.

70 *QHXZ* 1855, "Tushuo," *juan* 1.

71 Alexander 1792–94, 28v–29; Ellis [1817], 268–88; Staunton 1797, 2:415–16.

72 Zheng 1966, 65–92.

73 Zheng 1966, 144–59.

74 See Feng 1840, 1:7b–8.

75 Gandar [1894], 33–43; *XXSJJ* 1832, 1131–41; Zheng 1966, 144–59.

76 *Gongbu celi* 1815, 44:8.

77 Liao 1987, 115–16; Tong 1861, 33:1–33; Zheng 1966, 136–37; Zhu 1962, 88.

78 Feng 1840, 1:5b–6; Tong 1861, 33:33–55b

79 Dodgen 1989, 36–38.

80 Gandar [1894], 33–43; Needham 1971, 362–63; Zhu 1962, 105–30.81

81 *Gongbu celi* 1815, *juan* 44–55, 61–62.

82 Zhu 1962, 124–30.

83 S4.12.18b.

84 Wang Jingyang 1984, 190–91.

Notes to Chapter 2

1 The first two characters of this phrase, *guoji*, refer to the state's strategic responsibilities, or plans, as well as the fiscal resources to carry them out. They will be defined and translated slightly differently throughout this study according to context.

2 *CHC* 10, 107–62.

3 Crossley 1985, 3–24; 1989a/b; 1990a, 13–30; Kahn 1971, 138–43; Spence 1974, xiv–xv.

4 Crossley 1994; Kahn 1965, 29–43; 1967a, 15–44; 1967b, 197–203.

5 These writings are a valuable source for his views on emperorship in the year just prior to his succession. Qing Xuanzong. 1824.

6 Naquin 1976, 176–84, 339, n.107.

7 *DHL* 14, 1:1–12b; *ECCP*, 574–76; *QS*, 17:231–44; 215:3499–3500; 222:3571–75.

8 Bartlett 1991, 257–78; Cahill 1982, 146–225; Crossley 1990, 13–30; Fisher, Thomas 1974, 210–75, 289–308; Guy 1987, 16–37; Kahn 1965, 29–43; 1967b, 197–203; 1971, 115-67; Kessler 1971, 190–200; 1976, 112–71; Lee, Sherman 1954, 97–133; Shyrock [1932]; Spence 1967, 206; 1974, xiv–xv; Struve 1979, 321-65; Wakeman 1985, 2, 1074–1127.

9 Dardess 1993, 1–108; Fisher, Thomas 1974, 210–75; 1990, 82–86.

10 *DOT*, 62–80.

Notes 265

11 *CHC* 7, 107–81, 508–84; *DOT*, 70–96; Fisher, Carney 1990, 82–86; Huang, Ray 1964, 38–63; Hucker 1961, 3–7, 38–60; 1975, 307–15.

12 Dardess 1993, 1–108.

13 Throughout this study, references to imperial action from the early Qianlong reign to the regency in 1861 indicate decisions and initiatives made by the emperor with his inner court advisers, or servitors, in the Grand Council (Bartlett 1991, 169–228).

14 Bartlett 1991, 1–64; Wu, Silas 1967, 7–75; 1968, 275–87; 1970a, 52–65.

15 Bartlett 1991, 17–134; 257–78; Chu and Saywell 1984, 1–25; Dennerline 1975, 86–120; 1981, 278–301; DOT 75–82,88–89, nos. 67–68; Huang Pei 1974, 113–61; 1985, 502–15; Kessler 1976, 112–36, 167–71; Oxnam 1975, 166–98; Spence 1966; Wu, Silas 1967, 7–75; 1968, 275–87; 1970a, 27–65, 52–106; 1970b, 210–27; 1972, 230–39. See also Huang Pei's recent article on the historiography of the secret communications system 1994, 329–38.

16 Bartlett 1991, 169–99, 231–55, 257–78.

17 Leonard 1986, 1-28.

18 Leonard and Watt 1992b, 1–7; Leonard 1993, 1–4.

19 Leonard 1986, 1-28.

20 Chu and Saywell 1984, 1–25, 87–90; Huang Pei 1967, 105–48; 1974, 187–308; Metzger 1973, 95–164, 168–232; Smith 1968, 10–15; Wu, Silas 1967, 7–75; 1970b, 210–27; 1972, 230–39.

21 Bartlett 1991, 278; *CHC* 10, 415–25, 504–7; Kwong 1983, 221–38; Yu 1982–83, 1:3–16; 2:70–85.

22 Huang, Ray 1981, 223–34.

23 Dardess 1993, 1–108.

24 Chang Hao 1974, 36–61; 1983, 3–19; Leonard 1992a, 47–68.

25 Farquhar 1968, 198–205; Fletcher 1968, 206–24; 1978a, 35–106; 1978b, 351–408; Lamb 1968, 54–75, 190–213; Lee, Robert 1970, 1–77; Leonard 1984, 121–44; 1987, 63–97; Mancall 1971, 1–32; 1984, 13–64; Rossabi 1979, 167–99.

26 Leonard 1984, 121–44, 153–83; Wang Gungwu 1968, 34–62; 1970, 375–401.

27 Chen Wenshi 1981, 11–46; Im 1981; Lee, Robert 1970; Liu Jiaju 1981, 47–75.

28 Borei 1988; *ECCP*, 67–69, 584–87, 691–92; Fairbank and Teng 1961d, 130–35; Fletcher 1978a, 35–106; 1978b, 351–408; Hsu 1964a, 688–700; 1964b, 142–49; 1965a, 212–28; 1965b, 16–29.

29 Fletcher 1978a, 35–106; 1978b, 351–408; Millward 1991.

30 Borei 1987, 26–45; 1992, 21–46; Fletcher 1978b, 351–408; Hsu 1964b, 142–49; 1965a, 212–28; Petech 1950; Rossabi 1975; 1979, 167–99.

31 S4.12.18b.

32 Hsi 1975, 443–53; Kessler 1971, 181–84; 1976, 74–111; Struve 1984, 1–14, 167–95; Wakeman 1985, 1:414–680, 2:717–83.

33 Crozier 1977; Leonard 1984, 63–77; Wills 1974, 11–28; 1979, 201–38.

34 Chang Te-ch'ang 1933, 264–82; Cushman 1975, 160–87; Leonard 1988b, 230–36; Lin Renchuan 1987, 1–39, 176–214; Ng 1983, 184–212. See also Chen Wenshi 1966 and Wang Gungwu 1964, 1968, 1970 for background on the Ming.

35 *CHC* 10, 163–212; Dermigny 1964, 1:276–369; Fairbank [1953], 23–53; Morse 1910–18,1:63–92; Ng 1983, 42–94; Pritchard 1936.

36 Ng 1983, 42–94, 184–222.

37 Cushman 1975, 160–98; Fairbank [1953], 114–32; Murray 1987, 6–17, 151–58; Wei Peh-t'i 1979, 83–112.

38 *CHC* 7, 182–304; Elvin 1973, 91–110; Farmer 1976, 98–133; Wang Gungwu 1964, 87–104; 1968, 34–62; 1970, 375–401.

39 Leonard 1984, 63–77; 1988b, 230–36.

40 Chen, Kenneth 1939, 325–59; 1942, 218–26.

41 Leonard 1979, 23–57; 1987, 63–97.

42 Liu Danian 1981, 76–107; Liu Deren 1981, 115–20; Liu Lu 1983, 70–79; Shang 1981a, 111–20; 1981b, 19–61.

43 Leonard and Watt, 1992b, 1–7.

44 Feuerwerker 1984, 297–326; King 1965, 91–143; Lee, James 1982, 711–45; Perdue 1987a, 59–135; 1989, 1–37; 1991, 1–20; Perdue and Wong 1983, 291–332;

Notes 267

Quan and Kraus 1975, 17–39; Shulman 1989; Vogel 1983, 381–93; 1987, 1–52; Wang Yeh-chien 1973b; Will 1980, 261–87; 1985, 295–352; 1990, 97–301; Zelin 1984, 116–66. See also Edkins 1903 for an early account of the Qing tax system.

45 Ch'u 1962, 1–13,130–47; Dennerline 1975, 73–128; 1981, 278–301; Hsiao 1960, 43–258; Watt 1972, 11–22, 138–59; Zelin 1984, 116–166.

46 Leonard 1992a, 59–68.

47 Cushman 1975, 1–133; Guo Songyi 1985, 24–40; Huang Pei 1981, 3–10; Johnson 1993b, 151–81; Ng 1983, 184–212; Perdue 1987a, 59–135; Tien Ju-kang 1956, 1–21; 1982, 31–44.

48 Borei 1992, 21–46; *CHC* 10, 58–90; Lipman 1981; Millward 1991.

49 Gardella, 1992, 97–118; Ng 1983, 184–212 ; Perdue 1987a, 164–233.

50 Perdue 1987a, 136–63, 234–52; Rowe 1984, 177–210.

51 Will 1985, 295–352.

52 Will 1990, 269–301.

53 Vogel 1983, 381–96.

54 Shulman 1989; Sun 1968, 835–45.

55 Rowe 1991, 1–34.

56 Kelley 1986, 338, n.59.

57 King 1965, 91–117.

58 Dermigny 1964, 1:276–369; McElderry 1992, 119–37; Ng 1983, 153–212.

59 Shulman 1989; Sun 1962–63, 175–227; 1968, 835–45; 1992, 9–20; Vogel 1983, 381–96.

60 Borei 1992, 21–40; Fletcher 1978a, 35–106; Perdue 1991, 1–20.

61 Elvin 1975a, 82–103; Kelley 1982, 361–91; 1987; Leonard 1989, 1–22; Liu, T.J. 1970, 1–28; Schoppa 1987, 13–29; Will 1980, 261–87; 1985, 295–352.

62 Metzger 1962, 1–39; 1970, 23–46; 1972, 9–45; Rowe 1984, 90–121.

63 Chiang Tao-chang 1983, 197–219; King 1965, 121–43; Metzger 1962, 1–39; Quan and Kraus 1975, 72–78; Vogel 1987, 1–52; Wang Yeh-chien 1973b, 110–33.

64 Will 1985, 295–352; Zheng 1966, 224–33; Zhu 1962, 92–147.

65 Elvin 1975a, 82–103; Liu, T.J. 1970, 1–28; Pasternak 1972b, 193–213; Perdue 1987a, 164–96; 1987b, 1–12; Schoppa 1987, 1–29; 1989; Watt 1972, 161–209; Will 1985, 295–352.

66 Gandar [1894], 33–43; Wu Tongju [1928], 683–753; Zheng 1966, 224–33, 241–45; Zhu 1962, 92–147.

67 Perdue 1982, 747–65; 1987a, 164–219; Will 1980, 261–87; 1985, 295–352.

68 P5.3.17c.

69 Chuan 1981, 536–49; Gandar [1894], 33–43; Liu Danian 1981, 76-107; Liu Daren 1981, 115–20; Liu Lu 1983, 70–79; Shang 1981a, 113–19; 1981b, 19–61; Zhu 1962, 92–147.

70 Kelley 1986, 12–20.

71 Johnson 1993a; 1993b, 151–81; Marks 1991, 64–116; Metzger 1977; Myers 1974, 77–93; Yang Zhengtai 1986, 104–29; See also Fu Zhonglan 1985 for a further discussion of the cities along the Grand Canal.

72 *DOT* no. 7409; Kelley 1986, 304–11.

73 See below in chap. 6.

Notes to Chapter 3

1 P4.1.13; P4.4.4a; P4.4.4b; P4.*run* 7.1; P4.10.16c; P4.3.7; P4.1.27; P4.5.22; P4.1.21.

2 For two examples of routine authorization of proposals made by the new Shandong Canal director, Zhang Jing, see P5.2.28; P5.3.17b.

3 Leonard 1988a, 665–99.

4 Bartlett 1991, 94–112.

5 S4.10.25a.

Notes

6   *ECCP*, 936.

7   S4.10.16b.

8   Liu Danian 1981, 5–21; Liu Deren 1981, 115–20; Liu Lu 1983, 70–79; Shang 1981b, 19–61; Zheng 1966, 224–33; Zhu 1962, 105–19.

9   Chu and Saywell 1984, 1–25; Kelley 1986, 11–91; Zheng 1966, 325–40; Leung 1990, 1–34.

10 *BH* 1912, 395–437; Chu and Saywell 1984, 1–25; *DOT*, 88–91; Mayers [1897], 33–47.

11 TJ5.6.17b.

12 Chu and Saywell 1984, 87–90.

13 Bao 1982, 29–32; *ECCP* 1967, 938; Shang 1981b,15,1–2:19–61.

14 Staunton 1797, 2:1–46. See Van-Braam Houckgeest 1798 for a late seventeenth-century account of the canal.

15 TJ4.11.24b.

16 *QDCJCK*, 092: 532; 100: 516; 157: 165; 194: 291.

17 TJ5.3.6.

18 TJ4.11.24c; TJ4.12.27.

19 Dodgen 1989, 16–65; Zhu 1962, 92–147.

20 Leonard 1989, 8–10. For a discussion of transfer-shipping, see chap. 6.

21 TJ4.12.10; TJ4.12.25a.

22 TJ4.12.25a.

23 Rowe 1983, 33–86.

24 *BH*, 820D; P5.2.28; P5.3.17a/b.

25 *BH*, 417–19; Ch'u 1962, 6–14, 155; *DOT*, 89:2191; Leung 1990, 1–34.

26 The location of numerous local waterways and water-control facilities along the Yellow River and the canal in the Qinghe district can be seen in the map

section of the Qinghe county gazeteer. *QHXZ* 1855, *juan* 1:2b–4; *BH*, 417–19, 423, 425–29; Ch'u 1962, 4–13, 155–56; *DOT* 88–91; Mayers [1897], 33–47.

27 *BH*, 749; Kelley 1986, 54–69.

28 *Grand Canal* 1984, 30–31.

29 Perdue 1987b, 1–13.

30 P5.2.23.

31 P4.11.23.

32 Wang Yeh-chien 1973b, 67–83.

33 *CAT*, 727–29; Hinton 1970, 14–15; Quan and Kraus 1975, 84–92.

34 Hinton 1970, 2–3; Quan and Kraus 1975, 36–39.

35 Hinton 1970, 9a; Kelley 1986, 20–31.

36 Wang Yeh-chien 1973b, 20–109.

37 *CAT* 511–12; Hinton 1970, 8–9; Quan and Kraus 1975, 28–39; Rowe 1983, 33–49; Wang Yeh-chien 1973b, 60–61; Zhang Zhelang 1942, 22–24.

38 Wang Yeh-chien 1973b, 67–109, 110–33.

39 Wang Yeh-chien 1973b, 5–19.

40 Kelley 1986, 36–41.

41 Hinton 1970, 12–12a.

42 Needham 1971, 409–17, 621–22, 659, 662–64; Sun and Sun, trans. 1966, 172–73.

43 Hinton 1970, 10–11; Needham 1971, 409–17, 621–22; Playfair 1875, 354ff.; Sun and Sun, trans. 1966, 172–73; Worcester 1971, 320–21.

44 Hinton 1970, 8–9; Kelley 1986, 40–41; Zhang Zhelang 1942, 33–54.

45 See Playfair 1875, 354ff. for an account of the shipment process in 1874 after the shift of the Yellow River.

46 Dodgen 1989, 16–65; Kelley 1986, 56–76; Leonard 1989, 15–30.

47 *CHC* 10, 119–28; Hinton 1970, 1–15; Hoshi 1971, 165–79; Hu 1954–55, 505–13; Meng 1960, 330-90; Zhang Zhelang 1942, 55–60.

48 Dodgen 1989, 16–65; Kelley 1986, 41–54; Zhang Zhelang 1942, 11–54.

Notes to Chapter 4

1 S4.12.3b.

2 *XXSJJ*, head *juan*, 24.

3 Their function is described in the explanatory text on an early eighteenth-century Grand Canal scroll, BLOC 2362.

4 TJ4.9.29; S4.10.12; S4.10.16a/b; S4.10.25a; S4.10.26a; P4.10.26b; P4.11.15; P4.11.19.

5 S4.10.12.

6 *ECCP*, 683–85.

7 S4.10.12.

8 S4.10.16a

9 S4.10.16a

10 S4.10.25a.

11 S4.10.25a.

12 S4.10.25a.

13 P4.11.15; P4.11.19.

14 P4.10.26b.

15 S4.12.3b.

16 P4.11.23.

17 S4.12.3.

18 TJ4.12.9; *XXSJJ*, head *juan*, 50–56.

19 Gandar [1894], 33–43; *XXSJJ*, head *juan*, 23–28; Zheng 1966, 136–44.

20 P4.11.23; TJ4.11.26a/b; S4.12.3b; S4.12.5; TJ4.12.9; S4.12.18; TJ4.12.21; TJ4.12.25; TJ5.1.6; TJ5.1.12a. Sites near the junction and lakes that sustained damage can be seen on a map in *XXSJJ*, head *juan*, 27.

21 P4.11.23.

22 P4.11.23; TJ4.11.24a/b; TJ4.11.26a/b.

23 P4.11.15; P4.11.19; QDCJCK 56:164; 92:563–64; 157:465; 198:467.

24 P4.11.23.

25 TJ4.11.26a.

26 *ECCP*, 776; QDCJCK [Wang] 12:699; 16:230; 18:185; 19:395; 92:342; 100:161; 115:159; 140:255; 193:062; [Wen] 17:924; 92:325; 100:356.

27 TJ4.11.26a/b.

28 QDCJCK 16:241; 150:850; 56:68; 92:564–67; 157:097.

29 TJ4.11.24b.

30 While serving as Southern Canal director in 1830–31, Zhang undertook the completion of a valuable source book on Qing water-control management, *Xuxingshui jinjian (XXSJJ)*. It contains a head *juan* devoted to maps, plus 156 *juan* of text. The Huaiyang section of the Grand Canal is covered in *juan* 131: 2979–3000. This work had been initiated by the renowned Li Shixu (to whom the hapless Zhang Wenhao had been compared unfavorably), and it supplemented the early Qing collection on China's waterways from antiquity to 1721 by Fu Zehong. Fu Zehong 1725; *ECCP*, 936; QDCJCK 32:468; 56:170; 92:567; 100:309; 116:739; 121:085–90; 157:255–68.

31 This is a case where the lower ranking governor (2b) has supervisory responsibility over the higher-ranking canal director (2a).

32 TJ4.11.24b.

33 P5.1.5.

34 *ECCP*, 683–86; QDCJCK 57:657; 92:417; 100:791–806; 195:270; 100:316–21.

35 S/TJ5.1.12a.

36 S4.12.18.

37 See explanatory note near the depiction of the Xiangfu and Wushui channels on scroll map of the Grand Canal. BLOC 2362.

38 P4.12.1.

39 P4.11.23; P4.12.1; P4.12.3a/b; TJ4.12.9; TJ4.12.21.

40 P4.12.1.

41 P4.12.1.

42 TJ4.12.5.

43 Finnane 1984a, 168; Polachek 1976, pt. 1, chap. 4; *ECCP*, 347; *QDCJCK* 16:284; 56:172; 92:576; 116:775.

44 S4.12.15.

45 TJ4.12.5.

46 TJ4.11.26b; S4.12.3b; TJ4.12.9; TJ4.12.21.

47 S4.12.3; TJ4.12.5; S4.12.15; TJ4.12.24; TJ4.12.27.

Notes to Chapter 5

1 *CHC* 10, 108–32; Hoshi 1971, 165–79; Hu 1954–55, 505–13 See chap. 1 for a discussion of the growing complexity and cost of the canal hydraulic system. See chap. 8 for a discussion of structural corruption.

2 S4.12.3.

3 See explanation of backflows in chap. 1, pp. 41, 48.

4 TJ4.12.9.

5 Polachek 1976, pt.1, chap. 4.

6 S4.12.9.

7 S4.12.9; TJ4.12.21.

8   S4.12.9.

9   TJ4.12.21.

10 S4.12.18b.

11 S4.12.18b.
12 S4.12.18b.

13 S4.12.18b.

14 S5.1.6.

15 S/TJ5.4.27.

16 S5.1.6.

17 P5.1.23a.

18 S5.1.6.

19 TJ5.1.12c; P5.1.12b; P5.1.24; S/TJ5.1.28; S/TJ5.3.10; P5.10.17a; TJ5.11.3a.

20 S/TJ5.1.12c.

21 S5.1.6.

22 P5.1.5.

23 S/TJ5.1.29b.

24 TJ5.2.20.

25 S5.2.7; P5.2.14; P5.2.23.

26 P5.2.19; P5.3.16; S5.3.20; P5.3.23; S5.3.24a/b.

Notes to Chapter 6

1   TJ4.12.18.

Notes 275

2. A beautifully drawn scroll of the Yellow River, held in the British Library, Oriental Collection, actually shows this anchorage on the south bank of the Yellow River, complete with tiny junks drawn in. BLOC 13990.

3. Kelley 1986, 338, n.59.

4. P5.1.29b.

5. S/TJ5.4.2a.

6. S/TJ5.4.2a.

7. S/TJ5.4.2b.

8. S/TJ5.4.2a.

9. S/TJ5.4.2a.

10. S/TJ5.4.2a; S/TJ5.4.2b.

11. S/TJ5.4.2b.

12. The 1766 edition discusses the reduction in the number of regular grain boats and procedures for hiring private lighters (*juan* 18); the 1845 collection, compiled by Pan Xi'en, reviews the disaster beginning in the early Daoguang reign and outlines the procedures for transfer-shipping as well as sea transport (*juan* 89, 90); the 1875 edition contains information about changes in grain shipping following the shift of the Yellow River (*juan* 89–96).

13. Leonard 1992a, 47–73.

14. TJ5.3.6.

15. TJ4.12.10; TJ4.12.25a.

16. TJ4.12.25a.

17. S/TJ5.4.15.

18. S/TJ5.4.15.

19. P5.2.19; P5.3.16; P5.3.23a/b; S5.3.24b; TJ5.6.6b.

20. Kelley 1982, 361.

21. TJ5.6.6b.

22 TJ5.6.6b.

23 S5.7.19b; P5.8.3; P5.8.8; PM5.9.10 (*SL*:1587).

24 S/TJ5.4.18.

25 S/TJ5.4.18.

26 S/TJ5.5.2.

27 S/TJ5.5.2.

28 S/TJ5.4.27; S/TJ5.5.10a; S/TJ5.5.19a/b; TJ5.6.10a.

29 S/TJ5.5.19b.

30 S/TJ5.5.25a.

31 S/TJ5.5.25a.

32 S/TJ5.5.25a.

33 TJ5.6.28c.

34 S5.8.25; S5.8.28.

35 TJ5.6.17c.

36 TJ5.6.3.

37 TJ5.6.3.

38 TJ5.6.17e.

39 TJ5.6.17e.

40 P5.7.16.

41 P5.7.26a; PM5.10.13(*SL*:1622).

42 PM5.10.5 (*SL*: 1616–1617); PM5.10.6 (*SL*:1619); P5.9.8c; S5.9.11a; S5.10.15.

43 S5.9.11b; S5.10.15; P5.10.16; S5.10.25; P5.11.1.

44 P5.11.3b; PM5.11.15 (*SL*:1644); S5.11.24b; P5.11.25.

45 S5.11.14.

46 P5.11.3b.

47 S/TJ5.2.20.

48 Lieberthal and Oksenberg 1988, 135–68, 339–90; Nickum 1974, 12, 26–30, 31–56; 1981, 3–40. See also Greer 1979 for an assessment of water resource management in the Yellow River basin.

49 Lai 1992, 139–55; Harding 1987, 99–171; Lieberthal and Oksenberg 1988, 243–68; Sun E-tu Zen 1968, 835–45; 1992, 9–20.

50 Leonard 1992b, 1–16; 1993, 7–16.

51 Lai 1992, 139–55; Sun E-tu Zen 1992, 9–20; Zelin 1984, 1–24, 116–166.

Notes to Chapter 7

1 S/TJ5.4.27; S/TJ5.5.10a; S/TJ5.5.19a; S/TJ5.5.19b; TJ5.6.10a.

2 S/TJ5.4.27.

3 S/TJ5.4.27.

4 S/TJ5.5.10a.

5 This notion is related to the late imperial view that the institutions of government, their functions, and the funds necessary to perform their functions were fixed. When the functions could no longer be performed with existing budgetary allocations, then changes in the institutions and functions were thought to be appropriate and timely. The idea of the fixed prerogatives of government is discussed in the 1826 statecraft collection (He Changling 1826a, 1:15b), and the importance of timely change is raised frequently in the introductory essays on "Learning" and "Principles of Governance" as well as in the proposals for specific reforms in the body of the collection.

6 S/TJ5.5.10a.

7 S/TJ5.4.2b.

8 S/TJ5.5.19a/b.

9   S/TJ5.5.19a.

10 S/TJ5.5.19a.

11 S/TJ5.5.19b.

12 S/TJ5.5.19b.

13 TJ5.6.10a/b.

14 S/TJ5.5.19b.

15 S/TJ5.5.22a.

16 *ECCP*, 932; S/TJ5.4.10a; S/TJ5.5.22a.

17 TJ4.12.9.

18 P4.12.15.

19 S4.12.18.

20 S4.12.18.

21 S/TJ5.2.5.

22 S/TJ5.2.5.

23 S/TJ5.4.2b.

24 S4.12.18; S5.1.6; S/TJ5.4.10a; TJ5.6.6a; S5.7.21; S5.11.28.

25 S/TJ5.4.2b.

26 S/TJ5.4.10a.

27 S/TJ5.4.10a.

28 S/TJ5.4.10a.

29 S/TJ5.4.10a.

30 *CHC* 10, 119–28; Hoshi 1971, 179; 1960, 181–82; Kelley 1982, 361–91; 1986, 232ff.; Metzger 1972, 32–33; Zhang Zhelang 1942, 55–60. Official views about the canal versus sea transport are contained in He Changling 1826a, *juan* 46–48 and He Changling 1826b.

31 It should be noted that earlier explanations of the failure of the canal–grain transport system in the early nineteenth century emphasize the corrupt and inefficient role of court and official patronage networks that assigned expectant officials to canal–grain transport posts (*CHC* 10, 119–28; Hu 1954–55, 505–13). While this approach to managing low-level administrative tasks may have contributed to some problems, this study regards the practice as a regular, routine part of governing at the lowest levels of regional bureaucracy where bureaucratic government was most thinly spread. Instead, greater emphasis is placed on low-level government's ties with, and the positive functional role of, private labor, shipping, and trade organizations on whom the yearly shipments and canal defense work depended.

32 S/TJ5.5.22a.

33 S/TJ5.5.22a; TJ5.6.6c.

34 S/TJ5.5.22a.

35 S/TJ5.5.22a.

36 TJ5.6.6c

37 S4.12.18b

38 TJ5.6.6c.

39 TJ5.6.6c.

40 TJ5.6.6c.

41 TJ5.6.6c.

42 TJ5.6.6c.

43 TJ5.6.10b.

44 TJ5.6.10b.

45 TJ5.6.13a.

Notes to Chapter 8

1 *ECCP*, 931–33; S/TJ5.4.10a; S/TJ5.5.22a.

2   *CAT* 512, 734; Hinton 1970, 8–9; Rowe 1983, 33–86; Wang Yeh-chien 1973b, 60–61.

3   Will 1990, 153–76, 294–301; Will and Wong 1991, 141–78. The management of granaries and famine relief raised concerns about the use of grain in kind versus money, as did grain tax commutation.

4   *CAT* 785; Hinton 1970, 7–8; Quan and Kraus 1975, 28–39.

5   TJ5.6.28c.

6   Leonard 1992a, 54–66.

7   TJ5.6.29a; TJ5.7.17.

8   King 1965, 121–43; Lin, M.H. 1989, chaps. 5–6; Quan and Kraus 1975, 1–39; Wang Yeh-chien 1973b, 115; 1973c, 541–50; 1979, 441–45; 1986a, 23–30, plus tables.

9   *CHC* 10, 116–128; Hoshi 1960; 1971; Kelley 1986, 11–91.

10 TJ5.6.6b.

11 S5.6.28c.

12 TJ5.6.29a.

13 S5.7.21.

14 P5.8.9a.

15 King 1965, 140–43; Lin, M. H. 1989, 19–205; Vogel 1983, 377–96; Wang Yeh-chien 1973b, 12–19, 60–61; Zhou 1982, 61–105.

16 Chang Hsin-pao 1964, 36–46; Lin, M. H. 1989, 72–115; Marks 1991, 64–116; Wang Yeh-chien 1979, 425–447.

17 Lin, M.H. 1991b, 1–35; Wang Yeh-chien 1973b, 110–115; 1986a, 1–30; 1979, 425–47.

18 Wang Yeh-chien 1973b, 102–3, 110–28.

19 S5.7.19c.

20 S/TJ5.6.22; TJ5.6.28c; S5.7.3b.

Notes 281

21 Lin Qing [1836], *juan* 2.
22 TJ5.6.13a; see also Zhang Jing's proposal, TJ5.10.1a.
23 TJ5.6.13b.
24 S5.5.19b. See maps in Feng 1840, 1:1b, 3.
25 P5.6.1.
26 P5.6.1.
27 P5.6.6c.
28 TJ5.6.9a.
29 S/TJ5.5.19b.
30 TJ5.6.28d.
31 P5.10.17; TJ5.11.3a.
32 S5.7.3a.
33 P5.7.19a; P5.7.26a; PM5.9.5 (*SL*:1582); P5.9.16; S5.10.1b; S5.10.7a; PM5.10.7b (*SL*:1619); PM5.10.13 (*SL*:1622); PM5.11.16 (*SL*:1645).
34 TJ5.10.1a; S5.10.28.
35 S5.10.1b; TJ6.3.12a.
36 P5.11.2.
37 P5.6.17a; S5.7.12; TJ5.11.3a.
38 P5.11.2.
39 TJ5.7.28.
40 TJ5.7.28.
41 S5.9.28b.
42 TJ5.10.1a.

43 Feng 1840, 1:3b–4; Gandar [1894], 40.

44 TJ5.11.24b.

45 TJ5.7.28.

46 TJ5.11.24b.

47 P5.6.17a.

48 P5.10.17a.

49 S5.10.1a.

50 See S5.9.28b for this report.

51 Polachek 1976, 207–62.

52 S6.9.6; S6.11.25.

Notes to Chapter 9

1 P6.8.13.

2 *Hubu caoyun quanshu* 1845, head *juan* 3–7.

3 S/TJ5.2.5; S/TJ5.4.10a; S/TJ5.5.22a.

4 S/TJ5.4.27; S/TJ5.5.10a; S/TJ5.5.19b; S/TJ5.6.10a.

5 S/TJ5.2.5; S/TJ5.4.10a.

6 S/TJ5.4.2b.

7 S/TJ5.2.5; TJ5.6.22a.

8 S/TJ5.4.2b; S/TJ5.4.10a.

9 S/TJ5.2.5.

10 S/TJ5.5.22; P5.12.5d.

11 S/TJ5.2.5; S/TJ5.5.22a; P5.12.5a/c.

Notes

12 S/TJ5.5.22a.
13 TJ5.6.6c.
14 S/TJ5.6.28c.
15 S/TJ5.6.28c.
16 TJ5.6.29a.
17 TJ5.6.28c; TJ5.6.29a.
18 S/TJ5.6.28d.
19 TJ5.6.29a.
20 TJ5.7.3a.
21 S5.7.23.
22 Some of these issues are raised in Lojewski 1973; 1976, 128–36; Polachek 1976, 334–51.
23 This pattern of ameliorative action is also seen during the Yellow River floods from 1835–45. Dodgen 1989, 66–125.
24 TJ5.6.29a; P5.9.8b; P5.11.24a.
25 TJ5.6.29a; TJ5.7.26b; P5.11.4; P5.11.24a.
26 TJ5.7.26b.
27 P5.9.8b; P5.11.25; P5.12.5; S6.3.3; P6.3.19.
28 P5.9.8b.
29 P5.11.24a; P5.11.25a; P5.12.5a.
30 P5.11.25; P5.12.2; P6.2.18a.
31 S5.8.5.
32 P5.9.8b.
33 P5.9.8b; P5.11.24a; P5.12.51.

34 P5.11.28.

35 P5.11.28.

36 P5.11.28.

37 Previous studies tend to view regional officials as corrupt or careerist in their management of canal–grain transport issues without taking into consideration the limits of state power at the regional level that necessitated reliance on patronage networks, or the dangerous complexity of the hydraulic system in the 1820s that made large-scale reconstruction futile. *CHC* 10, 116–28; Polachek 1976, 207–62.

38 The emperor's fear of factionalism over the use of sea transport is clearly stated in 1827 in a fifty-one character rescript on a palace memorial sent by Tao Zhu. The emperor indicates his willingness to use sea transport when canal conditions warrant such use, but he cautions Tao to keep quiet about sea transport for fear of stirring up factional intrigue against it. PM7.9.30, no. 056986.

39 PM5.11.5 (*SL*:1640).

40 P6.2.11a/b; P6.2.15a; P6.2.18a/c; S6.3.3; P6.3.18; P6.3.19; P6.4.14; P6.4.19a/b. Most studies treat the Daoguang Emperor as weak and ineffective, bound to past precedents and incapable of innovative leadership. *CHC* 10, 125–26; *ECCP*, 574–76; Polachek 1976, 207–62.

41 P6.6.17a/b; P6.8.13.

42 P6.5.16.

43 P6.6.17b.

44 P6.6.17b.

45 P6.8.13.

46 P6.6.17a.

47 P6.8.13.

48 TJ6.8.15; P6.9.30b; P6.10.13; P6.10.16b/c; P6.10.27c.

49 P6.6.26.

Notes to Conclusion

1 Disciplined practicality also characterized the Qing leadership's approach to Yellow River control problems in the 1830s and 1840s. Dodgen 1989, 358–63.

2 Chang Hao 1974, 36–61; 1983, 3–19; Liu, K.C. 1983a, 1–15; Liu, K.C., ed. 1990; Metzger 1973, 21–71.

3 Dodgen 1989; King 1965; Metzger 1962; 1970; 1972; 1973; Perdue 1987a; 1992, 100–25; Quan and Kraus 1975; Vogel 1983; Will 1990; Will and Wong 1991.

4 Polachek 1976, 207–62.

5 *CHC* 10, 119–32; Hinton 1970, 1–15, 104–8; Hoshi 1971; Hu 1954–55; Meng 1960, 334–39; Zhang Zhelang 1942; Zheng 1966; Zhu 1962.

Glossary of Chinese Characters

Bai Chun	百春	*dongzhi*	冬至
Baima	白馬		
baozheng	保證	*fangyu*	防御
Baoshan	寶山	Feijiachang	裴家場
Baoying	報應	Feng Daoli	馮道立
Beihe	北河	Fuxing	福興
bochuan	剝船		
		gaidui	改兌
caobiao	漕標	Gaojia *yan/dadi*	高家堰/大隄
Caoliang guanxi	漕糧關係	Gaoyan *ting*	高堰廳
tianyu zhenggong	天庾正供	Gaoyou	高郵
Chapu	乍浦	*gong*	公
chaiqian	差遣	Guazhou	瓜州
Changhe	長河	*guan*	關
Changling	長齡	*guanbo*	官剝
changpingcang	常平倉	Guanhe	灌河
Chelo *ba*	車邏垻	Guanzhong	關中
Chen Xuan	陳瑄	*guoduminxiu*	國督民修
Chen Zhongfa	陳中孚	*guoji minsheng*	國計民生
Cheng Hanzhang	程含章		
Cheng Zuluo	程祖洛	Hangjiahu	杭嘉湖
Chuansha	川沙	*hebiao*	河標
chuangshi	創始	He Changling	賀長齡
		hedao	河道
dadi	大隄/堤	Hedong	河東
Dawenhe	大汶河	*hefu*	河夫
Dayang	大洋	*heshen*	河神
daofu	道府	Hongzehu	洪澤湖
de	德	Huangpu	黃浦
Dong'a	東阿	Huiji	惠濟

Jiang'an	江安	Nanguan *ba*	南關埧
Jiangbei	江北	Nanguanxin *ba*	南關新埧
Jin Fu	靳輔	Nanhe	南河
jintie	津貼	Nanwang	南旺
Jingjia	竟家	Nijia	倪家
jingshi	經世		
jiugui	舊規	*panba jieyun*	盤埧接運
jiuzhang	舊章	*panbo*	盤剝
		Pan Jixun	潘季馴
koumen	口門	Pan Xi'en	潘錫恩
		Pinghe *qiao*	平河橋
Lanhu *ba*	攔湖埧		
laoguan	老官	Qishan	琦善
li	里	Qinghe	清河
lishe	利涉	Qingjiangpu	清江浦
Li Shixu	黎世序	*quanyi*	權宜
Lixiahe	裡下河	*quanyi banli*	權宜辦理
Lizi *ba*	禮字埧	*quanyi zhi ji*	權宜之計
Lin Qing	麟慶		
Linjia *ba*	林家埧	Ren *ba*	仁埧
Liu Yinheng	劉尹衡	*ru chu yiche*	如出一轍
Luo jiao	羅教		
Luo Qing	羅清	*sao*	埽
		shachuan	沙船
Maochengpu	毛城鋪	Shanxu *ting*	山盱廳
Mianning	綿寧	Shaobo	邵伯
minchuan	民船	Shen Cheng	沈㳕
minnian	民埝	Shijia	侍家
minsheng	民生	Shisanbao	十三堡
Muzhang'a	穆彰阿	Shuqing *ba*	束清埧
		Sihe	泗河
Na'erjing'e	訥爾經額	Songyun	松筠
Nayancheng	那彥成	*sucui*	速催

Glossary

Suqian	宿遷	Xilang	息浪
Susong	蘇松	Xiahe	下河
Susongchangzhen	蘇松常鎮	Xiazhen	夏鎮
Sun Yuting	孫玉庭	*xiazhi*	夏至
		xianshi chouji	先事籌計
Tai'erzhuang	臺兒庄	*xianwei*	啣尾
Taihuang	汰黃	Xiangfu	祥符
Taiping	太平	Xin *ba*	新壩
tao	套	Xiong Yutai	熊遇泰
Tao Zhu	陶澍	*xun*	汛
tianlu	田廬		
Tianran	天然	*yan*	堰
ting	廳	Yanhe	鹽河
tongpan	通判	Yan Jian	顏檢
Tongji	通濟	Yan Lang	嚴烺
tongzhi	同知	Yangzhuang	楊庄
tuntian	屯田	*yaolu*	搖櫓
		yaozhi	遙制
Wangjia	王家	Yi *ba*	義壩
Wang Lin	汪琳	*yicang*	義倉
Wang Shifu	王世紱	Yizheng	儀徵
Wang Tingzhen	汪廷珍	*yinhe*	引河
Wangying *jianba*	王營減壩	Yinghe	英和
Weishanhu	微山湖	Yongdinghe	永定河
weiso	衛所	Yongfeng	永豐
Wei Yuanyu	魏元煜	*youtian*	由天
Wen Fu	文孚	Yu Chenglong	于成龍
Wulizhong *ba*	五里中壩	Yuhuang *ba*	藥黃壩
Wurui	五瑞	Yunti *guan*	雲梯關
Wusong	吳淞		
Wuzhi	武陟	Zhangfukou	張福口
		Zhangjiazhuang	張家庄
Xihechuan	西河船	Zhang Jing	張井

Zhang Ming 張銘
Zhang Shicheng 張師誠
Zhang Wenhao 張文浩
Zhaoguan *ba* 昭關壩
zhaolai 招徠
zhaoshang 招商
zhen 鎮
zhengdui 正兌
Zhengsi 嵊泗
Zhi *ba* 智壩
Zhou *qiao* 周橋
zhouxian 州縣
Zhujia 朱家
Zhu Shiyan 朱士彥

Reference List

Alexander, William. 1792–1802. Drawings. Add. Ms., 35,300. Department of Manuscripts. British Museum, London.

———. 1792–1794. Journal of voyage to China with drawings. Add. Ms., 35174:1–59. Department of Manuscripts. British Museum, London.

———. 1796. *Maps and plates to illustrate the fine large paper edition of Lord Macartney's embassy to China.* London: G. Nicol. Pressmark 92 D.57. Department of Prints. Victoria and Albert Museum, London.

———. 1798. *Views of headlands, islands, etc., taken during a voyage to China.* London.

———. N.d. Drawings. 3 vols.: WC 959:1–70; WC 960:1–66; WC 961:1–89. Department of Prints and Drawings. India Office Library and Records, London.

———. N.d. Drawings taken in China. Press no. 198 c.1. LB no. 22. 1865. 5.20:193–274. Department of Prints and Drawings. British Museum, London.

Archer, Mildred. 1969. *British drawings in the India Office Library.* Vol. 2, *Official and professional artists.* Her Majesty's Stationery Office, London.

Bao Hongzhang. 1982. Kangxi yu zhihe (The Kangxi Emperor and river management). *Beifang luncong* (Harbin) 5:29–32.

Bartlett, Beatrice S. 1991. *Monarchs and ministers: The Grand Council in mid-Ch'ing China (1723–1820).* Berkeley: University of California Press.

Bastin, John and R. Roolvink, eds. 1964. *Malayan and Indonesian Studies*: Essays presented to Sir Richard Winstedt. Oxford: Clarendon Press.

Binyon, Laurence. 1898. *Catalogue of drawings by British artists and artists of foreign origin working in Great Britain preserved in the Department of Prints and Drawings in the British Museum.* London: British Museum. Ref. to William Alexander, 15–27.

Borei, Dorothy V. 1987. Images of the northwest frontier: A study of the *Hsi-yu wen-chien lu* (1777). *The American Asian Review* 5, 2:26–45.

———. 1988. Economic implications of empire-building: The case of Sinkiang. Conference paper, Mid-Atlantic regional meeting, Association for Asian Studies, Indiana University of Pennsylvania, Indiana, Pa., October 21–23.

———. 1992. Beyond the Great Wall: Agricultural development in northern Xinjiang, 1780–1820. In Leonard and Watt 1992a, 21–46.

British Library Oriental Collection documents 2362, 13990, see below: Scroll maps.

Brunnert, H. S. and V. V. Hagelstrom. 1912. *Present day political organization of China*. Trans. A. Beltchenko and E. E. Moran. Shanghai: Kelly and Walsh.

Buchanan, Keith. 1970. *The transformation of the Chinese earth*. New York: Praeger.

Cahill, James. 1982. *The compelling image: Nature and style in seventeenth-century Chinese painting*. Cambridge, MA: Harvard University Press.

Carin, Robert E. 1962. *River control in communist China EC 31*. Hong Kong: Union Research Institute.

Reference List 293

Chang Hao. 1974. On the *ching-shih* ideal in Neo-Confucianism. *CSWT* 3, 1:36–61.

———. 1983. Song-Ming yilai rujia jingshi sixiang shishi (Explanation of Confucian statecraft thought since the Song-Ming periods). In *Jinshi Zhongguo jingshi sixiang yantao huilun wenji* (Proceedings of the international conference on modern Chinese statecraft thought). Taibei: Institute of Modern History, Academia Sinica. Pp. 3–19.

Chang Hsin-pao. 1964. *Commissioner Lin and the Opium War.* Cambridge, MA: Harvard University Press.

Chang Kwang-chih. 1986. *The archeology of ancient China.* 4th ed. New Haven: Yale University Press.

Chang Te-ch'ang. 1933. Maritime trade at Canton during the Ming dynasty. *Chinese Social and Political Science Review* 17.2:264–82.

Chen, Jerome and Nicholas Tarling, eds. 1970 *China and Southeast Asia.* Cambridge: Cambridge University Press.

Chen, Kenneth K. S. 1939. Matteo Ricci's contribution to, and influence on, geographical knowledge in China. *JAOS* 59:325–59.

———. 1942. Hai-lu: Forerunner of Chinese travel accounts of Western countries. *Monumenta Serica* 7:218–26.

Chen Wenshi. 1966. *Ming Hongwu Jiajing jiande haijin zhengce* (The policy of sea prohibitions in the Ming Hongwu to Jiajing reigns). Taibei.

———. 1981. The creation of the Manchu *niru. Chinese Studies in History* 14, 4:11–46.

Chi Ch'ao-ting. [1936] 1963. *Key economic areas in Chinese history as revealed in the development of public works for water control*. 2d ed. Reprint. New York: Paragon Books.

Chiang Tao-chang. 1983. The Salt Trade in Ch'ing China. *MAS* 17, 2:197–219.

China Pictorial. 1986–87 (July–February). Beijing.

Chu, Raymond W. and William G. Saywell. 1984. *Career patterns in the Ch'ing dynasty: The office of the governor–general*. Ann Arbor, MI: Center for Chinese Studies, University of Michigan.

Chu, Samuel C. 1965. *Reformer in modern China: Chang Chien 1853–1926*. Studies of the East Asian Institute. New York: Columbia University Press.

Ch'u T'ung-tsu. 1962. *Local government in China under the Ch'ing*. Cambridge, MA: Harvard University Press.

Chuan Shengshou. 1981. Mingdai Jiangnan shuili zhengce di fazhan (Development of water control policy in Jiangnan in Ming). In *MQSGJ*, 1981, 536–49.

Cohen, Paul A. and John E. Schrecker, eds. 1976. *Reform in nineteenth-century China*. Cambridge, MA: Harvard University Press.

Cressey, George Babcock. 1934. *China's geographic foundations: A survey of the land and its people*. New York: McGraw-Hill.

Crossley, Pamela K. 1985. An introduction to the Qing foundation myth. *LIC* 6, 2:3–24.

———. 1989. The Qianlong retrospect on the Chinese Martial *(Hanjian)* Banners. *LIC* 10, 1:1–26.

———. 1990. *Orphan warriors:: Three Manchu generations and the end of the Qing world*. Princeton: Princeton University Press.

———. 1994. Manchu education in the middle Ch'ing period. In *Education and society in late imperial China, 1600-1900.* Benjamin Elman and Alexander Woodside, eds. Berkeley: University of California Press, 340-78.

Crozier, Ralph C. 1977. *Koxinga and Chinese nationalism: History, myth, and hero.* Cambridge, MA: East Asian Research Center, Harvard University.

Cushman, Jennifer Wayne. 1975. Fields from the sea: Chinese junk trade with Siam during the late eighteenth and early nineteenth centuries. Ph.D. diss., Cornell University.

Czaya, Eberhard. 1981. *Rivers of the world.* New York: Van Nostrand Reinhold.

Dardess, John. 1993. Protest and its limits: Ming officials and modern intellectuals. Conference paper, Traditional Institutions and Values in Contemporary China, 20–22 May, East-West Center, University of Hawaii, Honolulu, HI.

Dennerline, Jerry. 1975. Fiscal reform and local control: The gentry-bureaucratic alliance survives the conquest. In Wakeman and Grant, eds. 1975, 73–128.

———. 1981. *The Chia-ting loyalists: Confucian leadership and social change in seventeenth-century China.* New Haven: Yale University Press.

Dermigny, Louis. 1964. *Le commerce à Canton au XVIIe siècle 1719–1833.* 3 vols. 1 album. Paris: École Pratique des Hautes Études.

Dodgen, Randall A. 1989. Controlling the dragon. Confucian engineers and the Yellow River in the late Daoguang reign (1835–1850). Ph. D. diss., Yale University.

———. 1991. Hydraulic evolution and dynastic decline: The Yellow River Conservancy, 1796–1855. *LIC* 12, 2: 36–63 (December).

Dreyer, Edward. 1982. *Early Ming China: A political history, 1355–1435.* Stanford: Stanford University Press.

Du Halde, Jean Baptiste. 1738. *A description of the empire of China and Chinese tartary together with the kingdom of Korea and Tibet.* London: Edward Cave.

Dunstan, Helen. 1992. Safely supping with the devil: The Qing state and its merchant suppliers of copper. *LIC* 13, 2:42–81.

Edkins, Joseph. 1903. *The revenue and taxation of the Chinese empire.* Shanghai: Presbyterian Mission Press.

Ellis, Henry. [1817] 1973. *Journal of the proceedings of the late embassy to China.* London: John Murray. Reprint. Wilmington, DE: Scholarly Resources.

Elvin, Mark. 1973. *The pattern of the Chinese past.* Stanford: Stanford University Press.

———. 1975a. On water control and management during the Ming and Ch'ing periods: A review article. *CSWT* 3, 3:82–103.

———. 1975b. Skills in late traditional China. In Perkins, ed. 1975, 85–113.

Fairbank, John K. [1953] 1964. *Trade and diplomacy on the China coast. The opening of the treaty ports 1842–1854.* 2d ed. Cambridge, MA: Harvard University Press.

———, ed. 1968. *The Chinese world order. Traditional China's foreign relations.* Cambridge, MA: Harvard University Press.

Fairbank, John K. and Teng Ssu-yu, eds. 1961a. *Ch'ing administration: Three studies.* Harvard-Yenching Institute Studies, no. 19. Cambridge, MA: Harvard University Press.

———. 1961b. On the transmission of Ch'ing documents. In Fairbank and Teng 1961a, 1–35.

———. 1961c. On the types and uses of Ch'ing documents. In Fairbank and Teng 1961a, 36–106.

———. 1961d. On the Ch'ing tributary system. In Fairbank and Teng 1961a, 107–245.

Fairbank, John K. and Kwang-ching Liu, eds. 1980. *The Cambridge History of China. Vol. 11. Late Ch'ing, 1800–1911, pt. 2.* Cambridge: Cambridge University Press.

Farmer, Edward L. 1976. *Early Ming government: The evolution of dual capitals.* Cambridge, MA: East Asian Research Center, Harvard University.

Farquhar, David M. 1968. The origins of the Manchus' Mongolian policy. In Fairbank, ed. 1968, 198–205.

Fay, Peter Ward. 1975. *The Opium War, 1840–1842.* Chapel Hill, NC: University of North Carolina Press.

Feng Daoli. 1840. *Huaiyang shuili tushuo* (Maps and explanations on water control in the Huaiyang region). 1 *juan.* N.p.

Feuerwerker, Albert. 1984. The state and the economy in late imperial China. *Theory and Society* 13, 3:297–326.

Feuerwerker, Albert, Rhoads Murphey, and Mary C. Wright, eds. 1967. *Approaches to modern Chinese history.* Berkeley: University of California Press.

Finnane, Antonia. 1984a. The administration of water control under the Qing: The case of Xiahe, 1684–1796. Conference paper, biennial meeting, Asian Studies Association of Australia, Adelaide University, Adelaide, Australia, 13–19 May.

———. 1984b. Bureaucracy and responsibility: A reassessment of the River Administration under the Qing. *Papers on Far Eastern History* (Australian National University) 30:161–98 (September).

———. 1993. Yangzhou: A central place in the Qing empire. In Johnson 1993a, 117–49.

Fisher, Carney T. 1977. The great ritual controversy in Ming China. Ph.D. diss. University of Michigan.

———. 1990. *The chosen one: Succession and adoption in the court of Ming Shizong*. Sydney: Allen and Unwin.

Fisher, Thomas Stephen. 1974. Lu Liu-Liang (1629–83) and the Tseng Ching case (1728–33). Ph.D. diss., Princeton University.

Fitzpatrick, Merrilyn. 1979. Local interests and the anti-pirate administration in China's South-east, 1555–1565. *CSWT* 4, 2:1–50

Flessel, Klaus. 1974. *Der Huang-ho und die historische Hydrotechnik in China*. Tubingen: IBM-Composersatz.

Fletcher, Joseph F. 1968. China and Central Asia, 1368–1884. In Fairbank, ed. 1968, 206–24.

———. 1978a. Ch'ing Inner Asia c. 1800. In *CHC* 10, 35–106.

———. 1978b. The heyday of the Ch'ing order in Mongolia, Sinkiang and Tibet. In *CHC* 10, 351–408.

Fu Zehong. 1725. *Xingshui jinjian* (China's river systems). 175 *juan*. British Library, Oriental Collection: 15275, c, 6, London.

Fu Zhonglan. 1985. *Zhongguo Yunhe chengshi fazhanshi* (History of the development of cities along the Grand Canal). 2 vols. Chengdu: Renmin.

Fuyin baokan ziliao (Reprinted materials from periodicals and newspapers). 1985–89 Beijing.

Gandar, Domin. [1894] 1903. *Le canal impérial: étude historique et descriptive*. Variétés sinologiques, no. 4. Shanghai: The Catholic Mission.

Gardella, Robert P. 1992. Qing administration of the tea trade: Four facets over three centuries. In Leonard and Watt, 1992a, 97–118.

[*Qinding*] *Gongbu celi* (Regulations of the Board of Works). Jiaqing 20 [1815]. 142 *juan*. N.p.

———. Jiaqing 24 [1819]. 136 *juan*. N.p.

Goodrich, Luther Carrington. 1935. *The literary inquisition of Ch'ien-lung*. Baltimore: Waverly Press.

Goodrich, L. Carrington and Fang Chaoying, eds. 1976. *Dictionary of Ming biography, 1368–1644*. 2 vols. New York: Columbia University Press.

Grand Canal of China, The. 1984. Ed. and comp. *New China News* and *South China Morning Post*. Hong Kong: *South China Morning Post*.

Greer, Charles. 1979. *Water management in the Yellow River basin of China*. Austin: University of Texas Press.

Gugong jikan (National Palace Museum Quarterly), Taibei.

Guo Shu. 1982. Hongze Hu liangbainian de shuiwei (Hongze Lake water levels during a two-hundred year period). *Kexue yanjiu taolun ji* 12:47–60.

Guo Songyi. 1985. Qing qianqi Tianjin de haishang jiaotong (Maritime transportation of Tianjin in the early Qing period). *Tianjin shizhi* (Historical records of Tianjin) 3:24–40.

Gutzlaff, Karl. [1852] 1972. *The life of Taou-Kwang, late emperor of China.* . . . Reprint. Wilmington, DE: Scholarly Resources.

Guy, R. Kent. 1987. *The emperor's Four Treasuries: Scholars and the state in the late Ch'ien- lung era*. Cambridge, MA: Council on East Asian Studies, Harvard University.

Harding, Harry. 1987. *China's second revolution: Reform after Mao.* Washington, D.C.: The Brookings Institution.

He Changling. [1826a]. 1965. *Huangchao jingshi wenbian* (Essays on statecraft during the Qing dynasty). Comp. Wei Yuan. 120 *juan*. Prefaces dated 1826 and 1873. Reprint. Taibei: Shijie.

———. 1826b. *Jiangsu Daoguang Liunian fen haiyun quan'an* (Complete record of Jiangsu sea transport in Daoguang six). 12 *juan*. N.p. Microfilm.

———. 1826c. *Jiangsu haiyun quan'an* (Complete record of Jiangsu sea transport). 12 *juan*.

———. 1827. *Huangchao jingshi wenbian* (Essays on statecraft during the Qing dynasty) Wei Yuan, comp. 120 *juan* . Compiler's preface, 1826. N.p.

Hinton, Harold C. 1970. *The grain tribute system of China (1845–1911).* Cambridge, MA: East Asian Research Center, Harvard University.

Ho Ping-ti and Tsou Tang, eds. 1968. *China in crisis.* 3 Vols. Chicago: University of Chicago Press.

Hoshi Ayao. 1938. Early Ming grain transport. Edwin O. Reischauer, trans. *HJAS* 3, 2:183–85.

———. 1960. Shinmatsu kōun yori kaiun eno tenkai (Late Qing change from canal to sea transport of tribute grain). In *Tōyoshi ronso.* Tokyo: Kodansha.

———. 1970. *The Ming tribute grain system.* Trans. Mark Elvin. Michigan Abstracts of Chinese and Japanese History, no. 1. Ann Arbor: Center for Chinese Studies, University of Michigan.

———. 1971. *Tai unga: Chūgoku no sōun* (The Grand Canal and Chinese grain transport). Tokyo: Kōndo shuppansha.

―――. 1980. Transportation in the Ming dynasty. *Acta Asiatica* 38: 1–30.

Hou Chi-ming and Tzong-shian Yu, eds. 1979. *Modern Chinese economic history*. Taibei: Institute of Economics, Academia Sinica.

Hsi, Angela. 1975. Wu San-kuei in 1644: A reappraisal. *JAS* 34, 2:443–53.

Hsiao Kung-chuan. 1960. *Rural China: Imperial control in the nineteenth century*. Seattle: University of Washington Press.

Hsu, Immanuel C. Y. 1964a. Russia's special position in China during the early Ch'ing period. *Slavic Review* 13, 4:688–700.

―――. 1964b. British mediation of China's war with Yakub Beg. 1877. *Central Asiatic Journal* (Leiden) 9:2:142–49 (June).

―――. 1965a. The great policy date in China, 1874: Maritime defense versus frontier defense. *HJAS* 25: 212–28.

―――. 1965b. *The Ili crisis: A study of Sino-Russian diplomacy, 1871–1881*. Oxford: Oxford University Press.

Hu Ch'ang-tu. 1954–55. The Yellow River administration in the Ch'ing dynasty. *FEQ* 14:505–513.

Huang Kuo-shu and Wang Yeh-chien. 1981. The secular movement of grain prices in China, 1763–1910. *Academia Economic Papers* 9, 1:1–27.

Huang Pei. 1967. Aspects of Ch'ing autocracy: An institutional study, 1644–1735. *Tsinghua Journal of Chinese Studies*, n.s. 6, 1–2 (combined issue):105–48.

―――. 1974. *Autocracy at work. A study of the Yung-cheng period, 1723–1735*. Bloomington, IN: Indiana University Press.

———, ed. 1981. The early Ch'ing dynasty: State and society, 1601–1722 (1). Introduction. *Chinese Studies in History* 14, 4:3–10.

———. 1985. The Grand Council of the Ch'ing dynasty: A historiographical study. *Bulletin of the School of Oriental and African Studies* (University of London) 48, 3:502–15.

———. 1994. The confidential memorial system of the Qing dynasty reconsidered. *Bulletin of the School of Oriental and African Studies* 57, 329–38.

Huang, Ray. 1964. The Grand Canal during the Ming dynasty, 1368–1644. Ph.D. diss., University of Michigan.

———. 1969. Fiscal administration during the Ming dynasty. In Hucker, ed. 1969, 73–128.

———. 1974. *Taxation and government finance in sixteenth century Ming China*. London: Cambridge University Press.

———. 1981. *1587. A year of no significance: The Ming dynasty in decline*. New Haven: Yale University Press.

Huanghe shuili shi shuyao (An outline history of Yellow River conservancy). 1982. Edited by Bureau of Water Conservancy Commission on Yellow River Water Conservancy. Beijing: Shuili dianli.

[*Qinding*] *Hubu caoyun quanshu* (The Board of Revenue's complete book on grain transport). [1766] 1969. 88 *juan*. Taibei: Chengwen.

———. 1845. Pan Shi'en, comp. 92 *juan*.

———. 1875 completed. 1876 printed. Cailing, comp. 96 *juan*.

Hubu celi (Regulations of the Board of Revenue). 1831. 99 *juan*.

[*Qingding*] *Hubu celi* (Regulations of the Board of Revenue). 1838. 15 *juan*.

———. 1865. 100 *juan*.

———. 1874. 100 *juan*; index 1 *juan*.

Hucker, Charles O. 1958. Governmental organization of the Ming dynasty. *HJAS* 21:1–66.

———. 1961. *The traditional Chinese state in Ming times*. Tucson, AZ: University of Arizona Press.

———. 1966. *The censorial system of Ming China*. Stanford: Stanford University Press.

———, ed. 1969. *Chinese government in Ming times: Seven studies*. New York: Columbia University Press.

———. 1975. *China's imperial past: An introduction to Chinese history and culture*. Stanford: Stanford University Press.

———. 1985. *A dictionary of official titles in imperial China*. Stanford: Stanford University Press.

Hummel, Arthur W., ed. [1943–44] 1967. *Eminent Chinese of the Ch'ing period, 1644–1912*. 2 vols. in one. Washington, D.C.: U.S. Government Printing Office. Reprint. Taibei: Chengwen.

Im, Kaye Soon. 1981. The rise and decline of the eight Banner garrisons in the Ch'ing period (1644–1911): A study of the Kuang-chou, Hang-chou, and Ching-chou garrisons. Ph.D. diss., University of Illinois, Champaign-Urbana.

Jiaobu tingjidang (Record book of court letter drafts). National Palace Museum, Taibei.

Jinshi Zhongguo jingshi sixiang yantao huilun wenji (Proceedings of the Conference on the Theory of Statecraft of Modern China). 25–27 August 1983. Taibei: Institute of Modern History, Academia Sinica.

Johnson, Linda Cook, ed. 1993a. *Cities of Jiangnan in late imperial China: Suny Series in Chinese local history*. Albany, NY: State University of New York Press.

Junjidang (Grand Council Archives). National Palace Museum, Taibei.

———. 1993b. Shanghai: An emerging Jiangnan port, 1683–1840. In Johnson 1993a, 151–81.

Kahn, Harold L. 1965. Some mid-Ch'ing views of the monarch. *JAS* 24, 2:29–43.

———. 1967a. The education of a prince: The emperor learns his roles. In Feuerwerker, Murphey and Wright, 1967, 15–44.

———. 1967b. The politics of filiality: Justification for imperial action in eighteenth-century China. *JAS* 26, 2:197–203.

———. 1971. *Monarchy in the emperor's eyes: Image and reality in the Ch'ien-lung reign*. Cambridge, MA: Harvard University Press.

Kelley, David E. 1982. Temples and tribute fleets: The Luo sect and boatmen's associations in the eighteenth century. *Modern China* 8, 3:361–91.

———. 1986. Sect and society: The evolution of the Luo sect among Qing dynasty grain tribute boatmen, 1700–1850. Ph.D. diss., Harvard University.

———. 1987. Mobilization and control of hired labor in the early Qing grain tribute and copper industries. Annual meeting, Association for Asian Studies, Boston, 10 April.

Kessler, Lawrence D. 1971. Chinese scholars and the early Manchu state. *HJAS* 31:179–200.

———. 1976. *K'ang-hsi and the consolidation of Ch'ing rule*. Chicago: University of Chicago Press.

King, F. H. H. 1965. *Money and monetary policy in China.* Cambridge, MA: Harvard University Press.

Kishimoto-Nakayama, Mio. 1984. The Kangxi depression and early Qing local markets. *Modern China* 10, 2:23, 1–32.

Knapp, Ronald, ed. 1980. *China's island frontier: Studies in the historical geography of Taiwan.* Honolulu: University Press of Hawaii.

Kuhn, Philip A. 1970. *Rebellion and its enemies in late Imperial China: militarization and social structure, 1796–1864.* Cambridge, MA: Harvard University Press.

———. 1975. Local self-governance under the Republic: Problems of control, autonomy and mobilization. In Wakeman and Grant 1975, 257–98.

Kwong, Luke S. 1983. Imperial authority in crisis: An interpretation of the coup d'etat. *MAS* 17, 2:221–38.

Lai Chi-kong. 1992. The Qing state and merchant enterprise: The China Merchants' Company, 1872–1902. In Leonard and Watt, 1992a, 139–55.

Lamb, Alistair. 1968. *Asian frontiers.* Sydney: F. W. Cheshire.

Lee, James. 1978. Migration and expansion in Chinese history. In *Human migration: Patterns and policies..* William H. McNeill and Ruth S. Adams, eds. 20–47. Bloomington: Indiana University Press.

———. 1982. Food supply and population growth in southwest China, 1250–1850. *JAS* 41, 4:711–45.

Lee, Robert H. G. 1970. *The Manchurian frontier in Ch'ing history.* Cambridge, MA: Harvard University Press.

Lee, Sherman E. 1954. *Chinese landscape painting*. New York: Harper and Row.

Leonard, Jane Kate. 1979. Wei Yuan and images of the Nanyang. *CSWT* 4, 1:23–57.

———. 1984. *Wei Yuan and China's rediscovery of the maritime world*. Cambridge, MA: Council on East Asian Studies, Harvard University.

———. 1986. A study of the court letter and the canal administration during the Ch'ing period. *The American Asian Review* 4, 3:1–28.

———. 1987. Qing perceptions of geopolitical reality in the 1820s. *The American Asian Review* 5, 2:63–97.

———. 1988a. "Controlling from afar": Open communications and the Tao-kuang Emperor's control of Grand Canal-grain transport management. *MAS* (Cambridge University) 22, 4:665–99 (October).

———. 1988b. Geopolitical reality and the disappearance of the maritime frontier in Qing times. *The American Neptune* 48, 4:230–36.

———. 1989. Economic and strategic imperatives in Grand Canal-grain transport management in the 1820s. Conference paper, northeast regional meeting, Association for Asian Studies, Harvard University, Cambridge, MA, 12 October.

———. 1992a. The state's resources and the people's livelihood (*Guoji minsheng*): The Daoguang Emperor's Dilemmas about Grand Canal restoration, 1825. In Leonard and Watt 1992a, 47–73.

———. 1992b. Qing recruitment of private shippers in the 1826 sea transport experiment. Proceedings of the American Historical Association, Reference no. 10485, session no. 107.

———. 1993. Boundaries of state power in late Qing grain transport. Conference paper, Traditional Institutions and Values in Contemporary China, East–West Center, University of Hawaii, Honolulu, HI, 20–22 May.

Leonard, Jane Kate and John R. Watt, eds. 1992a. *To achieve security and wealth: The Qing imperial state and the economy, 1644–1911.* Cornell East Asia Series. Ithaca, NY: East Asia Program.

———. 1992b. Introduction. In Leonard and Watt 1992a, 1–7.

Leung Yuen-sang. 1990. *The Shanghai taotai: Linkage in a changing society, 1843–90.* Honolulu, HI: University of Hawaii Press.

Li Shixu with Zhang Jing and Pan Xi'en. 1832. *Xuxingshui jinjian* (An account of waterways). 1 *juan* maps; 156 *juan*. In *Guoxue jiben congshu.* N.p. Reprint: 1970. Taibei: Wenhai.

Li Wenzhi. 1989. Qing Daoguanghou gaige caozhi yi (Post-Daoguang [reign] reforms in the grain system). *Zhongguo jingjishi yanjiu* 1:29–44.

Liao Pin. 1987. *The Grand Canal: An odyssey.* Beijing: Foreign Language Press.

Lieberthal, Kenneth and Michael Oksenberg. 1988. *Policy making in China: Leaders, structures, and processes.* Princeton: Princeton University Press.

Lieberthal, Kenneth, Joyce Kallgren, Roderick MacFarquhar, and Frederic Wakeman, Jr., eds. 1991. *Perspectives on modern China. Four anniversaries.* Armonk, NY: M.E. Sharpe.

Lin Man-houng. 1989. Currency and society: The monetary crisis and political-economic ideology of early nineteenth-century China. Ph.D. diss., Harvard University.

———. 1991a. A time in which grandsons beat their grandfathers: The rise of liberal political-economic ideas in the monetary crisis of the early nineteenth-century China. Circulated paper, Symposium on the Qing Imperial State and the Economy, 1644–1911, 22–23 February, University of Akron.

———. 1991b. Two social theories revealed: Statecraft controversies over China's monetary crisis, 1808–1854. *LIC* 12, 2:1–35.

Lin Qing. [1836] 1937. *Hegong qiju tushuo* (Illustrations and explanations of techniques of water conservancy and civil engineering). 4 *juan*. Shanghai: Shangwu.

———. 1841. *Huang yunhe kou qujin tushuo* (Maps of the Yellow River–Grand Canal junction, past and present). N.p., 337 pp. in 1 box.

Lin Renchuan. 1987. *Mingmo Qingchu siren haishang maoyi* (Private sea trade in late Ming-early Qing). Shanghai.

Lipman, Jonathan. 1981. The border world of Gansu, 1895–1935. Ph.D. diss., Stanford University.

Liu Danian. 1981. On the K'ang-hsi Emperor. Pamela Crossley, trans.*Chinese Studies in History* 14, 4:76–107.

Liu Deren. 1981. Lun Kangxi de zhihe gongji (On the Kangxi Emperor's achievements in river management). *FYBKZL*, K2, 14:115–20.

Liu Jiaju. 1981. The creation of the Chinese Banners in the early Ch'ing. *Chinese Studies in History* 14, 4:47–75 (Summer).

Liu Kwang-ching. 1962. *Anglo-American steamship rivalry in China, 1862–1874*. Cambridge, MA: Harvard University Press.

———. 1964. British-Chinese steamship rivalry in China, 1873–1885. In *The Economic development of China and Japan: Studies in economic history and political economy.* C.D. Cowan, ed., 49–78. London: Allen and Unwin.

———. 1968. Nineteenth-century China: The disintegration of the old order and the impact of the West. In Ho Ping-ti and Tsou Tang, eds. 1968, 1:93–178.

———. 1983a. Xu (Preface). In *Jinshi Zhongguo jingshi sixiang yantao huilun wenji* (Proceedings of the international conference on modern Chinese statecraft thought). Taibei: Institute of Modern History, Academia Sinica, 1–15.

———. 1983b. Wei Yuan zhi zhexue yu jingshi sixiang (Wei Yuan's philosophy and statecraft thought). In *Jinshi Zhongguo jingshi sixiang yantao huilun wenji* (Proceedings of the international conference on modern Chinese statecraft thought). Taibei: Institute of Modern History, Academia Sinica, 359–90.

———, ed. 1990. *Orthodoxy in late imperial China*. Berkeley: University of California Press.

Liu Lu. 1983. Kangxi nanxun jianlun (A discussion of the Kangxi Emperor's southern tours). *Gugong bowuyuan yuankan* (Beijing) 2:70–79.

Liu, T. J. 1970. Dike construction in Ching-chow. Harvard East Asian Research Center. *Papers on China* 23:1–28.

Lo Jung-pang. 1953. The controversy over grain conveyance during the reign of Khubilai Khan 1260 to 1294. *FEQ* 13:262–85.

———. 1955. The emergence of China as a sea power during the late Sung and early Yuan periods. *FEQ* 14, 4:489–503.

———. 1958. The decline of the early Ming navy. *Oriens Extremus* 5:149–68.

Lojewski, Frank A. 1973. Confucian reformers and local vested interests: The Su-Sung-T'ai tax reduction of 1863 and its aftermath. Ph.D. diss. University of California-Davis.

———. 1976. Local reform and its opponents: Feng Kuei-fen's struggle for equality in taxation. In Cohen and Schrecker, 128–36.

Lowdermilk, W. C. 1924. Erosion and floods in the Yellow River watershed. *Journal of Forestry* 22, 6:11–18 (October).

———. 1925. A forester's search for forests in China. *American Forests and Forest Life* 31: 379–90.

———. 1926. Forest destruction and slope denudation in the province of Shansi. *China Journal of Science and Arts* 4, 127–35.

Lu Yitong and Wu Tang, comps. 1855. *Qinghe* [Jiangsu] *xianzhi* (Gazeteer of Qinghe district). 24 *juan*; one head *juan*.

Ma Xinyi, ed. 1867. *Zhejiang haiyun caoliang quan'an* (Compendium on sea transport of tribute grain from Zhejiang). 20 *juan*.

Mancall, Mark. 1971. *Russia and China: Their diplomatic relations to 1728*. Harvard East Asian Series. Cambridge, MA: Harvard University Press.

———. 1984. *China at the center*. New York: Free Press.

Marks, Robert B. 1991. Rice prices, food supply, and market structure in eighteenth-century South China. *LIC* 12, 2:64–116.

Masato Matsui. 1969. The 'Wo-k'ou disturbances' of the 1550s. *East Asian Occasional Papers*, University of Hawaii 1:97–109.

Mayers, William Frederick. [1897] 1966. *The Chinese government: A manual of Chinese titles, categorically arranged and explained, with an appendix*. 3d ed. Reprint. Taibei: Chengwen.

McElderry, Andrea. 1976. *Shanghai old-style banks (Ch'ien-chuang), 1800–1937*. Michigan Papers in Chinese Studies. Ann Arbor, MI: Center for Chinese Studies, University of Michigan.

———. 1992. Guarantors and guarantees in Qing government-business relations. In Leonard and Watt 1992a, 119–37.

Meng Sen. 1960. *Qingdai shi* (History of the Qing dynasty). 2d ed. Taibei: Zhengzhong.

Metzger, Thomas. 1962. T'ao Chu's reform of the Huaipei salt monopoly. Harvard East Asian Research Center. *Papers on China* 16:1–39.

———. 1970. The state and commerce in imperial China. *Asian and African Studies* 6:23–46.

———. 1972. The organizational capabilities of the Ch'ing state in the field of commerce: The Liang-Huai salt monopoly 1740–1840. In Willmott, ed. 1972, 9–45.

———. 1973. *The internal organization of Ch'ing bureaucracy: Legal, normative, and commercialization aspects.* Harvard Studies in East Asian Law, no. 7. Cambridge, MA: Harvard University Press.

———. 1977. On the roots of economic modernization in China: The increasing differentiation of the economy from the polity during late Ming and early Ch'ing times. In Institute of Economics, Academia Sinica, *Conference on Modern Chinese Economic History.* Taibei.

Miller, Harold L. 1974. Factional conflict and the integration of Ch'ing politics, 1660–1690. Ph.D. diss., George Washington University.

Millward, James A. 1991. Qing silk-horse trade with the Qazaqs in Yili and Tarbaghatai, 1758–1853. Annual meeting, Association for Asian Studies, New Orleans, LA, 13 April.

Morse, Hosea B. 1910–18. *The international relations of the Chinese empire.* 3 vols. London: Longmans, Green.

Murray, Dian H. 1987. *Pirates of the South China coast, 1790–1810*. Stanford: Stanford University Press.

Myers, Ramon H. 1974. Merchants and economic organization during the Ming and Ch'ing period: A review article. *CSWT* 3, 2:77–93.

Naquin, Susan. 1976. *Millenarian rebellion in China: The Eight Trigrams of 1813*. New Haven: Yale University Press.

Needham, Joseph. 1971. *Science and civilization in China*. Vol. 4, pt. 3, *Physics and physical technology: Civil engineering and nautics*. Cambridge: Cambridge University Press.

Ng Chin-keong. 1983. *Trade and society: The Amoy network on the China coast, 1683–1735*. Singapore: Singapore University Press.

Nickum, James E. 1974. *Hydraulic engineering and water resources in the People's Republic of China: Report of the U.S. Water Resources Delegation (August–September 1974)*. Stanford: U.S.-China Relations Program, Stanford University.

———, ed. 1981. *Water management organization in the People's Republic of China*. Armonk, NY: M. E. Sharpe.

Nieuhoff, P. E. 1665. *L'Ambassade [1655–1657] de la Compagnie Orientale des Provinces Unies vers l'Empereur de la Chine, ou Grand cam de Tartarie, faite par les Sieurs*. Pierre de Goyer and Jacob de Keyser... 2 pts. Leiden: de Meurs.

Nivison, David S. and Arthur F. Wright, eds. 1959. *Confucianism in action*. Stanford: Stanford University Press.

Oxnam, Robert B. 1975. *Manchu politics in the Oboi regency, 1661–1669*. Chicago: University of Chicago Press.

Parish, Henry William. [1792–93]. Drawings on Lord Macartney's embassy to China, 1792–93. Add. Ms. 33,931. Department of Manuscripts. British Library, London. Published by John

Barrow [1804] 1806. *Travels in China*. Second edition. London: T. Cadell.

———. 1792–1794. Maps of China, 1792–1794. Add. Ms. 19,822. Department of Manuscripts, British Library, London.Published by John Barrow [1804] 1806. *Travels in China*. Second edition. London: T. Cadell.

Pasternak, Boris. 1972a. *Kinship and community in two Chinese villages*. Stanford: Stanford University Press.

———. 1972b. The sociology of irrigation: Two Taiwanese villages. In Willmott, ed. 1972, 193–213.

Perdue, Peter C. 1982. Water control in the Dongting Lake region during the Ming and Qing periods. *JAS* 41, 4:747–65.

———. 1987a. *Exhausting the earth: State and peasant in Hunan, 1500–1850*. Cambridge, MA: Council on East Asian Studies, Harvard University.

———. 1987b. Dike labor in the Ming and Qing dynasties. Annual meeting, Association for Asian Studies, Boston, 9 April.

———. 1989. The West Route Army and the Silk Road: Grain supply and Qianlong's military campaigns in Northwest China (1755–1760). Unpublished ms.

———. 1991. Three Qing emperors and the northwest. Annual meeting, Association for Asian Studies, New Orleans, LA, 13 April.

———. 1992. The Qing state and the Gansu grain marker, 1739–1864. In Rawski and Li, eds., 100–25.

Perdue, Peter C. and R. Bin Wong. 1983. Famine's foes in Ch'ing China. *HJAS* 43, 1:291–332.

Petech, Lucien. 1950. *China and Tibet in the early 18th century: History of the establishment of the Chinese protectorate in Tibet.* Monographies du *T'oung Pao.* Leiden: E. J. Brill.

Playfair, George M. H. 1875. The grain transport system of China. Notes and statistics taken from the "Ta Ch'ing Hui Tien." *China Review* 3, 6:354–64.

Polachek, James M. 1976. Literati groups and literati politics in early nineteenth-century China. Ph.D. diss., University of California, Berkeley.

———. 1992. *The inner Opium War.* Cambridge, MA: Council on East Asian Relations, Harvard University.

Pritchard, Earl H. 1936. *The crucial years of early Anglo-Chinese relations, 1750–1800.* Pullman, WA: State College of Washington.

Proceedings of the Conference on the Theory of Statecraft of Modern China. (Jinshi Zhongguo jingshi sixiang yantao huilun wenji) 25–27 August 1983. Taibei: Institute of Modern History, Academia Sinica.

Qing Xuanzong. 1824. *Yangzheng shuwu quanji dingben* (Collected literary works of Minning). 40 *juan.* Collected 1822.

Qingdai changjiang liu yu xi'nanguo Yuanhe liu Honglao dang'an shiliao. (Historical materials on the Yangzi River's flow from the southwest border to the Hongze marshes). 1991. 16 vols.

Qingdai chuanji congkan (Collection of Qing dynasty biographies). 1985. 205 vols. Taibei: Mingwen.

Qinghe [Jiangsu] *xianzhi* (Gazeteer of Qinghe district). 1855. Lu Yitong and Wu Tang, comps. 24 *juan;* 1 head *juan.*

Qingshi (History of the Qing dynasty). 1961. Taibei: Guofang yanjiu yuan.

Quan Hansheng, and Richard A. Kraus. 1975. *Mid-Ch'ing rice markets and trade: An essay in price history*. Cambridge, MA: East Asian Research Center, Harvard University.

Rawski, Thomas G., and Lillian M. Li, eds. 1992. *Chinese history in economic perspective*. Berkeley: University of California Press.

Reischauer, Edwin O., trans. 1955a. *Ennin's diary: The record of a pilgimage to China in search of the law*. New York: Ronald Press.

———. 1955b. *Ennin's travels in T'ang China*. New York: Ronald Press.

Reynolds, Graham. 1947. British artists abroad. II. Alexander and Chinnery in China. *The Geographical Magazine* 20, 5:203–12 (September).

Rossabi, Morris. 1975. *China and Inner Asia from 1368 to the present day*. London: Thames and Hudson, 1975.

———. 1979. Muslim and Central Asian revolts. In Spence and Wills, eds. 1979, 167–99.

———. 1988. *Khubilai Khan: His life and times*. Berkeley: University of California Press.

Rowe, William T. 1983. Hu Lin-i's reform of the grain tribute system in Hupeh, 1855–1858. *CSWT* 4, 10:33–86.

———. 1984. *Hankow: Commerce and society in a Chinese city, 1796–1889*. Stanford: Stanford University Press.

———. 1991. State and market in mid-Qing economic thought: The career of Chen Hongmou (1696–1771). Symposium on the Qing Imperial State and the Economy, University of Akron, 22–23 February.

Schoppa, R. Keith. 1987. Power, legitimacy, and symbol: Local elites and the Jute Creek embankment case. Conference on Chinese Local Elites and Patterns of Dominance, 20–24 August. N.p.

———. 1989. *Xiang Lake: Nine centuries of Chinese life.* New Haven: Yale University Press.

Schram, Stuart, ed. 1985. *The scope of state power in China.* New York: St. Martin's Press.

Scroll map of Grand Canal. 18C. British Library, Oriental Collection: 2362, London.

Scroll map of Yellow River. 18C. British Library, Oriental Collection: 13990 (35A), London.

Shang Hongkui. 1981a. Kangxi nanxun yu zhili Huanghe (The Kangxi Emperor's southern tours and harnessing the Yellow River). *FYBKZL*, K2, 16:111–20.

———. 1981b. The process of economic recovery, stabilization, and the accomplishments of the early Ch'ing, 1681–1735. *Chinese Studies in History* 15, 1–2; 19–61.

Shangyudang fangben (Record book of ordinary Grand Council affairs). Grand Council Archives, National Palace Museum, Taibei.

Shen Bing. 1960. *Huanghe tongkao* (A comprehensive examination of the Yellow River). Taibei: Zhonghua.

Shulman, Anna See Ping Leon. 1989. Copper, copper cash, and government controls in Ch'ing China (1644–1795). Ph.D. diss. University of Maryland.

Shyrock, John K. [1932] 1966. *The origin and development of the state cult of Confucius.* New York: Paragon Book Reprint Corp.

Sinclair, Kevin. 1987. *The Yellow River: A 4000 year journey through Chinese history.* San Francisco: China Books and Periodical.

Skinner, G. William. 1976. Mobility strategies in late imperial China: A regional systems analyses. In *Regional analyses, vol. 1: Economic systems*. Carol A. Smith, ed. New York: Academic Press, 327–64.

Smith, Kent C. 1968. O-erh-t'ai and the Yung-cheng Emperor. *CSWT* 1, 8:10–15.

So Kwan-wai. 1975. *Japanese piracy in Ming China during the sixteenth century*. East Lansing: Michigan State University Press.

Spence, Jonathan D. 1966. *Ts'ao Yin and the K'ang-hsi Emperor: Bondservant and master*. New Haven: Yale University Press.

———. 1967. The seven ages of K'ang-hsi (1654–1722). *JAS* 26, 2:205–11.

———. 1974. *Emperor of China: A self-portrait of K'ang-hsi*. New York: Vintage.

Spence, Jonathan D. and John E. Wills, Jr., eds. 1979. *From Ming to Ch'ing: Conquest, region, and continuity in seventeenth-century China*. New Haven: Yale University Press.

Staunton, George. 1797. *An authentic account of an embassy from the King of Great Britain to the Emperor of China*. 2 vols. 1 folio. London: George Nicol.

Struve, Lynn A. 1979. Ambivalence and action. Some frustrated scholars of the K'ang-hsi period. In Spence and Wills, eds., pp. 321–65.

———. 1984. *The southern Ming, 1644–1662*. New Haven: Yale University Press.

———. 1989. Early Qing officials as chroniclers of the conquest. *LIC* 10, 1:1–26.

Sun E-tu Zen. 1961. *Ch'ing administrative terms: A translation of the terminology of the Six Boards with explanatory notes.* Cambridge, MA: Harvard University Press.

———. 1962–63. The Board of Revenue in 19th-century China. *HJAS* 24:175–227.

———. 1967. Mining labor in the Ch'ing period. In Feuerwerker, Murphey, and Wright, eds. 1967, 45–67.

———. 1968. Ch'ing government and the mineral industries before 1800. *JAS* 27, 4:835–45.

———. 1992. The Finance Ministry (Hubu) and its relationship to the private economy in the Qing times. In Leonard and Watt 1992a, 9–20.

Sun E-tu Zen and John deFrancis. 1956. *Chinese social history: Translations of selected studies.* Washington, D.C., American Council of Learned Societies.

Sun E-tu Zen and Sun Shiou-chuan, trans. 1966. *"Thien Kung Khai Wu": Chinese technology in the seventeenth century.* By Song Ying-xing. University Park, PA: Pennsylvania State University Press.

Sung Lien. 1956. *Economic structure of the Yuan dynasty: Translation of chapters 93 and 94 of the "Yuan shih."* Herbert Franz Schurman, trans. Harvard-Yenching Institute Studies 16. Cambridge, MA: Harvard University.

Ta Qing lichao shilu (Veritable records of the successive reigns of the Qing dynasty). [1937] 1964. Mukden. Reprint. Taibei.

Tien Ju-kang. 1956. Shiqi shiji zhi shijiu shiji Zhongguo fanchuan zai Dongnan yazhou hangyun he shangye shang de diwei (The position of Chinese junks in shipping and trade with Southeast Asia from the seventeenth century to the middle of the nineteenth century). *LSYJ* 8:1–21.

———. 1982. Causes of the decline in China's overseas trade between the 15th and 18th centuries. *Papers on Far Eastern History* (Australian National University), 25:31–44.

Tong Xun. 1861. *Jiangbei yun cheng* (The Jiangbei transport journey). 40 *juan*; 1 head *juan*.

Toyama Gunji. 1938. Water transportation in T'ang times. Edwin Reischauer, trans. *HJAS* 3, 2:202–4.

Tregear, Thomas R. 1965. *A geography of China*. Chicago: Aldine Press.

———. 1980. *China: A geographical survey*. New York: Halsted Press.

Ts'ao Kai-fu. 1965. The rebellion of the Three Feudatories against the Manchu throne in China, 1673–1681: Its setting and significance. Ph.D. diss., Columbia University.

Twitchett, Denis. 1957. The fragment of the T'ang ordinances of the Department of Waterways discovered at Tun-huang. *Asia Major* 6:23–79.

———. 1961. Some remarks on irrigation under the T'ang. *T'oung Pao* 48:175–94.

———. 1963. *Financial administration under the T'ang dynasty*. Cambridge: Cambridge University Press.

———. 1979. *The Cambridge history of China. 3, Sui-T'ang China, 589–906, pt. 1*. Cambridge: Cambridge University Press.

Twitchett, Denis and John K. Fairbank, eds. 1978. *The Cambridge history of China. 10, Late Ch'ing 1800–1911, pt. 1*. Cambridge: Cambridge University Press.

Twitchett, Denis and Michael Loewe, eds. 1986. *The Cambridge history of China. 1, The Ch'in-Han empires, 221 B.C.–A.D. 220*. Cambridge: Cambridge University Press.

Twitchett, Denis and Frederick W. Mote. 1988. *The Cambridge history of China. 7, The Ming Dynasty, 1368–1644, pt. 1*. Cambridge: Cambridge University Press.

Van-Braam Houckgeest, Andre Everard. 1798. *An authentic account of the Dutch East-India Company to the Court of the Emperor of China, 1794 and 1795;* (subsequent to that of the Earl of Macartney). M. L. E. Moreau de Saint-Merg, trans. London: R. Phillips.

Van Slyke, Lyman P. 1988. *Yangtze: Nature, history, and the river*. Reading, MA: Addison-Wesley.

Vogel, Hans Ulrich. 1983. Chinese central monetary policy and Yunnan copper mining in the early Qing (1644–1800). Ph.D. diss., University of Zurich.

———. 1987. Chinese monetary policy, 1644–1800. *LIC* 8, 2:1–52.

Wakeman, Frederic, Jr. 1985. *The great enterprise: The Manchu reconstruction of the imperial order in seventeenth century China*. 2 vols. Berkeley: University of California Press.

Wakeman, Frederic, Jr. and Carolyn Grant, eds. 1975. *Conflict and control in late imperial China*. Berkeley: University of California Press.

Waldron, Arthur. 1990. *The Great Wall of China*. Cambridge: Cambridge University Press.

Wang Gungwu. 1958. The Nanhai trade. A study of the early history of Chinese trade in the South China Sea. *Journal of the Malayan Branch, Royal Asiatic Society* 31, 2:1–135.

———. 1964. The opening of relations between China and Malacca, 1403–5. In John Bastin and R. Roolvink, eds., 87–104.

———. 1968. Early Ming relations with Southeast Asia: A background essay. In Fairbank, 1968, 34–62.

———. 1970. China and Southeast Asia, 1402–1424. In Jerome Ch'en and Nicholas Tarling, eds., 375–401.

———. 1973. The middle Yangtse in T'ang politics. In Wright and Twitchett, eds., 193–235.

Wang Jingyang. 1984. Qingdai Tongwaxiang gaidao qian de hehuan jiqi zhili (River disasters and their control in the Qing period prior to the change of course at Tongwaxiang). *Huanghe shi luncong.* Shanghai: Fudan University Press.

Wang Xianqian and Jiang Liangqi, comps. N.d. *Shi'er chao donghualu* (Record [of important documents of the twelve reigns of Qing] from the [State Historiographer's Office inside the] Donghua Gate). Taibei: Wenhai.

Wang Yeh-chien. 1971. The fiscal importance of the land tax during the Ch'ing period. *JAS* 30, 4:829–42.

———. 1973a. *An estimate of the land tax collection in China, 1753 and 1908.* Cambridge, MA: East Asian Research Center, Harvard University.

———. 1973b. *Land taxation in imperial China, 1750–1911.* Cambridge, MA: Harvard University Press.

———. 1973c. Some reflections on the economy of China under the Ch'ing 1644–1911. *Shihuo yuekan* 2, 11:541–50 (February).

———. 1973d. The secular trend of prices during the Ch'ing period. *Xianggang Zhongwen daxue, Zhongguo wenhua yanjiu so xuebao* (Journal of the Institute of Chinese Studies, Chinese University of Hong Kong) 5, 2:441–45.

———. 1978. Jindai Zhongguo nongye de chengzhang ji qi weiji (The growth and crisis of agriculture in modern China). *Bulletin of the Institute of Modern Chinese History, Academia Sinica* 7:355–70.

———. 1979. Evolution of the Chinese Monetary System, 1644–1850. In Hou and Yu, eds. 1979, 425–52.

———. 1986a. Secular trends of rice prices in the Yangzi delta 1638–1935. Workshop on International Price History, Ninth International Economic History Congress, Bern, Switzerland.

———. 1986b. Food supply in eighteenth-century Fukien. *LIC* 7, 2:80–117 (December).

———. 1992. Secular trends in rice prices in the Yangzi delta, 1638–1935. In Rawski and Li, eds., 35–68.

———. 1993. Grain prices and market regions in Qing China. Midwest Conference, Association for Asian Studies, Cleveland, Ohio. 1–3 October. 1–35.

Watt, John R. 1972. *The district magistrate in late imperial China.* New York: Columbia University Press.

———. 1977. The yamen and urban administration. In Skinner, ed. 1977b, 354–90.

Wechsler, Howard J. 1974. *Mirror to the Son of Heaven: Wei Cheng at the court of T'ang T'ai- tsung.* New Haven: Yale University Press.

Wei Peh-t'i. 1979. Internal security and coastal control: Juan Yuan and pirate suppression in Chekiang 1799–1809. *CSWT* 4, 2:83–112.

Wei Yuan. [1878] 1964. *Guweitang neiwaiji* (Collected writings from the Guwei Hall). 10 *juan*. Reprint. Taibei: Wenhai.

Widmer, Eric. 1976. *The Russian ecclesiastical mission in Peking during the eighteenth century.* Cambridge, MA: East Asian Research Center, Harvard University.

Wiens, Herold. 1955. Riverine and coastal junks in China's commerce. *Economic geography* 31:248–64.

Will, Pierre-Etienne. 1980. Un cycle hydraulique en Chine: La province du Hubei du XVIe au XIXe siècles. *Bulletin de l'École française d'extrême-orient* 68:261–87.

———. 1985. State intervention in the administration of a hydraulic infrastructure: The example of Hubei province in premodern times. In Schram, ed. 1985, 295–352.

———. 1990. *Bureaucracy and famine in eighteenth-century China.* Elborg Forster, trans. Rev. ed. Stanford: Stanford University Press.

Will, Pierre-Etienne, and R. Bin Wong with James Lee. 1991. *Nourish the people: The state civilian granary system in China, 1650–1850.* Ann Arbor, MI: Center for Chinese Studies, University of Michigan.

[Williams, S. Wells.] 1850. Course and topography of the Hwang-ho or Yellow River. *Chinese Repository* 19:499–509.

Williamson, A. 1866. Notes of a journey from Peking to Chefoo via Grand Canal, Yen-chow-foo, etc. JRAS:NCB, n.s. no. 3:1–25 (December).

———. 1867. Notes on the north of China, its production and communications. *JRAS:NCB,* n.s. no. 4:33–63 (December).

Willmott, W. E., ed. 1972. *Economic organization in Chinese society.* Stanford: Stanford University Press.

Wills, John E. 1974. *Pepper, guns, and parleys: The Dutch East India Company in China, 1622–1681.* Cambridge, MA: Harvard University Press.

———. 1979. Maritime China from Wang Chih to Shih Lang: Themes in peripheral history. In Spence and Wells, eds. 1979, 201–238.

Wong, R. Bin and Peter Perdue. 1983. Famine's foes in Ch'ing China. *HJAS* 43, 1:291–332.

Wolters, O. W. 1967. *Early Indonesian commerce*. Ithaca, NY: Cornell University Press.

———. 1970. *The fall of Srivijaya in Malay history*. Ithaca: Cornell University Press.

Worcester, G. R. G. 1966. *Sail and sweep in China*. London: Her Majesty's Stationery Office.

———. 1971. *The junks and sampans of the Yangtze*. Annapolis, MD: Naval Institute Press.

Wright, Arthur F. 1978. *The Sui dynasty*. New York: Alfred Knopf.

Wright, Arthur F. and Denis Twitchett, eds. 1973. *Perspectives on the T'ang*. New Haven: Yale University Press.

Wu Han. 1936. Shilun shiji qian zhi Zhongguo yu Nanyang (China and the Nanyang before the sixteenth century). *Qinghua xuebao* 11, 1:137–86.

Wu Jihua. 1961. *Mingdai haiyun ji yunhe de yanjiu* (A study of sea transport and the Grand Canal in the Ming). Special publication no. 43, Academia Sinica, Institute of History and Philology. Taibei: Commercial Press.

———. 1971. *Mingdai shehui jingjishi luncong* (Collected essays on the social-economic history of the Ming dynasty). Taibei.

Wu, Silas H. L. 1967. The memorial systems of the Ch'ing dynasty (1644–1911). *HJAS* 27:7–75.

———. 1968. Transmission of Ming memorials. *T'oung Pao* 54, 4–5:275–87.

———. 1970a. *Communication and imperial control in China: Evolution of the palace memorial system, 1693–1735*. Cambridge, MA: Harvard University Press.

―――. 1970b. Emperors at work: The daily schedules of the K'ang-hsi and Yung-cheng emperors, 1661–1735. *Tsinghua Journal of Chinese Studies*, n.s. 8, 1–2:210–27 (August).

―――. 1972. A note on the proper use of documents for historical studies: A rejoinder. *HJAS* 32:230–39.

―――. 1979. *Passages to power: K'ang-hsi and his heir apparent, 1661–1722*. Cambridge, MA: Harvard University Press.

Wu Tongju, comp. [1928] 1969. *Huaixi nianbiao quan pian* (Complete collection of historical tables of the Huai River system). 2 vols., 1066 pp., maps. In *Zhongguo shuili yaoji congbian* (Collection of important works on Chinese water conservancy). Pt. 1, no. 5, vol. 1–2. Taibei: Wenhai.

Yang Lien-sheng. 1969a. Economic aspects of public works in imperial China. In his *Excursions in Sinology*. Cambridge, MA: Harvard University Press, 191–248.

―――. 1969b. Ming local administration. In Hucker, ed. 1969, 1–10.

Yang Yafei. 1968. Shilun Mingdai caoyun fangshi de biange (The revolution in grain transportation during the Ming). *Mingdai jingji shi* 2:162–68.

Yang Zhengtai. 1986. Ming Qing shiqi Changjiang erbei yunhe chengzhen de tedian yu bianqian (Characteristics and changes of cities and towns on the Grand Canal north of the Yangzi during the Ming and Qing dynasties). *Lishi dili* 1:104–29.

Yu Bing-kun. 1982–83. "Reho mizha" gaoshi (An analysis of the secret letters from Jehol), *Gugong bowuyuan yuankan* (The National Palace Museum Quarterly, Beijing). In 2 parts: 1982, 1:3–16, 61; 1982, 2:70–85.

Zelin, Madeleine. 1980. Obstacles to reform in the Yung-cheng period: Low-level corruption and the Kiangnan tax clearance case.

University Seminar on Modern China, Columbia University, 13 March.

———. 1984. *The magistrate's tael: Rationalizing fiscal reform in eighteenth-century Ch'ing China.* Berkeley: University of California Press.

———. 1991. The structure of the Chinese economy during the Qing period: Some thoughts on the 150th anniversary of the Opium War. In Lieberthal et. al, eds., 31–67.

Zhang Jinqi and Wang Qiaonian. 1918. *Hegong yaoyi* (Discussion of river and canal works). In *Zhongguo shuili yaoji congbian*, 4th series, no. 37. Taibei: Wenhai.

Zhang Zhelang. 1942. *Qingdai de caoyun* (Grain tribute in the Qing dynasty). Taibei.

Zhao Erxun, et. al., comps. 1972. *Qingshi hequ zhi* (Monographs on the rivers and canals from the *Qingshi*). 4 *juan*. Taibei.

Zheng Zhaojing. 1966. *Zhongquo shuili shi* (The history of water conservancy in China). Taibei.

Zhou Yuande. 1982. A study of China's population during the Qing dynasty. *Social Sciences in China* 3, 3:61–105 (September).

Zhu Xie. 1962. *Zhongguo yunhe shiliao xuanji* (Compilation on the Grand Canal of China). Beijing.

Zou Yilin. 1981. Shandong Yunhe lishi dili wenti chutan (Preliminary study of the historical geography of the Shandong Canal). *Lishi dili* 1:80–98.

Index

administrative code, 80–81, 84–86
autumn crossing emergency, 83, 85–86, 111–117
autumn seasonal cycle, 47–48, 84–85, 136–38, 177–78; floods, 146, 216; maintenance cycle, 177–78, 203; shipping cycle, 138

backflows. *See* Yellow River
backspills. *See* Yellow River
Banner military organization, 62–63, 101

canal. *See* Grand Canal
canal building: history, 12–14, 21–28, 31; technology, 9–21
canal–grain transport management, 79–108; critique by emperor, 177–94; debate on, 204–11
Canal of Gates, 31, 33, 73
capstan, 16–17
central-regional decision making. *See also* Qing decisional process, 54–60, 80–84, 111–17, 155–59, 165, 172–75, 194–202, 231–33, 248–51
Chen Xuan, 36
Chen Zhongfa, 204
Cheng Hanzhang, 190
Cheng Zuluo, 90–91, 122, 155–60, 164
circuit intendant, 95; canal-river, 94; grain transport, 101
Clear Passage (*Qinghe*), 42–44, 111, 140

clear water, 129-132, 137–40, 196; crossing, 47, 139–44, 185
"controlling from afar," 58, 81, 117, 144, 185, 194–202, 248-49
court letter, 57, 59, 81–83, 113–16, 132, 164, 195

Daoguang Emperor, 39, 49, 51–77, 179, 242
Dawen River, 6
department district officials (*zhouxian*), 69–70, 72, 75, 165, 205–11
dikes. *See also* Gaojia Great Dike, 7, 10–12, 18–20, 33, 46, 80, 94, 118; earthen, 18, 118, 129; flying, 19, 132; narrow-diking, 10–11, 34–35, 41–42, 214; stone, 119; wide-diking, 10
double stanch. *See* flash lock
drainage networks, 44–45, 90–94, 133, 217
dredging, 18–20, 47, 96, 111, 133, 145, 213–18
dredging boat, 19, 215

ecological degradation, 106–107, 172
edict. *See* Qing decisional process
embankments. *See* dikes

fascine, 18–19
feeder channels. *See* lead channels

Finance Ministry (*Hubu*), 35, 71, 84, 99, 158, 215, 239
fiscal system, 66–70, 75–77, 106, 129–35, 172, 217
flash lock, 15–17, 42, 90, 95, 118
flood control, 9–10, 41, 90, 218; at canal–Yellow River junction (Fuxing, Tongji, Huiji), 42
floods, 84–88, 129; Huai–Yellow River, 8–9
foreigners, 187

gabion, 18–19
Gaojia Great Dike (Gaojia *yan*), 33–34, 46, 111, 140, 218; disaster, 1, 49, 118–24, 123–26, 138, 178, 184; reconstruction, 88, 129, 136, 147–48, 177–78, 182–83, 218, 222–24
geophysical barriers, 109, 126, 195
glacis, 17
government grain boat, 101–105, 149–53, 161
grain tax (grain tribute), 75, 98–100, 120, 143, 183, 187, 227; collection, 107; commutation, 110, 175, 194, 203–11, 232; direct, 99; exemptions, 162; indirect, 99
grain transport: agencies, 92; cycle, 105; intendants, 101; management, 79–92, 98–108, 177–202, 214; reforms, 183
Grain Transport Directorate, 98–108

grain tribute. *See* grain tax
Grand Canal, 21–49, 65, 66; administration, 79–98; canal-river intendants, 101; canal-river troops (*hebiao*), 95–97, 101; communications, 12–14, 20–21, 29, 31, 33, 37–41; construction, 17–18, 22–26, 29–32, 34–35; crisis, 51, 109–134, 177; dikes, 45–46, 94, 118; directorates, 92–98, 135; directors, 86–87, 93–94, 97, 100; disaster, 1, 49, 97, 118–19; dredging, 18–20, 111; flood control, 41; grain transport, 22–36, 38–41, 47, 72–75, 98–108, 177; maintenance cycle, 47-48, 136–38, 177–78; management, 79–92; origins of, 21–28; overflow gates (Nanguan, Nanguanxin,Wulizhong, Chelo, Zhuaguan), 45; Qing dynasty, 37–49; reconstruction, 31, 121–24, 135–50; restoration, 180–82, 194, 203–26; Song dynasty, 28; Sui-Tang construction, 24–28; Yellow River junction, 42–44, 47, 74, 90, 137; Yuan-Ming redesign, 29–36
Grand Canal crisis, 109–34; causes, 124–34; turning point, 177–83
Grand Canal–Yellow River Directorates, 92–98
Greater China, 60–66
Guan River scheme, 221–22

guoji minsheng (state's resources and people's livelihood), 51, 60, 66–68

He Changling, 60, 203, 230–31
Henan-Shandong (Hedong), 89–90, 94
Hongze Lake, 9, 20, 41–42, 74, 83, 95, 111, 118, 129; dikes, 20, 33, 46, 94, 109, 137, 147, 211; lead channels (Zhangfukou, Tianran, Zhangjiazhuang, Feijiachang, Taiping), 142, 145–47; overflow gates (Zhi, Linjia, Xin, Jiang, Lanhu, Ren, Yi, Li, Lizi), 46; siltation, 34, 41, 48
Hongze policy, 131, 185, 200–201, 215
Hongze strategy, 42–44, 131, 186, 193, 215
Huaiyang Canal, 33–34, 41–49, 71, 73, 76, 87, 89, 94, 109, 136, 151

imperial commissioners, 81, 120–25, 128, 133, 135–36, 143–48
imperial leadership, 54–62, 72–77, 194–202, 231–33, 248–51

Jiaqing Emperor, 39, 48
Jin Fu, 86

Kangxi Emperor, 42, 57, 64, 73, 87, 214
koumen. *See* overflow gates

lake reservoirs (Baima, Baoying, Gaoyu, Shaobo), 9, 33–34, 42
lead channels (*yinhe*), 44, 74, 118, 142, 145–47, 217
Li Shixu, 85
lighterage (*panbo*), 49, 71, 75–77, 93, 106–107, 151–55, 172–75, 196, 237

lighters (*bochuan*), 74–77, 103, 142–45, 150–54, 172–75, 181, 237; private, 154, 173; official, 154
Liu Yinheng, 219, 224
Luo sect, 76, 104, 149, 162–63

Macartney mission, 17, 89, 240
Mianning. *See* Daoguang Emperor
Ming dynasty, 31–36, 38–39, 54–57
minsheng (people's livelihood), 67–68
monetary system, 58, 68–71, 101, 107, 205–209
"muddling through," 126, 143, 151–76, 192, 207, 247

narrow diking. *See* dikes
Na'erjing'e, 166–69
Nayancheng, 245
Northern Canal, 88–89, 93–94

Opium War, 65–66
overflow gates. *See also* Grand Canal, Hongze Lake, 19, 45, 94, 118–19, 136–38

palace memorial. *See* court letter, Qing decisional process
Pan Jixun, 11, 34–35, 42, 46
Pan Xi'en, 93, 130
people's hydraulic works, 68, 73–75; people's dikes, 80
people's livelihood, 51, 66–68, 208, 241
People's Republic of China, 173, 256

piracy, 38–40, 51, 65, 187, 235–36
pound lock, 15, 18
private shipping, 75–76, 152–162, 187–88, 192, 203, 236–40
public edict. *See* Qing decisional process

Qianlong Emperor, 48, 53, 57, 106, 114
Qing decisional process, 54-60; in Grand Canal–grain transport management, 80–86, 105–108; in Grand Canal Crisis, 179–202;
Qing dynasty, 37–49, 51–77; Grand Canal–grain transport management, 79–108
Qishan, 88, 91, 123, 155–77, 196, 204, 213–26, 230–31, 241, 243–44

reconstruction policy, 121–24, 148
retention basin, 10

Salt Canal, 44–45, 112, 216
sandboat (*shachuan*), 234
Sanmen Gorge, 14, 24–26
sculling oars, 103
sea transport, 29–30, 33, 36, 38–40, 110, 141, 157, 180, 182–83, 186–91, 193–200, 203, 209–12, 227–46
secret edict. *See* court letter, Qing decisional process
Shandong Canal, 31–32, 44, 89–91, 94
shipping. *See* grain tax, grain transport, private shipping
Shen Cheng, 200, 215
siltation, 1–12, 19–21, 41–44, 88, 109–11, 119, 126, 130–31, 145–46, 149–55, 192, 200, 211–22

silt scrapers, 20
sluice gate. *See* flash lock
Songyun, 62, 233, 240–43
Southern Canal. *See* Huaiyang Canal
spring seasonal cycle 47–48, 84–85, 136–138, 177–78; maintenance, 47–48, 84–85, 136–38; shipping cycle, 101–105, 136–38, 146
summit canal, 18
Sun Yuting, 114–16, 119–23, 126–28, 132–33, 141, 148, 154–55, 161–62, 182, 198–99

Tao Zhu, 60, 204, 230–31, 238, 245
Three Gorges project, 173
trackers, 37, 103, 152
tracking road, 145
transfer shipping (*panba jieyun*), 49, 90, 110, 151–76, 180, 188–89, 212, 227; assessment, 172–76; initiative, 155–66; management, 166–72
transport corps (*caobiao*), 101–102
tributary system, 60–66

Wang Shifu, 162–63
Wang Tingzhen. *See* imperial commissioners
Wangying drainage gate, 44–45, 73, 112, 116, 216
water control, 9–21, 125; *see also* dikes, drainage networks, flash lock, pound lock, retention basin, weirs

Index

Wei Yuanyu, 114, 123, 126, 142–44, 151, 153, 189, 196–99
weirs, 10, 118
Wen Fu. *See* imperial commissioners
West River boats, 154–55
wide-diking. *See* dikes
winch, 17
Wushui gate, 41, 43, 111–12

Xiahe region, 9, 45, 73, 119, 132
Xiangfu gate, 41–43, 111–12
Xiong Yutai, 235, 238

Yan Jian, 123, 148, 190, 199
Yan Lang, 88, 121–22
Yangzi River drainage outlets, 44–45, 90–94
Yellow River, 5–9; backflows, 41, 48–49, 129–33; backspills, 48, 139, 142–46, 151, 157, 167, 180, 184, 189, 196; canal junction, 42–47, 74, 90, 137; change of course, 1, 8–9, 35, 49, 77, 110, 125–26, 192; dikes, 7–9, 132, 224; dredging, 34, 224, 225; flooding, 8, 111, 182, 220; geography, 5–7; Huai River junction, 9, 125; opening (mouth of), 222; silt deposition, 5–9; straightening bends, 225; water control, 9–12
Yinghe, 182–83, 190–91, 194–95, 197, 203–11, 230–31, 245
Yongle Emperor, 32–33, 66
Yongzheng Emperor, 57, 93, 214
Yu Chenglong, 86
Yuhuang Lock gate, 44, 48, 111–12, 115, 118, 127–33, 144–46, 149, 151–53, 165–67, 177–81, 240–43
Yuan dynasty, 29–33

Zhang Jing, 93, 122–23, 158, 213, 219, 224–26
Zhang Wenhao, 85–86, 114, 117, 120, 127, 130
zhaoshang (recruiting), 71, 76–77, 107, 155–65, 173–75, 203–204, 236–39
Zheng regime, 39, 64, 66
Zhengguo canal, 13
zhouxian officials. *See* department district officials
Zhu Shiyan, 128–30, 133